The Life and Genius of Nathaniel Hawthorne

Frank Preston Stearns

Table of Contents

The Life and Genius of Nathaniel Hawthorne...1

   Frank Preston Stearns...1

   Preface...2

   CHAPTER I. SALEM AND THE HATHORNES: 1630–1800..................................3

   CHAPTER II. BOYHOOD OF HAWTHORNE: 1804–1821.................................17

   CHAPTER III. BOWDOIN COLLEGE: 1821–1825..31

   CHAPTER IV. LITTLE MISERY: 1825–1835..41

   CHAPTER V. EOS AND EROS: 1835–1839...56

   CHAPTER VI. PEGASUS AT THE CART: 1839–1841..67

   CHAPTER VII. HAWTHORNE AS A SOCIALIST: 1841–1842...........................75

   CHAPTER VIII. CONCORD AND THE OLD MANSE: 1842–1845......................85

   CHAPTER IX. "MOSSES PROM AN OLD MANSE": 1845.................................96

   CHAPTER X. FROM CONCORD TO LENOX: 1845–1849................................109

   CHAPTER XI. PEGASUS IS FREE: 1850–1852...124

   CHAPTER XII. THE LIVERPOOL CONSULATE: 1852–1854...........................138

   CHAPTER XIII. HAWTHORNE IN ENGLAND: 1854–1858.............................150

   CHAPTER XIV. ITALY...167

   CHAPTER XV. HAWTHORNE AS ART CRITIC: 1858....................................178

   CHAPTER XVI. "THE MARBLE FAUN": 1859–1860.......................................189

   CHAPTER XVII. HOMEWARD BOUND: 1860–1862.......................................205

   CHAPTER XVIII. IMMORTALITY..219

   APPENDIX A..241

   APPENDIX B..242

   APPENDIX C..243

The Life and Genius of Nathaniel Hawthorne

Frank Preston Stearns

- Preface
- CHAPTER I. SALEM AND THE HATHORNES: 1630–1800
- CHAPTER II. BOYHOOD OF HAWTHORNE: 1804–1821
- CHAPTER III. BOWDOIN COLLEGE: 1821–1825.
- CHAPTER IV. LITTLE MISERY: 1825–1835
- CHAPTER V. EOS AND EROS: 1835–1839
- CHAPTER VI. PEGASUS AT THE CART: 1839–1841
- CHAPTER VII. HAWTHORNE AS A SOCIALIST: 1841–1842
- CHAPTER VIII. CONCORD AND THE OLD MANSE: 1842–1845
- CHAPTER IX. "MOSSES PROM AN OLD MANSE": 1845
- CHAPTER X. FROM CONCORD TO LENOX: 1845–1849
- CHAPTER XI. PEGASUS IS FREE: 1850–1852
- CHAPTER XII. THE LIVERPOOL CONSULATE: 1852–1854
- CHAPTER XIII. HAWTHORNE IN ENGLAND: 1854–1858
- CHAPTER XIV. ITALY
- CHAPTER XV. HAWTHORNE AS ART CRITIC: 1858
- CHAPTER XVI. "THE MARBLE FAUN": 1859–1860
- CHAPTER XVII. HOMEWARD BOUND: 1860–1862
- CHAPTER XVIII. IMMORTALITY
- APPENDIX A
- APPENDIX B
- APPENDIX C

FRANK PRESTON STEARNS

AUTHOR OF "THE REAL AND IDEAL IN LITERATURE," "LIFE OF TINTORETTO," "LIFE OF BISMARCK," "TRUE REPUBLICANISM," "CAMBRIDGE SKETCHES," ETC.

[Illustration: Nathaniel Hawthorne. The Frances Osborne Portrait: by permission of the Essex Institute.]

INSCRIBED

TO EMILIA MACIEL STEARNS

> "In the elder days of art
> Builders wrought with greatest care
> Each minute and unseen part,—
> For the gods see everywhere."
> —*Longfellow*

> "Oh, happy dreams of such a soul have I,
> And softly to myself of him I sing,
> Whose seraph pride all pride doth overwing;
> Who stoops to greatness, matches low with high,
> And as in grand equalities of sky,
> Stands level with the beggar and the king."
> —*Wasson*

Preface

The simple events of Nathaniel Hawthorne's life have long been before the public. From 1835 onward they may easily be traced in the various Note-books, which have been edited from his diary, and previous to that time we are indebted for them chiefly to the recollections of his two faithful friends, Horatio Bridge and Elizabeth Peabody. These were first systematised and published by George P. Lathrop in 1872, but a more complete and authoritative biography was issued by Julian Hawthorne twelve years later, in which, however, the writer has modestly refrained from expressing an opinion as to the quality of his father's genius, or from attempting any critical examination of his father's literary work. It is in order to supply in some measure this deficiency, that the present volume has been written. At the same time, I trust to have given credit where it was due to my predecessors, in the good work of making known the true character of so rare a genius and so exceptional a personality.

The publication of Horatio Bridge's memoirs and of Elizabeth Manning's account of the boyhood of Hawthorne have placed before the world much that is new and valuable concerning the earlier portion of Hawthorne's life, of which previous biographers could not very well reap the advantage. I have made thorough researches in regard to Hawthorne's American ancestry, but have been able to find no ground for the statements of Conway and Lathrop, that William Hathorne, their first ancestor on this side of the ocean, was directly connected with the Quaker persecution. Some other mistakes, like Hawthorne's supposed connection with the duel between Cilley and Graves, have also been corrected.

F. P. S.

CHAPTER I. SALEM AND THE HATHORNES: 1630–1800

The three earliest settlements on the New England coast were Plymouth, Boston, and Salem; but Boston soon proved its superior advantages to the two others, not only from its more capacious harbor, but also from the convenient waterway which the Charles River afforded to the interior of the Colony. We find that a number of English families, and among them the ancestors of Gen. Joseph Warren and Wendell Phillips, who crossed the ocean in 1640 in the "good ship Arbella," soon afterward migrated to Watertown on Charles River for the sake of the excellent farming lands which they found there. Salem, however, maintained its ascendency over Plymouth and other neighboring harbors on the coast, and soon grew to be the second city of importance in the Colony during the eighteenth century, when the only sources of wealth were fishing, shipbuilding, and commerce. Salem nourished remarkably. Its leading citizens became wealthy and developed a social aristocracy as cultivated, as well educated, and, it may also be added, as fastidious as that of Boston itself. In this respect it differed widely from the other small cities of New England, and the exclusiveness of its first families was more strongly marked on account of the limited size of the place. Thus it continued down to the middle of the last century, when railroads and the tendency to centralization began to draw away its financial prosperity, and left the city to small manufactures and its traditional respectability.

The finest examples of American eighteenth century architecture are supposed to exist in and about the city of Salem, and they have the advantage, which American architecture lacks so painfully at the present time, of possessing a definite style and character—edifices which are not of a single type, like most of the houses in Fifth Avenue, but which, while differing in many respects, have a certain general resemblance, that places them all in the same category. The small old country churches of Essex County are not distinguished for fine carving or other ornamentation, and still less by the costliness of their material, for they are mostly built of white pine, but they have an indefinable air of pleasantness about them, as if they graced the ground they stand on, and their steeples seem to float in the air above us. If we enter them on a Sunday forenoon—for on week-days they are like a sheepfold without its occupants—we meet with much the same kind of pleasantness in the assemblage there. We do not find the deep religious twilight of past ages, or the noonday glare of a fashionable synagogue, but a neatly attired congregation of weather-beaten farmers and mariners, and their sensible looking wives, with something of the original Puritan hardness in their faces, much ameliorated by the liberalism and free thinking of the past fifty years. Among them too you will see some remarkably pretty young women; and young men like those who dug the trenches on Breed's Hill in the afternoon of June 16, 1775. There may be veterans in the audience who helped Grant to go to Richmond. Withal there is much of the spirit of the early Christians among them, and virtue enough to save their country in any emergency.

These old churches have mostly disappeared from Salem city and have been replaced by more aristocratic edifices, whose square or octagonal towers are typical of their leading parishioners,—a dignified class, if somewhat haughty and reserved; but they too will soon belong to the past, drawn off to the great social centres in and about Boston. In the midst of Salem there is a triangular common, "with its never-failing elms," where the boys large and small formerly played cricket—married men too—as they do still on the village greens of good old England, and around this enclosure the successful merchants and navigators of the city built their mansion houses; not half houses like those in the larger cities, but with spacious halls and rooms on either side going up three stories. It is in the gracefully ornamented doorways and the delicate interior wood–work, the carving of wainscots, mantels and cornices, the skilful adaptations of classic forms to a soft and delicate material that the charm of this architecture chiefly consists,—especially in the staircases, with their carved spiral posts and slender railings, rising upward in the centre of the front hall, and turning right and left on the story above. It is said that after the year eighteen hundred the quality of this decoration sensibly declined; it was soon replaced by more prosaic forms, and now the tools no longer exist that can make it. Sir Christopher Wren and Inigo Jones would have admired it. America, excepting in New York City, escaped the false rococo taste of the eighteenth century.

The Salem sea–captains of old times were among the boldest of our early navigators; sailing among the pirates of the Persian Gulf and trading with the cannibals of Polynesia, and the trophies which they brought home from those strange regions, savage implements of war and domestic use, clubs, spears, boomerangs, various cooking utensils, all carved with infinite pains from stone, ebony and iron–wood, cloth from the bark of the tapa tree, are now deposited in the Peabody Academy, where they form one of the largest collections of the kind extant. Even more interesting is the sword of a sword–fish, pierced through the oak planking of a Salem vessel for six inches or more. No human force could do that even with a spear of the sharpest steel. Was the sword–fish roused to anger when the ship came upon him sleeping in the water; or did he mistake it for a strange species of whale?

There is a court–house on Federal Street, built in Webster's time, of hard cold granite in the Grecian fashion of the day, not of the white translucent marble with which the Greeks would have built it. Is it the court–house where Webster made his celebrated argument in the White murder case, or was that court–house torn down and a plough run through the ground where it stood, as Webster affirmed that it ought to be? Salem people were curiously reticent in regard to that trial, and fashionable society there did not like Webster the better for having the two Knapps convicted.

Much more valuable than such associations is William Hunt's full–length portrait of Chief Justice Shaw, which hangs over the judge's bench in the front court–room. "When I look at your honor I see that you are homely, but when I think of you I know that you are great." it is this combination of an unprepossessing physique with rare dignity of character which Hunt has represented in what many consider the best of American portraits. It is perhaps too much in the sketchy style of Velasquez, but admirable for all that.

Time has dealt kindly with Salem, in effacing all memorials of the witchcraft persecution, except a picturesque old house at the corner of North and Essex Streets, where there are said to have been preliminary examinations for witchcraft,—a matter which concerns us now but slightly. The youthful associations of a genius are valuable to us on account of the influence which they may be supposed to have had on his early life, but associations which have no determining consequences may as well be neglected. The hill where those poor martyrs to superstition were executed may be easily seen on the left of the city, as you roll in on the train from Boston. It is part of a ridge which rises between the Concord and Charles Rivers and extends to Cape Ann, where it dives into the ocean, to reappear again like a school of krakens, or other marine monsters, in the Isles of Shoals.

New England has not the fertile soil of many sections of the United States, and its racking climate is proverbial, but it is blessed with the two decided advantages of pure water and fine scenery. There is no more beautiful section of its coast than that between Salem Harbor and Salisbury Beach, long stretches of smooth sand alternating with bold rocky promontories. A summer drive from Swampscott to Marblehead reminds one even of the Bay of Naples (without Vesuvius), and the wilder coast of Cape Ann, with its dark pines, red–roofed cottages, and sparkling surf, is quite as delightful. William Hunt went there in the last sad years of his life to paint "sunshine," as he said; and Whittier has given us poetic touches of the inland scenery in elevated verse:

> "Fleecy clouds casting their shadows
> Over uplands and meadows;
> And country roads winding as roads will,
> Here to a ferry, there to a mill."

Poets arise where there is poetic nourishment, internal and external, for them to feed on; and it is not surprising that a Whittier and a Hawthorne should have been evolved from the environment in which they grew to manhood.

It is a common saying with old Boston families that their ancestors came to America in the "Arbella" with Governor Winthrop, but as a matter of fact there were at least fifteen vessels that brought colonists to Massachusetts in 1630, and I cannot discover that any lists of their passengers have been preserved. The statement that certain persons came over at the same time with Governor Winthrop might soon become a tradition that they came in the same ship with him; but all that we know certainly is that Governor Winthrop landed about the middle of June, 1630, and that his son arrived two weeks later in the "Talbot," and was drowned July 2, while attempting to cross one of the tide rivers at Salem. Who arrived in the thirteen other vessels that year we know not. Ten years later Sir Richard Saltonstall emigrated to Boston with the Phillips and Warren families in the "Arbella" (or "Arabella"), and there is no telling how much longer she sailed the ocean.

Hawthorne himself states that his ancestors came from Wig Castle in Wigton in Warwickshire, [Footnote: Diary, August 22, 1837.] but no such castle has been discovered, and the only Wigton in England appears to be located in Cumberland. [Footnote: Lathrop's "Study of Hawthorne," 46.] He does not tell us where he obtained this information, and it certainly could not have been from authentic documents,—more likely from conversation with an English traveller. Hawthorne never troubled himself much concerning his ancestry, English or American; while he was consul at Liverpool, he had exceptional advantages for investigating the subject, but whatever attempt he made there resulted in nothing. It is only recently that Mr. Henry F. Waters, who spent fifteen years in England searching out the records of old New England families, succeeded in discovering the connecting link between the first American Hawthornes and their relatives in the old country. It was a bill of exchange for one hundred pounds drawn by William Hathorne, of Salem, payable to Robert Hathorne in London, and dated October 19, 1651, which first gave Mr. Waters the clue to his discovery. Robert not only accepted his brother's draft, but wrote him this simple and business–like but truly affectionate epistle in return:

"GOOD BROTHER: Remember my love to my sister, my brother John and sister, my brother Davenport and sister and the rest of our friends.

> "In haste I rest
> "Your loving brother,

"From Bray this 1 April, 1653. ROBERT HATHORNE."

From this it appears that Major William Hathorne not only had a brother John, who established himself in Lynn, but a sister Elizabeth, who married Richard Davenport, of Salem. Concerning Robert Hathorne we only know further that he died in 1689; but in the probate records of Berkshire, England, there is a will proved May 2, 1651, of William Hathorne, of Binfield, who left all his lands, buildings and tenements in that county to his son Robert, on condition that Robert should pay to his father's eldest son, William, one hundred pounds, and to his son John twenty pounds sterling. He also left to another son, Edmund, thirty acres of land in Bray, and there are other legacies; but it cannot be doubted that the hundred pounds mentioned in this will is the same that Major William Hathorne drew for five months later, and that we have identified here the last English ancestor of Nathaniel Hawthorne. His wife's given name was Sarah, but her maiden name still remains unknown. The family resided chiefly at Binfield, on the borders of Windsor Park, and evidently were in comfortable circumstances at that time. From William Hathorne, senior, their genealogy has been traced back to John Hathorne (spelled at that time Hothorne), who died in 1520, but little is known of their affairs, or how they sustained themselves during the strenuous vicissitudes of the Reformation. [Footnote: "Hawthorne Centenary at Salem," 81.]

Emmerton and Waters [Footnote: "English Records about New England Families."] state that William Hathorne came to Massachusetts Bay in 1630, and this is probable enough, though by no means certain, for they give no authority for it. We first hear of him definitely as a freeholder in the settlement of Dorchester in 1634, but his name is not on the list of the first twenty-four Dorchester citizens, dated October 19, 1630. All accounts agree that he moved to Salem in 1636, or the year following, and Nathaniel Hawthorne believed that he came to America at that time. Upham, the historian of Salem witchcraft, who has made the most thorough researches in the archives of old Salem families, says of William Hathorne:

"William Hathorne appears on the church records as early as 1636. He died in June, 1681, seventy-four years of age. No one in our annals fills a larger space. As soldier, commanding important and difficult expeditions, as counsel in cases before the courts, as judge on the bench, and innumerable other positions requiring talent and intelligence, he was constantly called to serve the public. He was distinguished as a public speaker, and is the only person, I believe, of that period, whose reputation as an orator has come down to us. He was an Assistant, that is, in the upper branch of the Legislature, seventeen years. He was a deputy twenty years. When the deputies, who before sat with the assistants, were separated into a distinct body, and the House of Representatives thus came into existence, in 1644, Hathorne was their first Speaker. He occupied the chair, with intermediate services on the floor from time to time, until raised to the other House. He was an inhabitant of Salem Village, having his farm there, and a dwelling–house, in which he resided when his legislative, military, and other official duties permitted. His son John, who succeeded him in all his public honors, also lived on his own farm in the village a great part of the time." [Footnote: "Salem Witchcraft," i. 99.]

Evidently he was the most important person in the colony, next to Governor Winthrop, and unequalled by any of his descendants, except Nathaniel Hawthorne, and by him in a wholly different manner; for it is in vain that we seek for traits similar to those of the great romance writer among his ancestors. We can only say that they both possessed exceptional mental ability, and there the comparison ends.

The attempt has been made to connect William Hathorne with the persecution of the Quakers, [Footnote: Conway's "Life of Hawthorne," 15.] and it is true that he was a member of the Colonial Assembly during the period of the persecution; it is likely that his vote supported the measures in favor of it, but this is not absolutely certain. We do not learn that he acted at any time in the capacity of sheriff; the most diligent researches in the archives of the State House at Boston have failed to discover any direct connection on the part of William Hathorne with that movement; and the best authorities in regard to the events of that time make no mention of him. [Footnote: Sewel, Hallowell, Ellis.] It was the clergy who aroused public opinion and instigated the prosecutions against both the Quakers and the supposed witches of Salem, and the civil authorities were little more than passive instruments in their hands. Hathorne's work was essentially a legislative one,—a highly important work in that wild, unsettled country,—to adapt English statutes and legal procedures to new and strange conditions. He was twice Speaker of the House between 1660 and 1671, and as presiding officer he could exert less influence on measures of expediency than any other person present, as he could not argue either for or against them. And yet, after Charles II. had interfered in behalf of the Quakers, William Hathorne wrote an elaborate and rather circuitous letter to the British Ministry, arguing for non–intervention in the affairs of the colony, which might have possessed greater efficacy if he had not signed it with an assumed name. [Footnote: J. Hawthorne's "Nathaniel Hawthorne," i. 24.] However strong a Puritan he may have been, William Hathorne evidently had no intention of becoming a martyr to the cause of colonial independence. Yet it may be stated in his favor, and in that of the colonists generally, that the fault was not wholly on one side, for the Quakers evidently sought persecution, and would have it, cost what it might. [Footnote: Hallowell's "Quaker Invasion of New England."] Much the same may be affirmed of his son John, who had the singular misfortune to be judge in Salem at the time of the witchcraft epidemic. The belief in witchcraft has always had its stronghold among the fogs and gloomy fiords of the North. James I. brought it with him from Scotland to England, and in due course it was transplanted to America. Judge Hathorne appears to have been at the top of affairs at Salem in his time, and it is more than probable that another in his place would have found himself obliged to act as he did. Law is, after all, in exceptional cases little more than a reflex of public opinion. "The common law," said Webster, "is common–sense," which simply means the common opinion of the most influential people. Much more to blame than John Hathorne were those infatuated persons who deceived themselves into thinking that the pains of rheumatism, neuralgia, or some similar malady were caused by the malevolent influence of a neighbor against whom they had perhaps long harbored a grudge. *They* were the true witches and goblins of that epoch, and the only ones, if any, who ought to have been hanged for it.

What never has been reasoned up cannot be reasoned down. It seems incredible in this enlightened era, as the newspapers call it, that any woman should be at once so inhuman and so frivolous as to swear away the life of a fellow–creature upon an idle fancy; and yet, even in regard to this, there were slightly mitigating conditions. Consider only the position of that handful of Europeans in this vast wilderness, as it then was. The forests came down to the sea–shore, and brought with them all the weird fancies, terrors and awful forebodings which the human mind could conjure up. They feared the Indians, the wild beasts, and most of all one another, for society was not yet sufficiently organized to afford that repose and contentment of spirit which they had left behind in the Old World. They had come to America to escape despotism, but they had brought despotism in their own hearts. They could escape from the Stuarts, but there was no escape from human nature.

It is likely that their immediate progenitors would not have carried the witchcraft craze to such an extreme. The emigrating Puritans were a fairly well–educated class of men and women, but their children did not enjoy equal opportunities. The new continent had to be subdued physically and reorganized before any mental growth could be raised there. Levelling the forest was a small matter beside clearing the land of stumps and stones. All hands were obliged to work hard, and there was little opportunity for intellectual development or social culture. As a logical consequence, an era ensued not unlike the dark ages of Europe. But this was essential to the evolution of a new type of man, and for the foundation of American nationality; and it was thus that the various nationalities of Europe arose out of the ruins of the Roman Empire.

The scenes that took place in Judge Hathorne's court-room have never been equalled since in American jurisprudence. Powerful forces came into play there, and the reports that have been preserved read like scenes from Shakespeare. In the case of Rebecca Nurse, the Judge said to the defendant:

"'You do know whether you are guilty, and have familiarity with the Devil; and now when you are here present to see such a thing as these testify,—and a black man whispering in your ear, and devils about you,—what do you say to it?'"

To which she replied:

"'It is all false. I am clear.' Whereupon Mrs. Pope, one of the witnesses, fell into a grievous fit." [Footnote: Upham's "Salem Witchcraft," ii. 64.]

Alas, poor beleaguered soul! And one may well say, "What imaginations those women had!" Tituba, the West Indian Aztec who appears in this social–religious explosion as the chief and original incendiary,— verily the root of all evil,—gave the following testimony:

"Q. 'Did you not pinch Elizabeth Hubbard this morning?'

"A. 'The man brought her to me, and made me pinch her.'

"Q. 'Why did you go to Thomas Putnam's last night and hurt his child?'

"A. 'They pull and haul me, and make me go.'

"Q. 'And what would they have you do?'

"A. 'Kill her with a knife.'

"(Lieutenant Fuller and others said at this time, when the child saw these persons, and was tormented by them, that she did complain of a knife,—that they would have her cut her head off with a knife.)

"Q. 'How did you go?'

"A. 'We ride upon sticks, and are there presently.'

"Q. 'Do you go through the trees or over them?'

"A. 'We see nothing, but are there presently.'

"Q. 'Why did you not tell your master?'

"A. 'I was afraid. They said they would cut off my head if I told.'

"Q. 'Would you not have hurt others, if you could?'

"A. 'They said they would hurt others, but they could not.'

"Q. 'What attendants hath Sarah Good?'

"A. 'A yellow–bird, and she would have given me one.'

"Q. 'What meat did she give it?'

"A. 'It did suck her between her fingers.'".

This might serve as an epilogue to "Macbeth," and the wonder is that an unlettered Indian should have had the wit to make such apt and subtle replies. It is also noteworthy that these strange proceedings took place after the expulsion of the royal governor, and previous to the provincial government of William III. If Sir Edmund Andros had remained, the tragedy might have been changed into a farce.

After all, it appears that John Hathorne was not a lawyer, for he describes himself in his last will, dated June 27, 1717, as a merchant, and it is quite possible that his legal education was no better than that of the average English squire in Fielding's time. It is evident, however, from the testimony given above, that he was a strong believer in the supernatural, and here if anywhere we find a relationship between him and his more celebrated descendant. Nathaniel Hawthorne was too clear-sighted to place confidence in the pretended revelations of trance mediums, and he was not in the least superstitious; but he was remarkably fond of reading ghost stories, and would have liked to believe them, if he could have done so in all sincerity. He sometimes felt as if he were a ghost himself, gliding noiselessly in the walks of men, and wondered that the sun should cast a shadow from him. However, we cannot imagine him as seated in jurisdiction at a criminal tribunal. His gentle nature would have recoiled from that, as it might from a serpent.

In the Charter Street burial-ground there is a slate gravestone, artistically carved about its edges, with the name, "Col. John Hathorne Esq.," upon it. It is somewhat sunken into the earth, and leans forward as if wishing to hide the inscription upon it from the gaze of mankind. The grass about it and the moss upon the stone assist in doing this, although repeatedly cut and cleaned away. It seems as if Nature wished to draw a kind of veil over the memory of the witch's judge, himself the sorrowful victim of a theocratic oligarchy. The lesson we learn from his errors is, to trust our own hearts and not to believe too fixedly in the doctrines of Church and State. It must be a dull sensibility that can look on this old slate-stone without a feeling of pathos and a larger charity for the errors of human nature.

It is said that one of the convicted witches cursed Judge Hathorne,— himself and his descendants forever; but it is more than likely that they all cursed him bitterly enough, and this curse took effect in a very natural and direct manner. Every extravagant political or social movement is followed by a corresponding reaction, even if the movement be on the whole a salutary one, and retribution is sure to fall in one shape or another on the leaders of it. After this time the Hathornes ceased to be conspicuous in Salem affairs. The family was not in favor, and the avenues of prosperity were closed to them, as commonly happens in such cases. Neither does the family appear to have multiplied and extended itself like most of the old New England families, who can now count from a dozen to twenty branches in various places. Of John Hathorne's three sons only one appears to have left children. The name has wholly disappeared from among Salem families, and thus in a manner has the witch's curse been fulfilled.

Joseph Hathorne, the son of the Judge, was mostly a farmer, and that is all that we now know of him. His son Daniel, however, showed a more adventurous spirit, becoming a shipmaster quite early in life. It has also been intimated that he was something of a smuggler, which was no great discredit to him in a time when the unfair and even prohibitory measures of the British Parliament in regard to American commerce made smuggling a practical necessity. Even as the captain of a trading vessel, however, Daniel Hathorne was not likely to advance the social interests of his family. It is significant that he should have left the central portion of Salem, where his ancestors had lived, and have built a house for himself close to the city wharves,—a house well built and commodious enough, but not in a fashionable location.

But Daniel Hathorne had the advantage over fashionable society in Salem, in being a thorough patriot. Boston and Salem were the two strongholds of Toryism during the war for Independence, which was natural enough, as their wealthy citizens were in close mercantile relations with English houses, and sent their children to England to be educated. Daniel Hathorne, however, as soon as hostilities had begun, fitted out his bark as a privateer, and spent the following six years in preying upon British merchantmen. How successful he was in this line of business we have not been informed, but he certainly did not grow rich by it; although he is credited with one engagement with the enemy, in which his ship came off with honor, though perhaps not with a decisive victory. This exploit was celebrated in a rude ballad of the time, which has been preserved in "Griswold's Curiosities of American Literature," and has at least the merit of plain unvarnished language. [Footnote: Also in Lathrop's "Hawthorne."]

There is a miniature portrait of Daniel Hathorne, such as was common in Copley's time, still in the possession of the Hawthorne family, and it represents him as rather a bullet–headed man, with a bright, open, cheery face, a broad English chin and strongly marked brows,—an excellent physiognomy for a sea–captain. He appears besides to have had light brown or sandy hair, a ruddy complexion and bright blue eyes; but we cannot determine how truthful the miniature may be in respect to coloring. At all events, he was of a very different appearance from Nathaniel Hawthorne, and if he resembled his grandson in any external respect, it was in his large eyes and their overshadowing brows. He has not the look of a dare–devil. One might suppose that he was a person of rather an obstinate disposition, but it is always difficult to draw the line between obstinacy and determination.

The Life and Genius of Nathaniel Hawthorne

A similar miniature of his son Nathaniel, born in 1775, and who died at Surinam in his thirty–fourth year, gives us the impression of a person somewhat like his father, and also somewhat like his son Nathaniel. He has a long face instead of a round one, and his features are more delicate and refined than those of the bold Daniel. The expression is gentle, dreamy and pensive, and unless the portrait belies him, he could not have been the stern, domineering captain that he has been represented. He had rather a slender figure, and was probably much more like his mother, who was a Miss Phelps, than the race of Judge Hathorne. He may have been a reticent man, but never a bold one, and we find in him a new departure. His face is more amiable and attractive than his father's, but not so strong. In 1799 he was married to Miss Elizabeth Clarke Manning, the daughter of Richard Manning, and then only nineteen years of age. She appears to have been an exceptionally sensitive and rather shy young woman—such as would be likely to attract the attention of a chivalrous young mariner—but with fine traits of intellect and character.

The maternal ancestry of a distinguished man is quite as important as the paternal, but in the present instance it is much more difficult to obtain information concerning it. The increasing fame of Hawthorne has been like a calcium–light, illuminating for the past fifty years everything to which that name attaches, and leaving the Manning family in a shadow so much the deeper. All we can learn of them now is, that they were descended from Richard Manning, of Dartmouth in Devonshire, England, whose son Thomas emigrated to Salem with his widowed mother in 1679, but afterwards removed to Ipswich, ten miles to the north, whence the family has since extended itself far and wide,—the Reverend Jacob M. Manning, of the Old South Church, the fearless champion of practical anti–slaveryism, having been among them. It appears that Thomas's grandson Richard started in life as a blacksmith, which was no strange thing in those primitive times; but, being a thrifty and enterprising man, he lived to establish a line of stage–coaches between Salem and Boston, and this continued in the possession of his family until it was superseded by the Eastern Railway. After this catastrophe, Robert Manning, the son of Richard and brother of Mrs. Nathaniel Hathorne, became noted as a fruit–grower (a business in which Essex County people have always taken an active interest), and was one of the founders of the Massachusetts Horticultural Society. The Mannings were always respected in Salem, although they never came to affluent circumstances, nor did they own a house about the city common. Robert Manning, Jr., was Secretary of the Horticultural Society in Boston for a long term of years, a pleasant, kindly man, with an aspect of general culture. Hawthorne's maternal grandmother was

Miriam Lord, of Ipswich, and his paternal grandmother was Rachel Phelps, of Salem. His father was only thirty–three when he died at Surinam.

In regard to the family name, there are at present Hawthornes and Hathornes in England, and although the two names may have been identical originally, they have long since become as distinct as Smith and Smythe. I have discovered only two instances in which the first William Hathorne wrote his own name, and in the various documents at the State House in which it appears written by others, it is variously spelled Hathorn, Hathorne, Hawthorn, Haythorne, and Harthorne,—from which we can only conclude that the a was pronounced broadly. It was not until the reign of Queen Anne, when books first became cheap and popular, that there was any decided spelling of either proper or common names. Then the printers took the matter into their own hands and made witch–work enough of it. The word "sovereign," for instance, which is derived from the old French *souvrain*, and which Milton spelled "sovran," they tortured into its present form,—much as the clerks of Massachusetts Colony tortured the name of William Hathorne. This, however, was spelled Hathorne oftener than in other ways, and it was so spelled in the two signatures above referred to, one of which was attached as witness to a deed for the settlement of the boundary between Lynn and Salem, [Footnote: Also in Lathrop's "Hawthorne."] and the other to a report of the commissioners for the investigation of the French vessels coming to Salem and Boston in 1651, the two other commissioners being Samuel Bradstreet and David Denison. [Footnote: Massachusetts Archives, x. 171.]The name was undoubtedly Hathorne, and so it continued with one or two slight variations during the eighteenth century down to the time of Nathaniel Hathorne, Jr., who entered and graduated at Bowdoin College under that name, but who soon afterward changed it to Hawthorne, for reasons that have never been explained.

All cognomens would seem to have been derived originally from some personal peculiarity, although it is no longer possible to trace this back to its source, which probably lies far away in the Dark Ages,—the formative period of languages and of families. Sometimes, however, we meet with individuals whose peculiarities suggest the origin of their names: a tall, slender, long–necked man named Crane; or a timid, retiring student named Leverett; or an over–confident, supercilious person called Godkin In the name of Hawthorne also we may imagine a curious significance: "When the may is on the thorn," says Tennyson. The English country people call the flowering of the hawthorn "the may." It is a beautiful tree when in full bloom. How sweet–scented and delicately colored are its blossoms! But it seems to say to us, "Do not come too close to me."

CHAPTER II. BOYHOOD OF HAWTHORNE: 1804–1821

Salem treasures the memory of Hawthorne, and preserves everything tangible relating to him. The house in which he was born, No. 27 Union Street, is in much the same style and probably of the same age as the Old Manse at Concord, but somewhat smaller, with only a single window on either side of the doorway—five windows in all on the front, one large chimney in the centre, and the roof not exactly a gambrel, for the true gambrel has a curve first inward and then outward, but something like it. A modest, cosy and rather picturesque dwelling, which if placed on a green knoll with a few trees about it might become a subject for a sketching class. It did not belong to Hawthorne's father, after all, but to the widow of the bold Daniel, It was the cradle of genius, and is now a shrine for many pilgrims. Long may it survive, so that our grandchildren may gaze upon it.

Here Nathaniel Hawthorne first saw daylight one hundred years ago [Footnote: 1804.] on the Fourth of July, as if to make a protest against Chauvinistic patriotism; here his mother sat at the window to see her husband's bark sail out of the harbor on his last voyage; and here she watched day after day for its return, only to bring a life–long sorrow with it. The life of a sea–captain's wife is always a half–widowhood, but Mrs. Hathorne was left at twenty–eight with three small children, including a daughter, Elizabeth, older than Nathaniel, and another, Louisa, the youngest. The shadow of a heavy misfortune had come upon them, and from this shadow they never wholly escaped.

Lowell criticised a letter which John Brown wrote concerning his boyhood to Henry L. Stearns, as the finest bit of autobiography of the nineteenth century.[Footnote: *North American Review*, April 1860.] It is in fact almost the only literature of the kind that we possess. A frequent difficulty that parents find in dealing with their children is, that they have wholly forgotten the sensations and impressions of their own childhood. The instructor cannot place himself in the position of the pupil. A naturalist will spend years with a microscope studying the development of a plant from the seed, but no one has ever applied a similar process to the budding of genius or even of ordinary intellect. We have the autobiography of one of the greatest geniuses, written in the calm and stillness of old age, when youthful memories come back to us involuntarily; yet he barely lifts the veil from his own childhood, and has much more to say of external events and older people than of himself and his young companions. How valuable is the story of George Washington and his hatchet, hackneyed as it has become! What do we know of the boyhood of Franklin, Webster, Seward and Longfellow? Nothing, or next to nothing.

[Illustration: WINDOW OF THIS CHAMBER]

Goethe says that the admirable woman is she who, when her husband dies, becomes a father to his children; but in the case of Hawthorne's mother, this did not happen to be necessary. Her brother, Robert Manning, a thrifty and fairly prosperous young man, immediately took Mrs. Hathorne and her three children into his house on Herbert Street, and made it essentially a home for them afterward. To the fatherless boy he was more than his own father, away from home ten months of the year, ever could have been; and though young Nathaniel must have missed that tenderness of feeling which a man can only entertain toward his own child, there was no lack of kindness or consideration on Robert Manning's part, to either the boy or his sisters.

It was Mrs. Hathorne who chiefly suffered from this change of domicile. She would seem to have been always on good terms with her brother's wife, and on the whole they formed a remarkably harmonious family,—at least we hear nothing to the contrary,—but she was no longer mistress of her own household. She had her daughters to instruct, and to train up in domestic ways, and she could be helpful in various matters, large and small; but the mental occupation which comes from the oversight and direction of household affairs, and which might have served to divert her mind from sorrowful memories, was now gone from her. Her widowhood separated her from the outside world and from all society, excepting a few devoted friends, [Footnote: *Wide Awake*, xxxiii. 502.] so that under these conditions it is not surprising that her life became continually more secluded and reserved. It is probable that her temperament was very similar to her son's; but the impression which has gone forth, that she indulged her melancholy to an excess, is by no means a just one. The circumstances of her case should be taken into consideration.

Rebecca Manning says:

"I remember aunt Hawthorne as busy about the house, attending to various matters. Her cooking was excellent, and she was noted for a certain kind of sauce, which nobody else knew how to make. We always enjoyed going to see her when we were children, for she took great pains to please us and to give us nice things to eat. Her daughter Elizabeth resembled her in that respect. In old letters and in the journal of another aunt, which has come into our possession, we read of her going about making visits, taking drives, and sometimes going on a journey. In later years she was not well, and I do not remember that she ever came here, but her friends always received a cordial welcome when they visited her."

This refers to a late period of Madam Hathorne's life, and if she absented herself from the table, as Elizabeth Peabody states, [Footnote: Lathrop's "Study of Hawthorne."] there was good reason for it.

Hawthorne himself has left no word concerning his mother, of favorable or unfavorable import, but it seems probable that he owed his genius to her, if he can be said to have owed it to any of his ancestors. In after life he affirmed that his sister Elizabeth, who appears to have been her mother over again, could have written as well as he did, and although we have no palpable evidence of this—and the letter which she wrote Elizabeth Peabody does not indicate it,—we are willing to take his word for it. With the shyness and proud reserve which he inherited from his mother, there also came that exquisite refinement and feminine grace of style which forms the chief charm of his writing. The same refinement of feeling is noticeable in the letters of other members of the Manning family. Where his imagination came from, it would be useless to speculate; but there is no good art without delicacy.

Doctor Nathaniel Peabody lived near the house on Herbert Street, and his daughter Elizabeth (who afterward became a woman of prodigious learning) soon made acquaintance with the Hathorne children. She remembers the boy Nathaniel jumping about his uncle's yard, and this is the first picture that we have of him. When we consider what a beautiful boy he must have been, with his wavy brown hair, large wistful eyes and vigorous figure, without doubt he was a pleasure to look upon. We do not hear of him again until November 10, 1813, when he injured his foot in some unknown manner while at play, and was made lame by it more or less for the three years succeeding. After being laid up for a month, he wrote this pathetic little letter to his uncle, Robert Manning, then in Maine, which I have punctuated properly so that the excellence of its composition may appeal more plainly to the reader.

"SALEM, Thursday, December, 1813.

"DEAR UNCLE:

"I hope you are well, and I hope Richard is too. My foot is no better. Louisa has got so well that she has begun to go to school, but she did not go this forenoon because it snowed. Mama is going to send for Doctor Kitridge to–day, when William Cross comes home at 12 o'clock, and maybe he will do some good, for Doctor Barstow has not, and I don't know as Doctor Kitridge will. It is about 4 weeks yesterday since I have been to school, and I don't know but it will be 4 weeks longer before I go again. I have been out of the office two or three times and have set down on the step of the door, and once I hopped out into the street. Yesterday I went out in the office and had 4 cakes. Hannah carried me out once, but not then. Elizabeth and Louisa send their love to you. I hope you will write to me soon, but I have nothing more to write; so good–bye, dear Uncle.

"Your affectionate Nephew,
"NATHANIEL HATHORNE." [Footnote: Elizabeth Manning in *Wide Awake*, Nov. 1891.]

This is not so precocious as Mozart's musical compositions at the same age, but how could the boy Hawthorne have given a clearer account of himself and his situation at the time, without one word of complaint? It is worth noting also that his prediction in regard to Doctor Kitridge proved to be correct and even more.

It is evident that neither of his doctors treated him in a physio–logical manner. Kitridge was a water–cure physician, and his method of treatment deserves to be recorded for its novelty. He directed Nathaniel to project his naked foot out of a sitting–room window, while he poured cold water on it from the story above. This, however, does not appear to have helped the case, and the infirmity continued so long that it was generally feared that his lameness would be permanent.

Horatio Bridge considered this a fortunate accident for Nathaniel, since it prevented him from being spoiled by his female relatives, as there is always danger that an only son with two or more sisters will be spoiled. But it was an advantage to the boy in a different manner from this. He learned from it the lesson of suffering and endurance, which we all have to learn sooner or later; and it compelled him, perhaps too young, to seek the comfort of life from internal sources. There were excellent books in the house,—Shakespeare and Milton, of course, but also Pope's "Iliad," Thomson's "Seasons," the "Spectator," "Pilgrim's Progress," and the "Faerie Queene," and the time had now come when these would be serviceable to him. He was not the only boy that has enjoyed Shakespeare at the age of ten, but that he should have found interest in Spenser's "Faerie Queene" is somewhat exceptional. Even among professed *litterateurs* there are few that read that long allegory, and still fewer who enjoy it; and yet Miss Manning assures us that Hawthorne would muse over it for hours. Its influence may be perceptible in some of his shorter stories, but "Pilgrim's Progress" evidently had an effect upon him; and so had Scott's novels, as we may judge from the first romance that he published.

At the age of twelve years and seven months he composed a short poem, so perfect in form and mature in judgment that it is difficult to believe that so young a person could have written it. Not so poetic as it is philosophical, it is valuable as indicating that the boy had already formed a moral axis for himself,—a life principle from which he never afterward deviated; and it is given herewith: [Footnote: A facsimile of the original can be found in *Wide Awake*, November, 1891.]

> "MODERATE VIEWS.
>
> "With passions unruffled, untainted by pride,
>   By reason my life let me square;
> The wants of my nature are cheaply supplied,
>   And the rest are but folly and care.
> How vainly through infinite trouble and strife,
>   The many their labours employ,
> Since all, that is truly delightful in life,
>   Is what all if they please may enjoy.
>
> "NATHANIEL HATHORNE.
> "SALEM, February 13, 1817."

He wrote this with the greatest nicety, framing it in broad black lines, and ornamenting the capitals in a manner that recalls the decoration of John Hathorne's gravestone. He composed a number of poems between his thirteenth and seventeenth years, quite as good as those of Longfellow at the same age; but after he entered Bowdoin College he dropped the practice altogether and never resumed it, although one would suppose that Longfellow's example would have stimulated him to better efforts. Neither does he appear to have tried his hand in writing tales, as boys who have no thought of literary distinction frequently do. During the years of his lameness he sometimes invented extemporaneous stories, which invariably commenced with a voyage to some foreign country, from which his hero never returned. This shows how continually his father's fate was in his mind, although he said nothing of it.

Robert Manning's interest in the stage-company afforded the boy fine opportunities for free rides, and he probably also frequented the stables; although neither as youth nor as man did he take much interest in driving or riding. He was more fond of playing upon the wharves, a good healthy place,—and watching the great ships sailing forth to far-off lands, and returning with their strange cargoes,—enough to stimulate any boy's imagination, if he has it in him. It is likely that if Nathaniel's father had lived, he would also have followed a seafaring life, and would never have become useful to the world in the way that he did.

Somewhere about the close of the eighteenth century, Richard Manning, the father of Mrs. Hathorne, purchased a large tract of land in Cumberland County, Maine, between Lake Sebago and the town of Casco; and in 1813 Robert Manning built a house near the lake, in the township of Raymond, and his brother Richard, who had become much of an invalid, went to live there, partly for his health and partly to keep an oversight on the property. In 1817 Mrs. Hathorne also went there, taking her children with her, and remaining, with some intermissions, until 1822. Meanwhile the Mannings sold some thousands of acres of land, although not, as we may suppose, at very good prices, and the name of Elizabeth Hathorne was repeatedly attached to the deeds of conveyance. The house that Robert built was the plainest sort of structure, of only two stories, and with no appearance of having been painted; but the farmers in the vicinity criticised it as "Manning's folly,"—exactly why, does not appear clearly, unless they foresaw what actually happened, that the house could be neither sold nor rented after the Mannings had left it. For many years, it served as a meeting-house,—one could not call it a church,—and now it has become a Hawthorne museum, the town of Raymond very laudably keeping it in repair.

Although none of the events in the early life of Hawthorne ought to be considered positive misfortunes, as they all contributed to make him what he was, yet upon general principles it is much to be regretted that he should have passed the best years of his boyhood in this out-of-the-way place. His good uncle supplied him with a boat and a gun, and he enjoyed the small shooting, fishing, sailing and skating that the place afforded; but in later years he wrote to Bridge, "It was at Sebago that I learned my cursed habit of solitude," and this pursued him through life like an evil genius, placing him continually at a disadvantage with his fellow–men. It has been supposed that this mode of life assisted in developing his individuality, but quite as strong individualities have been developed in the midst of large cities. "Speech is more refreshing than light."

When will parents learn wisdom in regard to their children? A conscientious, tender–hearted boy will be sent to a rough country school, to be scoffed at and maltreated there, before he is twelve years old; while another of a coarser and harder nature will be kept at home, to be petted and pampered until all the vigor and manliness are sapped out of him. Parents who prefer to live in a modest, humble manner, in order that their children may have better advantages, deserve the highest commendation, but in this respect good instruction is less important than favorable associations. From fourteen to twenty–one is the formative period of character, and the influences which may be brought to bear on the growing mind are of the highest importance. Lake Sebago served as an excellent gymnasium for young Hawthorne, and may have helped to develop his sense of the beautiful, but he found few companions there, and those not of the most suitable kind. He was exceedingly fond of skating—so much so that when the ice was smooth he sometimes remained on the lake far into the night. This we can envy him, for skating is the poetry of motion.

The captain of the "Hawthorne," which plies back and forth across the lake in summer, regularly points out to his passengers the house where the Hathornes lived. It is easily seen from the steamer,—a severely plain, unpainted building, in appearance much like the Manning house on Herbert Street. Nearly in line with it a great cliff–like rock juts out from the centre of the lake, on which the Indians centuries ago etched and painted great warlike figures, whose significance is now known to no one. It is said that Hawthorne frequently sailed or rowed to Indian Rock, and to a sort of grotto there which was large enough for his boat to enter. Both the rock and the Manning house are now difficult of access. Longfellow wrote a pretty descriptive poem of a voyage on Sebago, and it is remarkable how he has made use of every feature of the landscape, every incident of the excursion, to fill his verses. The lake has much the shape of an hour–glass, the northern and southern portions being connected by a winding strait, so crooked that it requires the constant effort of the pilot to prevent the little steamer from running aground. There used to be fine fishing in it,—large perch, bass, and a species of fresh–water salmon often weighing from six to eight pounds.

Strangely enough, one of Hawthorne's acquaintances on the shores of Sebago was a mulatto boy named William Symmes, the son of a Virginia slave, foisted by his father upon a Maine sea–captain named Britton, who lived in the half–wilderness around Raymond. Symmes afterwards became a sailor, and continued in that vocation until the Civil War, when he went to live in Alexandria, Va. In 1870 he published in the Portland *Transcript* what pretended to be a series of extracts from a diary which young Hawthorne had kept while at Raymond, and which was found there, after the departure of the Manning family, by a man named Small, while moving a load of furniture which had been sold to another party. Small preserved it until 1864, and then made a present of it to Symmes.

Doubts have been cast on the genuineness of this diary, as was natural enough under the circumstances; for the original manuscript was never produced by Symmes, who died the following year, and no one knows what has become of it. It may also be asked, why should Small have disposed so readily of this manuscript to Symmes after preserving it sedulously for more than forty years? Why did he not return it to its rightful owner; or, if he felt ashamed of his original abstraction, why did not Symmes restore it to the Hawthorne family after Hawthorne's death, when every newspaper in the country was celebrating Hawthorne's genius? It also might have occurred to one of them that such property would have a marketable value, and could be disposed of at a high price to some collector of literary curiosities; but Symmes did not even ask to be remunerated for the portion that he contributed to the Portland Transcript. Neither did he harbor the slightest ill feeling toward Hawthorne, whom he claimed to have met several times in the course of his wanderings,—once at Salem, and again at Liverpool,—and was always treated by him with exceptional kindness and civility.

The only answer that can be made to these queries is, that men in Symmes's position in life do not act according to any method that can be previously calculated. In a case like the present, there could be no predicting it; and it is possible that this mulatto valued the diary above all price, as a souvenir of the one white man who had ever been kind and good to him. Who knows what a heart there may have been in William Symmes?

The internal evidence of this diary is so strongly in its favor as to be almost conclusive. Lathrop, who made a special study of it, says:

The Life and Genius of Nathaniel Hawthorne

"The fabrication of the journal by a person possessed of some literary skill and familiar with the localities mentioned, at dates so long ago as 1816 to 1819, might not be an impossible feat, but it is an extremely improbable one."

To which it might be added, that it could be only a Hawthorne that could accomplish such a fabrication. Few things in literature are more difficult than to make a boy talk *like* a boy, and the tone of this Sebago journal is not only boyish, but sweet and pleasant to the ear, such as we might imagine the talk of the youthful Hawthorne. Not only this, but there is a gradated improvement of intelligence in the course of it,—rather too much so for entire credibility. It is quite possible that there is more of it than Hawthorne ever wrote, but that does not prevent us from having faith in the larger portion of it. The purity of its diction, the nice adaptation of each word to its purpose, and the accuracy of detail are much in its favor; besides which, the personal reflections in it are exactly like Hawthorne. The published portion of the diary in Mr. Pickard's book makes about fifty rather small pages, but no dates are given except at the close, and that is August, 1818; and as Hawthorne went to Sebago for the first time the preceding year, we may presume that this note–book represents a winter and summer vacation, during which he would seem to have enjoyed himself in a healthy boyish fashion. We have only space for a few extracts from this publication, which serve both to exemplify Hawthorne's mode of life at Raymond and to illustrate the preceding statement concerning the book.

The first observation in the diary is quoted by Lathrop, and has a decidedly youthful tone.

"Two kingbirds have built their nest between our house and the mill–pond. The male is more courageous than any creature that I know about. He seems to have taken possession of the territory from the great pond to the small one, and goes out to war with every fish–hawk that flies from one to the other over his dominion. The fish–hawks must be miserable cowards to be driven by such a speck of a bird. I have not yet seen one turn to defend himself."

Kingbirds are the knights–errant of the feathered tribes. They never attack another bird unless it is three times their own size; but when a few years older, the boy Hawthorne would probably have noticed that the kingbirds' powers of flight are so superior that all other birds are practically at their mercy. This fixes the date of the entry in the early summer of 1817, for kingbirds are not belligerent except during the nesting season. Somewhat later in the year he writes:

25

"Went yesterday in a sail–boat on the Great Pond with Mr. Peter White, of Windham. He sailed up here from White's Bridge to see Captain Dingley, and invited Joseph Dingley and Mr. Ring to take a boat–ride out to the Dingley Islands and to the Images. He was also kind enough to say that I might go, with my mother's consent, which she gave after much coaxing. Since the loss of my father, she dreads to have any one belonging to her go upon the water. It is strange that this beautiful body of water is called a 'pond.' The geography tells of many in Scotland and Ireland, not near so large, that are called 'Lakes.'"

Notice his objection to bad nomenclature, and his school–boy argument against it. In his account of this excursion he says further:

"After we got ashore, Mr. White allowed me to fire his long gun at a mark. I did not hit the mark, and am not sure that I saw it at the time the gun went off, but believe rather that I was watching for the noise that I was about to make.

"Mr. Ring said that with practice I could be a gunner, and that now, with a very heavy charge, he thought I could kill a horse at eight paces!"

Here or nowhere do we recognize the budding of Hawthorne's genius. This clear introspective analysis is the foundation of all true mental power, and Hawthorne might have become a Platonic philosopher, if he had not preferred to be a story–teller.

These sports came to an end in the autumn when he was sent to study with the Reverend Caleb Bradley, a somewhat eccentric graduate of Harvard, who resided at Stroudwater, Maine, and with whom he remained during the winter. [Footnote: S. T. Pickard's "Hawthorne's First Diary."]He refers to this period of tuition in the short story of "The Vision of the Fountain," and whether or no any such vision appeared to him, we can fairly believe that the tale was suggested by some pretty school–girl who made an impression on him, only to disappear in a tantalizing manner. It is to be presumed that he returned to his mother at Raymond, for Christmas; and at that time he heard a story of how an Otisfield man named Henry Turner had killed three hibernating bears which he discovered in a cave near Moose Pond, not a difficult feat when one comes upon them in that torpid condition. This would place the killing of the bears at about the first of December, which would be probable enough, and the fact itself has been substantiated by Samuel Pickard. The next succeeding entry relates to the drowning of a boy while swimming, which could only have happened the following June. Mrs. Hathorne was greatly alarmed, and objected to Nathaniel's going in bathing with the other boys. He did not like the restriction, but writes that he shall obey his mother.

There is a ghost story in the diary, quite original, and told with an air of excellent credibility; and also a short anthropomorphic romance concerning a badly treated horse, full of genuine pathos and kindly sympathy,—more sympathetic, in fact, than Hawthorne's later stories, in which he is sometimes almost too reserved and unemotional:

"'Good morning, Mr. Horse, how are you to–day?' 'Good morning, youngster,' said he, just as plain as a horse can speak, and then said, 'I am almost dead, and I wish I was quite. I am hungry, have had no breakfast and stand here tied by the head while they are grinding the corn, and until master drinks two or three glasses of rum at the store, and then drag him and the meal up the Ben Ham hill, and home, and am now so weak that I can hardly stand. Oh, dear, I am in a bad way,' and the old creature cried,—I almost cried myself."

The only difficulty in believing this diary to be genuine is the question: If Hawthorne could write with such perspicuity at fourteen, why are there no evidences of it during his college years? But it sometimes happens so.

We cannot refrain from quoting one more extract from the last entry in the Sebago diary, so beautifully tender and considerate as it is of his mother's position toward her only son. He had been invited by a party of their neighbors to go on an all–day excursion, and though his mother grants his request to be allowed to join them, he feels the reluctance with which she does so and he writes:

"She said 'Yes,' but I was almost sorry, knowing that my day's pleasure would cost *her* one of anxiety. However, I gathered up my hooks and lines, with some white salted pork for bait, and with a fabulous number of biscuit, split in the middle, the insides well buttered, then skilfully put together again, and all stowed in sister's large work– bag, and slung over my shoulder, I started, making a wager with Enoch White, as we walked down to the boat, as to which could catch the largest number of fish." [Footnote: Appendix A.]

This is the only entry that is dated (August, 1818), and as it was on this same occasion that the black ducks were shot, it must have been on one of the last days of August. We may presume that Nathaniel returned to his studies at Stroudwater the following month, for we do not hear of him again at Raymond—or in Salem, either—until March 24, when he writes to his uncle, Robert Manning, who has evidently just returned from Raymond to Salem, and speaks of expecting to go to Portland with a Mr. Linch for the day. On May 16, 1819, he writes to his uncle Robert again:

"The grass and trees are green, the fences finished and the garden planted. Two of the goats are on the island and the other kept for the milk. I have shot a partridge and a hen–hawk and caught eighteen large trout [probably Sebago salmon]. I am sorry that my uncle intends sending me to school again, for my mother can hardly spare me."

From which it is easy to infer that he had not attended school very regularly of late, and Uncle Robert would seem to have concluded that it would be better to have his fine nephew where he could personally supervise his goings and comings. Accordingly, on July 26 we find Nathaniel attending school in Salem,—a most unusual season for it,— and although his mother remained at Raymond two years longer, he was not permitted to return there again, except possibly for short periods.

Emerson once pointed out to me on Sudbury Street, Boston, an extremely old man with long white locks and the face of a devoted scholar, advancing toward us with slow and cautious steps. "That," said he, "is Doctor Worcester, the lexicographer." Hawthorne's early education remains much of a mystery. In 1819 he complains in a letter to his mother that he has to go to a cheap school,—a good indication that he did not intend to trust to fortune for his future welfare; soon after this we hear that dictionary Worcester is his chief instructor. He could not have found a more amiable or painstaking pedagogue; nor is it likely that the fine qualities of his teacher were ever better appreciated. Hawthorne himself says nothing of this, for it was not his way to express admiration for man or woman, but we can believe that he felt the same affection for the doctor that well–behaved boys commonly do for their old masters. It was from Worcester that he derived his excellent knowledge of Latin, the single study of which he was fond; and it is his preference for words derived from the Latin which gives grace and flexibility to Hawthorne's style, as the force and severity of Emerson's style come from his partiality for Saxon words. During his last year at school, Hawthorne took private lessons of a Salem lawyer, Benjamin Oliver, and perhaps studied with him altogether at the finish.

The Life and Genius of Nathaniel Hawthorne

Hawthorne's life had been so irregular for years that it is creditable to him that he should have succeeded in entering college at all. We hear of him at Sebago in winter and at Salem in July. He writes to his Uncle Robert to look out for the shot–gun which he left in a closet at Sebago, and which has a rather heavy charge of powder in it. He appears to have found as little companionship in Salem as he did in that wilderness,—the natural effect of such a life. He may have been acquainted with half the boys in Salem, but he did not make any warm friends among them. His sister Louisa, who was a more vivacious person than Elizabeth, was his chief companion and comfort. Seated at the window with her on summer evenings, he elaborated the plan of an imaginary society, a club of two, called the "Pin Society," to which all fees, assessments and fines were paid in pins,—then made by hand and much more expensive than now. He constituted himself its secretary, and wrote imaginary reports of its proceedings, in which Louisa is frequently fined for absence from meetings. We do not hear of their going to parties or dances with other children.

In August, 1820, he started an imaginary newspaper called the *Spectator*, which he wrote himself with some help from Louisa, and of which there was only one copy of each number. He continued this through five successive issues, and we trace in its pages the commencement of Hawthorne's peculiar humor,—too quiet and gentle to make us laugh, but with a penetrating tinge of pathos. Take for instance the following:

"There is no situation in life more irksome than that of an editor who is obliged to find amusement for his Readers, from a head which is too often (as is the present predicament with our own) filled with emptiness. Since commencing this paper, we have received no communication of any kind, so that the whole weight of the business devolves upon our own shoulders, a load far too great for them to bear. We hope the Public will reflect on these grievances."

This is true fiction, and Nathaniel was not the first or the last editor to whom the statement has applied. His difficulties are imaginary, but he realizes what they might be in reality.

In another number he says:

"We know of no news, either domestic or foreign, and we hope our readers will excuse our not inserting any. The law which prohibits paying debts when a person has no money will apply in this case."

Then he makes this quiet hit against the people of Maine for having separated themselves and their territory from Massachusetts:

"By a gentleman in the state of Maine, we learn that a famine is seriously apprehended owing to the want of rain. Potatoes could not be procured in some places. When children break their leading strings, and run away from their Parent, (as Maine has done) they may expect sometimes to suffer hunger." [Footnote: *Wide Awake*, xxxiii. 512.]

Of his religious instruction we hear nothing; but church–going in New England during the first forty years of the nineteenth century was wellnigh universal, and it makes little difference now to which of the various forms of Calvinistic worship the Manning family subscribed. That young Hawthorne was seriously impressed in this way is evident from the following ode, which he may have composed as early as his fifteenth year:

> "Oh, I have roamed in rapture wild
> Where the majestic rocks are piled
> In lonely, stern, magnificence around
> The troubled ocean's steadfast bound;
> And I have seen the storms arise
> And darkness veil from mortal eyes
> The Heavens that shine so fair and bright,
> And all was solemn, silent night.
> Then I have seen the storm disperse,
> And Mercy hush the whirlwind fierce,
> And all my soul in transport owned
> There is a God, in Heaven enthroned."

There is more of a rhetorical flourish than of serious religious feeling in this; but genuine piety is hardly to be expected, and not greatly to be desired, in a boy of that age. It represents the desire to be religious, and to express something, he knows not what.

Nathaniel Hawthorne had already decided on his vocation in life before he entered Bowdoin College,—a decision which he afterwards adhered to with inflexible determination, in spite of the most discouraging obstacles. In a memorable letter to his mother, written March 13, 1821, he says:

"I am quite reconciled to going to college, since I am to spend my vacations with you. Yet four years of the best part of my life is a great deal to throw away. I have not yet concluded what profession I shall have. The being a minister is of course out of the question. I shall not think that even you could desire me to choose so dull a way of life. Oh, no, mother, I was not born to vegetate forever in one place, and to live and die as tranquil as—a puddle of water. As to lawyers, there are so many of them already that one–half of them (upon a moderate calculation) are in a state of actual starvation. A physician, then, seems to be 'Hobson's choice'; but yet I should not like to live by the diseases and infirmities of my fellow–creatures. And it would weigh very hardly on my conscience, in the course of my practice, if I should chance to send any unlucky patient 'ad infernum,' which, being interpreted, is 'to the realms below.' Oh that I was rich enough to live without profession! What do you think of my becoming an author, and relying for support upon my pen? Indeed, I think the illegibility of my hand is very author–like." [Footnote: Conway, 24.]

Such were the Ides of March for Hawthorne. It was no boyish ambition for public distinction, nor a vain grasping at the laurel wreath, but a calmly considered and clear–sighted judgment.

CHAPTER III. BOWDOIN COLLEGE: 1821–1825.

The life of man is not like a game of chess, in which the two players start upon equal terms and can deliberate sufficiently over every move; but more like whist, in which the cards we hold represent our fortunes at the beginning, but the result of the game depends also on the skill with which we play it. Life also resembles whist in this, that we are obliged to follow suit in a general way to those who happen to have the lead.

Why Hawthorne should have entered Bowdoin College instead of Harvard has not been explained, nor is it easily explained. The standard of scholarship maintained at Harvard and Yale has always been higher than that at what Doctor Holmes designated as the "freshwater colleges," and this may have proved an unfavorable difference to the mind of a young man who was not greatly inclined to his studies; but Harvard College is only eighteen miles from Salem, and he could have returned to his home once a week if he had chosen to do so, and this is a decided moral and social advantage to a young man in those risky years. If Hawthorne had entered Harvard in the next class to Emerson, he could not well have escaped the latter's attention, and would have come in contact with other vigorous and stimulating minds; but it is of little use to speculate on what might have been.

Boys are encouraged to study for college by accounts of the rare enjoyment of university life, but they commonly find the first term of Freshman year both dismal and discouraging. Their class is a medley of strangers, their studies are a dry routine, and if they are not hazed by the Sophomores, they are at least treated by them with haughtiness and contempt. It is still summer when they arrive, but the leaves soon fall from the trees, and their spirits fall with them.

Hawthorne may have felt this more acutely than any other member of his class, and in addition to the prevailing sense of discomfort he was seized early in November with that disgusting malady, the measles, which boys usually go through with before they are old enough to realize how disagreeable it is. It appears to have been a light attack, however, and in three weeks he was able to attend recitations again. He made no complaint of it, only writing to his uncle for ten dollars with which to pay the doctor. He likes his chum, Mason, of Portsmouth, and does not find his studies so arduous as at Salem before entering. Neither are the college laws so strict as he anticipated.

In the following May he received the present of his first watch, presumably from Uncle Robert, and he writes to his mother, who is still at Sebago, that he is mightily pleased with it, and that it enables him "to cut a great dash" at college. His letters to his relatives are not brilliant, but they indicate a healthful and contented mind.

We will now consider some of the distinguished personages who were Hawthorne's friends and associates during these four years of his apprenticeship to actual life; and there were rare characters among them.

In the same coach in which Hawthorne left Portland for Brunswick, in the summer of 1821, were Franklin Pierce and Jonathan Cilley. [Footnote: Bridge's Memoir of Hawthorne, 3.] Two men seated together in a modern railway–carriage will often become better acquainted in three hours than they might as next–door neighbors in three years; and this was still more likely to happen in the old days of coach journeys, when the very tedium of the occasion served as an inducement to frank and friendly conversation. Pierce was the right man to bring Hawthorne out of his hard shell of Sebago seclusion. He had already been one year at Bowdoin, and at that time there was not the same caste feeling between Sophomores and Freshmen—or at least very little of it—that has since arisen in American colleges. He was amiable and kindly, and possessed the rare gift of personal magnetism. Nature sometimes endows men and women with this quality in lieu of all other advantages, and such would seem to have been the case with Franklin Pierce. He was not much above the average in intellect, and, as Hawthorne afterward confessed, not particularly attractive in appearance; with a stiff military neck, features strong but small, and opaque gray eyes,—a rather unimpressive face, and one hardly capable of a decided expression. Yet with such abilities as he had, aided by personal magnetism and the lack of conspicuous faults, he became United States Senator at the age of thirty–five, and President fifteen years later. The best we can say of him is, that he was always Hawthorne's friend. From the first day that they met he became Hawthorne's patron and protector—so far as he may have required the latter. There must have been some fine quality in the man which is not easily discernible from his outward acts; a narrow–minded man, but of a refined nature.

Jonathan Cilley was an abler man than Pierce, and a bold party–leader, but not so attractive personally. He always remained Hawthorne's friend, but the latter saw little of him and rarely heard from him after they had graduated. The one letter of his which has been published gives the impression of an impulsive, rough–and–tumble sort of person, always ready to take a hand in whatever might turn up.

On the same day, Horatio Bridge, who lived at Augusta, was coming down the Kennebec River to Brunswick. Hawthorne did not make his acquaintance until some weeks later, but he proved to be the best friend of them all, and Hawthorne's most constant companion during the four years they remained together. Pierce, Cilley and Bridge were all born politicians, and it was this class of men with whom it would seem that Hawthorne naturally assimilated.

On the same day, or the one previous, another boy set out from Portland for Brunswick, only fourteen years old, named Henry W. Longfellow,—a name that is now known to thousands who never heard of Franklin Pierce. Would it have made a difference in the warp and woof of Hawthorne's life, if he had happened to ride that day in the same coach with Longfellow? Who can tell? Was there any one in the breadth of the land with whom he might have felt an equal sympathy, with whom he could have matured a more enduring fellowship? It might have been a friendship like that of Beaumont and Fletcher, or, better still, like that of Goethe and Schiller,—but it was not written in the book of Fate. Longfellow also had tried his hand on the Sebago region, and was fond of the woods and of a gun; but he was too precocious to adapt himself easily to persons of his own age, or even somewhat older. He had no sooner arrived at Bowdoin than he became the associate and favorite of the professors. In this way he missed altogether the storm–and–stress period of youthful life, which is a useful experience of its kind; and if we notice in his poetry a certain lack, the absence of a close contact with reality,—as if he looked at his subject through a glass casement,—this may be assigned as the reason for it.

[Illustration: HORATIO BRIDGE. FROM THE PORTRAIT BY EASTMAN JOHNSON]

During the four years they went back and forth to their instruction together, Hawthorne and Longfellow never became cordially acquainted. They also belonged to rival societies. There were only two principal societies at Bowdoin, which continued through the college course—the Peucinian and the Athenaan, and the difference between them might be described by the words "citified" and "countrified," without taking either of those terms in an objectionable sense. Pierce was already a leading character in the Athenaan, and was soon followed by Cilley, Bridge and Hawthorne. The Peucinian suffered from the disadvantage of having members of the college faculty on its active list, and this must have given a rather constrained and academic character to its meetings. There was much more of the true college spirit and classmate feeling in the Athenaan.

Horatio Bridge is our single authority in regard to Bowdoin College at this time, and his off–hand sketches of Hawthorne, Pierce and Longfellow are invaluable. Never has such a group of distinguished young men been gathered together at an American college. He says of Hawthorne:

"Hawthorne was a slender lad, having a massive head, with dark, brilliant, and most expressive eyes, heavy eyebrows, and a profusion of dark hair. For his appearance at that time the inquirers must rely wholly upon the testimony of friends; for, I think, no portrait of him as a lad is extant. On one occasion, in our senior years, the class wished to have their profiles cut in silhouette by a wandering artist of the scissors, and interchanged by

34

all the thirty–eight. Hawthorne disapproved the proposed plan, and steadily refused to go into the Class Golgotha, as he styled the dismal collection. I joined him in this freak, and so our places were left vacant. I now regret the whim, since even a moderately correct outline of his features as a youth would, at this day, be interesting.

"Hawthorne's figure was somewhat singular, owing to his carrying his head a little on one side; but his walk was square and firm, and his manner self–respecting and reserved. A fashionable boy of the present day might have seen something to amuse him in the new student's appearance; but had he indicated this he would have rued it, for Hawthorne's clear appreciation of the social proprieties and his great physical courage would have made it as unsafe to treat him with discourtesy then as at any later time.

"Though quiet and most amiable, he had great pluck and determination. I remember that in one of our convivial meetings we had the laugh upon him for some cause, an occurrence so rare that the bantering was carried too far. After bearing it awhile, Hawthorne singled out the one among us who had the reputation of being the best pugilist, and in a few words quietly told him that he would not permit the rallying to go farther. His bearing was so resolute, and there was so much of danger in his eye, that no one afterward alluded to the offensive subject in his presence." [Footnote: Horatio Bridge, 5.]

Horatio Bridge is a veracious witness, but we have to consider that he was nearly ninety years of age at the time his memoirs were given to the public. It is difficult to imagine Hawthorne as a slender youth, for his whole figure was in keeping with the structure of his head. It is more likely that he had a spare figure. Persons of a lively imagination have always been apt to hold their heads on one side, but not commonly while they are walking. It is for this reason that phrenologists have supposed that the organ of ideality is located on the side of the head,—if there really is any such organ.

Bridge says of Longfellow precisely what one might expect:

"He had decided personal beauty and most attractive manners. He was frank, courteous, and affable, while morally he was proof against the temptations that beset lads on first leaving the salutary restraints of home. He was diligent, conscientious, and most attentive to all his college duties, whether in the recitation–room, the lecture–hall, or the chapel. The word 'student' best expresses his literary habit, and in his intercourse with all he was conspicuously the gentleman."

In addition to those already mentioned, James W. Bradbury of Portland, afterwards United States Senator, and the Reverend Dr. George B. Cheever, the vigorous anti–slavery preacher, were members of this class. Three others, Cilley, Benson and Sawtelle, were afterward members of the United States House of Representatives. Surely there must have been quite a fermentation of youthful intellect at Bowdoin between 1821 and 1825.

Franklin Pierce was so deeply interested in military affairs that it was a pity he should not have had a West Point cadetship. He was captain of the college militia company, in which Hawthorne and Bridge drilled and marched; a healthy and profitable exercise, and better than a gymnasium, if rather monotonous. Pierce was the popular hero and *magnus Apollo* of his class, as distinguished foot–ball players are now; but just at this time he was neglecting his studies so badly that at the close of his second year he found himself at the very foot of the rank list. The fact became known through the college, and Pierce was so chagrined that he concluded to withdraw from Bowdoin altogether, and it was only by the urgent persuasion of his friends that he was induced to continue his course. "If I remain, however," he said, "you will witness a change in me." For months together he burned midnight oil in order to recover lost ground. During his last two years at college, he only missed two recitations, both for sufficient reasons. His conduct was unexceptionable, he incurred no deductions, and finally graduated third in his class. It is an uncommon character that can play fast–and–loose with itself in this manner. The boy Franklin had departed, and Pierce the man had taken his place. [Footnote: Professor Packard's "History of Bowdoin College."] Horatio Bridge gives a rather more idealized portrait of him than he does of Hawthorne. He says:

"In person Pierce was slender, of medium height, with fair complexion and light hair, erect, with a military bearing, active, and always bright and cheerful. In character he was impulsive, not rash; generous, not lavish; chivalric, courteous, manly, and warm–hearted,—and he was one of the most popular students in the whole college."

The instruction in American colleges during the first half of the nineteenth century was excellent for Greek, Latin and mathematics,— always the groundwork of a good education,—but the modern languages were indifferently taught by French and German exiles, and other subjects were treated still more indifferently. The two noble studies of history and philosophy were presented to the young aspiring soul in narrow, prejudiced text-books, which have long since been consigned to that bourn from which no literary work ever returns. As already stated, Hawthorne's best study was Latin, and in that he acquired good proficiency; but he was slow in mathematics, as artistic minds usually are, and in his other studies he only exerted himself sufficiently to pass his examinations in a creditable manner. We may presume that he took the juice and left the rind; which was the sensible thing to do. As might be expected, his themes and forensics were beautifully written, although the arguments in them were not always logical; but it is significant that he never could be prevailed upon to make a declamation. There have been sensitive men, like Sumner and George W. Curtis, who were not at all afraid of the platform, but they were not, like Hawthorne, bashful men. The college faculty would seem to have realized the true difficulty in his case, and treated him in a kindly and lenient manner. No doubt he suffered enough in his own mind on account of this deficiency, and it may have occurred to him what difficulties he might have to encounter in after-life by reason of it. If a student at college cannot bring himself to make a declamation, how can the mature man face an audience in a lecture-room, command a ship, or administer any important office? Such thoughts must have caused Hawthorne no slight anxiety, at that sensitive age.

The out-door sports of the students did not attract Hawthorne greatly. He was a fast runner and a good leaper, but seemed to dislike violent exercise. He much preferred walking in the woods with a single companion, or by the banks of the great river on which Brunswick is situated. There were fine trout-brooks in the neighborhood, and formerly the woods of Maine were traversed by vast flocks of passenger pigeons, which with the large gray squirrels afforded excellent shooting. How skilful Hawthorne became with his fowling-piece we have not been informed, but it is evident from passages in "Fanshawe" that he learned something of trout-fishing; and on the whole he enjoyed advantages at Bowdoin which the present student at Harvard or Oxford might well envy, him. The fish we catch in the streams and lakes of Maine only represent a portion of our enjoyment there. Horatio Bridge says:

"There was one favorite spot in a little ravine, where a copious spring of clear, cold water gushed out from the sandy bank, and joined the larger stream. This was the Paradise Spring, which deserves much more than its present celebrity for the absolute purity of its waters. Of late years the brook has been better known as a favorite haunt of the great romance writer, and it is now often called the Hawthorne Brook.

"Another locality, above the bridge, afforded an occasional stroll through the fields and by the river. There, in spring, we used to linger for hours to watch the giant pine–logs (for there were giants in those days) from the far–off forests, floating by hundreds in the stream until they came to the falls; then, balancing for a moment on the brink, they plunged into the foamy pool below."

At the lower end of the town there was an old weather–beaten cot, where the railroad track now runs, inhabited by a lone woman nearly as old and time–worn as the dwelling itself. She pretended to be a fortune– teller, and to her Hawthorne and Bridge sometimes had recourse, to lift the veil of their future prospects; which she always succeeded in doing to their good entertainment. The old crone knew her business well, especially the art of giving sufficient variety of detail to the same old story. For a nine–pence she would predict a beautiful blond wife for Hawthorne, and an equally handsome dark–complexioned one for Bridge. Riches were of course thrown in by the handful; and Bridge remarks that although these never came to pass they both happened to be blessed with excellent wives. It is not surprising that the handsome Hawthorne and his tall, elegant–looking companion should have stimulated the old woman's imagination in a favorable manner. The small coin they gave her may have been the least happiness that their visits brought into her life.

Close by the college grounds there was a miserable little inn, which went by the name of Ward's Tavern, and thither the more uproarious class of students consorted at intervals for the purpose of keeping care at a distance, and singing, "Landlord, fill your flowing bowls." Strange to say, the reserved, thoughtful Hawthorne was often to be found among them. It does not seem quite consistent with the gravity of his customary demeanor, but youth has its period of reckless ebullition. Punch–bowl societies exist in all our colleges, and many who disapprove of them join them for the sake of popularity. Hawthorne may have been as grave and well–behaved on these occasions as he was customarily. We have Bridge's word for this; and the matter would hardly be worth mentioning if it had not led to more serious proceedings. May 29, 1822, President Allen wrote to Mrs. Hathorne at Salem that her son had been fined fifty cents for gaming at cards. [Footnote: In 1864 a Harvard student was fined three dollars for writing on the woodwork with a lead–pencil—erased with a sponge.] Certainly this was not very severe treatment; and if the Bowdoin faculty, being on the spot, concluded that young Hawthorne had only injured his moral nature fifty cents' worth, I think we shall do well to agree with their decision. At the same time Nathaniel wrote his mother the following manly letter:

The Life and Genius of Nathaniel Hawthorne

"BRUNSWICK, May 30th, 1822.

"MY DEAR MOTHER:—I hope you have safely arrived in Salem. I have nothing particular to inform you of, except that all the card–players in college have been found out, and my unfortunate self among the number. One has been dismissed from college, two suspended, and the rest, with myself, have been fined fifty cents each. I believe the President intends to write to the friends of all the delinquents. Should that be the case, you must show the letter to nobody. If I am again detected, I shall have the honor of being suspended. When the President asked what we played for, I thought it proper to inform him it was fifty cents, although it happened to be a quart of wine; but if I had told him of that, he would probably have fined me for having a blow. There was no untruth in the case, as the wine cost fifty cents. I have not played at all this term. I have not drank any kind of spirits or wine this term, and shall not till the last week." [Footnote: Horatio Bridge, 118.]

The clemency with which the college authorities treated Bridge and Hawthorne is a plain indication of the confidence which they felt in them, and speaks more highly for their respective characters than if they had been patterns of good behavior. Some of the others were not so fortunate. One young man, whose name is properly withheld from us, was expelled from the institution. He was supposed to have been the ringleader in this dubious business, but Hawthorne manfully resented the supposition that any one could have influenced him, or did influence him, in this matter. It is more likely that he was influenced by the spirit of investigation, and wished to know what the sensation was like from personal experience.

"Letters home" from college are not commonly interesting to the general public, and those which Hawthorne wrote to his mother and sisters do not differ essentially from such as other young men write under similar conditions. At the age when it is so difficult to decide whether we have become men or are still boys, all our actions partake of a similar uncertainty, and the result of what we do and say is likely to be a rather confused impression. Though college students appear different enough to one another, they all seem alike to the outside world.

University towns always contain more or less cultivated society, and young Hawthorne might have been welcome to the best of it if he had felt so inclined; but he was as shy of the fair sex as Goldsmith's bashful lover. M. D. Conway, who knew him, doubts if he ever became well acquainted with a young lady until his engagement to Miss Peabody. Considering this, it seems as if Jonathan Cilley made rather a hazardous wager with Hawthorne, before leaving Bowdoin,—a wager of a cask of Madeira, that Hawthorne would become a married man within the next twelve years. Papers to that effect were duly signed by the respective parties, sealed, and delivered for safe–keeping to Horatio Bridge, who preserved them faithfully until the appointed time arrived. Under ordinary conditions the chances of this bet were in Cilley's favor, for in those primitive days it was much easier for educated young men to obtain a start in life than it is at present, and early marriages were in consequence much more common.[Footnote: Horatio Bridge, 47. The contract was dated November 14, 1824.]

The year 1824 was a serious one in American politics. The Republican– Democratic party, having become omnipotent, broke to pieces of its own weight. The eastern interest nominated John Quincy Adams for the Presidency; the western interest nominated Henry Clay; and the frontier interest nominated Andrew Jackson. Unfortunately the frontier interest included all the unsettled and continually shifting elements in the country, so that Jackson had nearly as strong a support in the East as in the West. Bridge says, "We were all enthusiastic supporters of old Hickory." It was evidently Pierce who led them into this, and although it proved in a material sense for Hawthorne's benefit, it separated him permanently from the class to which he properly belonged—the enlightened men of culture of his time; and Cilley's tragical fate can be directly traced to it. The Jackson movement was in its essence a revolt against *civility*,—and it seems as if Hawthorne and Bridge might have recognized this.

Hawthorne was well liked in his class in spite of his reserved manners, but he held no class offices that we hear of, except a place on a committee of the Athenaan Society with Franklin Pierce. Class days and class suppers, so prolific of small honors, were not introduced at Bowdoin until some years later. He graduated eighteenth in a class of thirty–eight, but this was not sufficient to give him a part in the commencement exercises. [Footnote: The President informed him that his rank in the class would have entitled him to a part if it had not been for his neglect of declamations; and Hawthorne wrote to his mother that he was perfectly satisfied with this, for it saved him the mortification of appearing in public.] Accordingly Hawthorne, Bridge, and others who were in a like predicament, organized a mock Commencement celebration at Ward's Tavern, where they elected officers of a comical sort, such as boatswain and sea–cook, and concluded their celebration in a manner suitable to the occasion.

Hawthorne was commonly known among his classmates, as "Hath," and his friends addressed him in this manner long after he had graduated. His degree was made out in the name of Nathaniel Hathorne, above which he subsequently wrote "Hawthorne," in bold letters.

The question may well be raised here, how it happened that America produced so many men of remarkable intellect with such slight opportunities for education in former times, while our greatly improved universities have not graduated an orator like Webster, a poet like Longfellow, or a prose–writer equal to Hawthorne during the past forty years. There have been few enough who have risen above mediocrity.

It is the same, more or less, all over the civilized world. We have entered into a mechanical age, which is natural enough considering the rapid advances of science and the numerous mechanical inventions, but which is decidedly unfavorable to the development of art and literature. Everything now goes by machinery, from Harvard University to Ohio politics and the gigantic United States Steel Company; and every man has to find his place in some machine or other, or he is thrown out of line. Individual effort, as well as independence of thought and action, is everywhere frowned upon; but without freedom of thought and action there can be no great individualities, which is the same as saying that there can be no poets like Longfellow, or writers like Hawthorne and Emerson. Spontaneity is the life of the true artist, and in a mechanical civilization there can be neither spontaneity nor the poetic material which is essential to artistic work of a high order. There can be no great orators, for masses of men are no longer influenced by oratory, but by newspapers. Genius is like a plant of slow growth, which requires sunshine and Mother Earth to nourish it, not chemicals and electric lights.

CHAPTER IV. LITTLE MISERY: 1825–1835

During the War of the American Revolution, the officers of the French fleet, which was stationed at Newport, invented a game of cards, called "Boston," of which one peculiarity was, that under certain conditions, whoever held the lowest hand would win the count. This was called "Little Misery," and this was the kind of hand which Nathaniel Hawthorne had to play for fifteen years after leaving Bowdoin College. Only his indomitable will could have carried him through it.

The Life and Genius of Nathaniel Hawthorne

A college graduate who lacks the means to study a profession, and who has no influential relative to make a place for him in the world, finds himself in a most discouraging position. The only thing that his education has fitted him to do is, to teach school, and he may not be adapted to this, on account of some personal peculiarity. There was, and I suppose is still, a prejudice among mercantile men against college graduates, as a class of proud, indolent, neglectful persons, very difficult to instruct. Undoubtedly there are many such, but the innocent have to suffer with the guilty. It is natural that a man who has not had a liberal education should object to employing a subordinate who knows Latin and Greek. Whether Hawthorne's Uncle Robert, who had thus far proved to be his guardian genius, would have educated him for a profession, we have no means of knowing. This would mean of course a partial support for years afterward, and it is quite possible that Mr. Manning considered his duties to his own children paramount to it. What he did for Nathaniel may have been the best he could, to give him the position of book–keeper for the stage–company. This was of course Pegasus in harness (or rather at the hitching–post), but it is excellent experience for every young man; although the compensation in Hawthorne's case was small and there could be no expectation of future advancement.

In this dilemma he decided to do the one thing for which Nature intended him,—to become a writer of fiction,—and he held fast to this determination in the face of most discouraging obstacles. He composed a series of short stories,—echoes of his academic years,—which he proposed to publish under the title of Wordsworth's popular poem, "We Are Seven." One of these is said to have been based on the witchcraft delusion, and it is a pity that it should not have been preserved, but their feminine titles afford no indication of their character. He carried them to a publisher, who received him politely and promised to examine them, but one month passed after another without Hawthorne's hearing from him, so that he concluded at length to make inquiries. [Footnote: J. Hawthorne, i. 124.] The publisher confessed that he had not even undertaken to read them, and Nathaniel carried them back, with a sinking heart, to his little chamber in the house on Herbert Street,—where he may have had melancholy thoughts enough for the next few weeks.

Youth, however, soon outgrows its chagrins. In less than two years Hawthorne was prepared to enter the literary lists, equipped with a novelette, called "Fanshawe"; but here again he was destined to meet with a rebuff. After tendering it to a number of publishers without encouragement, he concluded to take the risk of publishing it himself. This only cost him a few hundred dollars, but the result was unsatisfactory, and he afterward destroyed all the copies that he could regain possession of.

Hawthorne's genius was of slow development. He was only twenty–four when he published this rather immature work, and it might have been better if he had waited longer. It was to him what the "Sorrows of Werther" was to Goethe, but while the "Sorrows of Werther" made Goethe famous in many countries, "Fanshawe" fell still–born. The latter was not more imitative of Scott than the "Sorrows of Werther" is of Rousseau, and now that we consider it in the cool critical light of the twentieth century, we cannot but wonder that the "Sorrows of Werther" ever produced such enthusiasm. It is quite as difficult to see why "Fanshawe" should not have proved a success. It lacks the grace and dignity of Hawthorne's mature style, but it has an ingenious plot, a lively action, and is written in sufficiently good English. One would suppose that its faults would have helped to make it popular, for portions of it are so exciting as to border closely on the sensational. It may be affirmed that when a novel becomes so exciting that we wish to turn over the pages and anticipate the conclusion, either the action of the story is too heated or its incidents are too highly colored. The introduction of pirates in a work of fiction is decidely sensational, from Walter Scott downward, and, though Hawthorne never fell into this error, he approaches closely to it in "Fanshawe." There is some dark secret between the two villains of the piece, which he leaves to the reader as an exercise for the imagination. This is a characteristic of all his longer stories. There is an unknown quantity, an insoluble point, in them, which tantalizes the reader.

What we especially feel in "Fanshawe" is the author's lack of social experience. His heroine at times behaves in a truly feminine manner, and at others her performances make us shiver. Her leaving her guardian's house at midnight to go off with an unknown man, whom her maidenly instinct should have taught her to distrust, even if Fanshawe had not warned her against him, might have been characteristic of the Middle Ages, but is certainly not of modern life. Bowdoin College evidently served Hawthorne as a background to his plot, although removed some distance into the country, and it is likely that the portrait of the kindly professor might have been recognized there. Ward's Tavern serves for the public–house where the various characters congregate, and there is a high rocky ledge in the woods, or what used to be woods at Brunswick, where the students often tried their skill in climbing, and which Hawthorne has idealized into the cliff where the would–be abductor met his timely fate. The trout–brook where Bridge and Hawthorne used to fish is also introduced.

43

Fanshawe himself seems like a house of which only two sides have been built. There are such persons, and it is no wonder if they prove to be short–lived. Yet the scene in which he makes his noble renunciation of the woman who is devoted to him, purely from a sense of gratitude, is finely and tenderly drawn, and worthy of Hawthorne in his best years. The story was republished after its author's death, and fully deserves its position in his works.

It was about this time (1827) that Nathaniel Hathorne changed his name to Hawthorne. No reason has ever been assigned for his doing so, and he had no legal right to do it without an act of the Legislature, but he took a revolutionary right, and as his family and fellow–citizens acquiesced in this, it became an established fact. His living relatives in the Manning family are unable to explain his reason for it. It may have been for the sake of euphony, or he may have had a fanciful notion, that such a change would break the spell which seemed to be dragging his family down with him. Conway's theory that it was intended to serve him as an incognito is quite untenable. His name first appears with a *w* in the Bowdoin Triennial Catalogue of 1828.

There are very few data existing as to Hawthorne's life during his first ten years of manhood, but it must have been a hard, dreary period for him. The Manning children, Robert, Elizabeth and Rebecca, were now growing up, and must have been a source of entertainment in their way, and his sister Louisa was always a comfort; but Horatio Bridge, who made a number of flying visits to him, states that he never saw the elder sister, even at table,—a fact from which we may draw our own conclusions. Hawthorne had no friends at this time, except his college associates, and they were all at a distance,—Pierce and Cilley both flourishing young lawyers, one at Concord, New Hampshire, and the other at Thomaston, Maine,—while Longfellow was teaching modern languages at Bowdoin. He had no lady friends to brighten his evenings for him, and if he went into society, it was only to be stared at for his personal beauty, like a jaguar in a menagerie. He had no fund of the small conversation which serves like oil to make the social machinery run smoothly. Like all deep natures, he found it difficult to adapt himself to minds of a different calibre. Salem people noticed this, and his apparent lack of an object in life,—for he maintained a profound secrecy in regard to his literary efforts,—and concluded that he was an indolent young man without any faculty for business, and would never come to good in this world. No doubt elderly females admonished him for neglecting his opportunities, and small wits buzzed about him as they have about many another under similar conditions. It was Hans Andersen's story of the ugly duck that proved to be a swan.

No wonder that Hawthorne betook himself to the solitude of his own chamber, and consoled himself like the philosopher who said, "When I am alone, then I am least alone." He had an internal life with which only his most intimate friends were acquainted, and he could people his room with forms from his own fancy, much more real to him than the palpable *ignota* whom he passed in the street. Beautiful visions came to him, instead of sermonizing ladies, patronizing money–changers, aggressive upstarts, grimacing wiseacres, and that large class of amiable, well–meaning persons that makes up the bulk of society. We should not be surprised if angels sometimes came to hover round him, for to the pure in heart heaven descends upon earth.

There is a passage in Hawthorne's diary under date of October 4, 1840, which has often been quoted; but it will have to be quoted again, for it cannot be read too often, and no biography of him would be adequate without it. He says:

"Here I sit in my old accustomed chamber where I used to sit in days gone by....This claims to be called a haunted chamber, for thousands upon thousands of visions have appeared to me in it; and some few of them have become visible to the world. If ever I should have a biographer, he ought to make great mention of this chamber in my memoirs, because so much of my lonely youth was wasted here, and here my mind and character were formed; and here I have been glad and hopeful, and here I have been despondent. And here I sat a long, long time, waiting patiently for the world to know me, and sometimes wondering why it did not know me sooner, or whether it would ever know me at all,—at least, till I were in my grave. And sometimes it seemed as if I were already in the grave, with only life enough to be chilled and benumbed. But oftener I was happy,—at least as happy as I then knew how to be, or was aware of the possibility of being. By and by, the world found me out in my lonely chamber, and called me forth,—not indeed, with a loud roar of acclamation, but rather with a still, small voice,—and forth I went, but found nothing in the world that I thought preferable to my solitude till now ... and now I begin to understand why I was imprisoned so many years in this lonely chamber, and why I could never break through the viewless bolts and bars; for if I had sooner made my escape into the world, I should have grown hard and rough, and been covered with earthly dust, and my heart might have become callous by rude encounters with the multitude.... But living in solitude till the fulness of time was come, I still kept the dew of my youth, and the freshness of my heart."

During these dismal years Horatio Bridge was Hawthorne's good genius. The letters that Hawthorne wrote to him have not been preserved, but we may judge of their character by Bridge's replies to him—always frank, manly, sympathetic and encouraging. Hawthorne evidently confided his troubles and difficulties to Bridge, as he would to an elder brother. Bridge finally destroyed Hawthorne's letters, not so much on account of their complaining tone as for the personalities they contained; [Footnote: Horatio Bridge, 69.] and this suggests to us that there was still another side to Hawthorne's life at this epoch concerning which we shall never be enlightened. A man could not have had a better friend than Horatio Bridge. He was to Hawthorne what Edward Irving was to Carlyle; and the world is more indebted to them both than it often realizes.

There is in fact a decided similarity between the lives of Carlyle and Hawthorne, in spite of radical differences in their work and characters. Both started at the foot of the ladder, and met with a hard, long struggle for recognition; both found it equally difficult to earn their living by their pens; both were assisted by most devoted friends, and both finally achieved a reputation among the highest in their own time. If there is sometimes a melancholy tinge in their writings, may we wonder at it? Pericles said, "We need the theatre to chase away the sadness of life," and it might have benefited the whole Hawthorne family to have gone to the theatre once a fortnight; but there were few entertainments in Salem, except of the stiff conventional sort, or in the shape of public dances open to firemen and shop–girls. Long afterward, Elizabeth Hawthorne wrote of her brother:

"His habits were as regular as possible. In the evening after tea he went out for about an hour, whatever the weather was; and in winter, after his return, he ate a pint bowl of thick chocolate—(not cocoa, but the old–fashioned chocolate) crumbed full of bread: eating never hurt him then, and he liked good things. In summer he ate something equivalent, finishing with fruit in the season of it. In the evening we discussed political affairs, upon which we differed in opinion; he being a Democrat, and I of the opposite party. In reality, his interest in such things was so slight that I think nothing would have kept it alive but my contentious spirit. Sometimes, when he had a book that he particularly liked, he would not talk. He read a great many novels." [Footnote: J. Hawthorne, i. 125.]

If Elizabeth possessed the genius which her brother supposed, she certainly does not indicate it in this letter; but genius in the ore is very different from genius smelted and refined by effort and experience. The one important fact in her statement is that

The Life and Genius of Nathaniel Hawthorne

Hawthorne was in the habit of taking solitary rambles after dark,—an owlish practice, but very attractive to romantic minds. Human nature appears in a more pictorial guise by lamplight, after the day's work is over. The groups at the street corners, the glittering display in the watchmaker's windows, the carriages flashing by and disappearing in the darkness, the mysterious errands of foot–passengers, all served as object–lessons for this student of his own kind.

Jonathan Cilley once said:

"I love Hawthorne; I admire him; but I do not know him. He lives in a mysterious world of thought and imagination which he never permits me to enter." [Footnote: Packard's "Bowdoin College," 306.]

Long–continued thinking is sure to take effect at last, either in words or in action, and Hawthorne's mind had to disburden itself in some manner. So, after the failure of "Fanshawe," he returned to his original plan of writing short stories, and this time with success. In January, 1830, the well–known tale of "The Gentle Boy" was accepted by S. G. Goodrich, the editor of a Boston publication called the *Token*, who was himself better known in those days under the *nom de plume* of "Peter Parley." "The Wives of the Dead," "Roger Malvin's Burial," and "Major Molineaux" soon followed. In 1833 he published the "Seven Vagabonds," and some others. The New York *Knickerbocker* published the "Fountain of Youth" and "Edward Fayne's Rosebud." After 1833 the *Token* and the *New England Magazine* [Footnote: J. Hawthorne, i. 175.] stood ready to accept all the short pieces that Hawthorne could give them, but they did not encourage him to write serial stories. However, it was not the custom then for writers to sign their names to magazine articles, so that Hawthorne gained nothing in reputation by this. Some of his earliest pieces were printed over the signature of "Oberon."

An autumn expedition to the White Mountains, Lake Champlain and Lake Ontario, and Niagara Falls, in 1832, raised Hawthorne's spirits and stimulated his ambition. He wrote to his mother from Burlington, Vermont, September 16:

"I have arrived in safety, having passed through the White Hills, stopping at Ethan Crawford's house, and climbing Mt. Washington. I have not decided as to my future course. I have no intention of going into Canada. I have heard that cholera is prevalent in Boston."

The Life and Genius of Nathaniel Hawthorne

It was something to have stood on the highest summit east of the Rocky Mountains, and to have seen all New England lying at his feet. A hard wind in the Crawford Notch, which he describes in his story of "The Ambitious Guest," must have been in his own experience, and as he passed the monument of the ill-fated Willey family he may have thought that he too might become celebrated after his death, even as they were from their poetic catastrophe. This expedition provided him with the materials for a number of small plots.

The ice was now broken; but a new class of difficulties arose before him. American literature was then in the bud and promised a beautiful blossoming, but the public was not prepared for it. Monthly magazines had a precarious existence, and their uncertainty of remuneration reacted on the contributors. Hawthorne was poorly paid, often obliged to wait a long time for his pay, and occasionally lost it altogether. For his story of "The Gentle Boy," one of the gems of literature, which ought to be read aloud every year in the public schools, he received the paltry sum of thirty-five dollars. Evidently he could not earn even a modest maintenance on such terms, and his letters to Bridge became more despondent than ever.

Goodrich, who was a writer of the Andrews Norton class, soon perceived that Hawthorne could make better sentences than his own, and engaged him to write historical abstracts for his pitiful Peter Parley books, paying him a hundred dollars for the whole work, and securing for himself all the credit that appertained to it. Everybody knew who Peter Parley was, but it has only recently been discovered that much of the literature which passed under his name was the work of Nathaniel Hawthorne.

The editor of a New York magazine to which Hawthorne contributed a number of sketches repeatedly deferred the payment for them, and finally confessed his inability to make it,—which he probably knew or intended beforehand. Then, with true metropolitan assurance, he begged of Hawthorne the use of certain unpublished manuscripts, which he still had in his possession. Hawthorne with unlimited contempt told the fellow that he might keep them, and then wrote to Bridge:

"Thus has this man, who would be considered a Macenas, taken from a penniless writer material incomparably better than any his own brain can supply." [Footnote: Horatio Bridge, 68, 69.]

The Life and Genius of Nathaniel Hawthorne

Whether this New York periodical was the *Knickerbocker* or some other, we are not informed; neither do we know what Bridge replied to Hawthorne, who had closed his letter with a malediction, on the aforesaid editor, but elsewhere in his memoirs he remarks:

"Hawthorne received but small compensation for any of this literary work, for he lacked the knowledge of business and the self–assertion necessary to obtain even the moderate remuneration vouchsafed to writers fifty years ago." [Footnote: Horatio Bridge, 77.]

If Horatio Bridge had been an author himself, he would not have written this statement concerning his friend. Magazine editors are like men in other professions: some of them are honorable and others are less so; but an author who offers a manuscript to the editor of a magazine is wholly at his mercy, so far as that small piece of property is concerned. The author cannot make a bargain with the editor as he can with the publisher of his book, and is obliged to accept whatever the latter chooses to give him. Instances have been known where an editor has destroyed a valuable manuscript, without compensation or explanation of any kind. Hawthorne was doing the best that a human being could under the conditions that were given him. Above all things, he was true to himself; no man could be more so.

Yet Bridge wrote to him on Christmas Day, 1836:

"The bane of your life has been self–distrust. This has kept you back for many years; which, if you had improved by publishing, would long ago have given you what you must now wait a long time for. It may be for the best, but I doubt it."

Nothing is more trying in misfortune than the ill–judged advice of well–meaning friends. There is no nettle that stings like it. To expect Hawthorne to become a literary genius, and at the same time to develop the peculiar faculties of a commercial traveller or a curb–stone broker, was unreasonable. In the phraseology of Sir William Hamilton, the two vocations are "non–compossible." Bridge himself was undertaking a grandly unpractical project about this time: nothing less than an attempt to dam the Androscoggin, a river liable to devastating floods; and in this enterprise he was obliged to trust to a class of men who were much more uncertain in their ways and methods than those with whom Hawthorne dealt. Horatio Bridge had not studied civil engineering, and the result was that before two years had elapsed the floods on the Androscoggin swept the dam away, and his fortune with it.

In the same letter we also notice this paragraph concerning another Bowdoin friend:

"And so Frank Pierce is elected Senator. There is an instance of what a man can do by trying. With no very remarkable talents, he at the age of thirty–four fills one of the highest stations in the nation. He is a good fellow, and I rejoice at his success." [Footnote: J. Hawthorne, i. 148.]

Pierce certainly possessed the cap of Fortunatus, and it seems as if there must have been some magic faculty in the man, which enabled him to win high positions so easily; and he continued to do this, although he had not distinguished himself particularly as a member of Congress, and he appeared to still less advantage among the great party leaders in the United States Senate. He illustrated the faculty for "getting elected."

In October, 1836, the time arrived for settling the matrimonial wager between Hawthorne and Jonathan Cilley, which they had made at college twelve years before. Bridge accordingly examined the documents which they had deposited with him, and notified Cilley that he was under obligation to provide Hawthorne with an octavo of Madeira.

Cilley's letter to Hawthorne on this occasion does not impress one favorably. [Footnote: J. Hawthorne, i. 144.] It is familiar and jocose, without being either witty or friendly, and he gives no intimation in it of an intention to fulfil his promise. Hawthorne appears to have sent the letter to Bridge, who replied:

"I doubt whether you ever get your wine from Cilley. His inquiring of you whether he had really lost the bet is suspicious; and he has written me in a manner inconsistent with an intention of paying promptly; and if a bet grows old it grows cold. He wished me to propose to you to have it paid at Brunswick next Commencement, and to have as many of our classmates as could be mustered to drink it. It may be Cilley's idea to pay over the balance after taking a strong pull at it; if so, it is well enough. But still it should be tendered within the month."

In short, Cilley behaved in this matter much in the style of a tricky Van Buren politician, making a great bluster of words, and privately intending to do nothing. He was running for Congress at the time on the Van Buren ticket, and it is quite likely that the expenses of the campaign had exhausted his funds. That he should never have paid the bet was less to Hawthorne's disadvantage than his own.

It was now that Horatio Bridge proved himself a true friend, and equally a man. In the spring of 1836 Goodrich had obtained for Hawthorne the editorship of the *American Magazine of Useful and Entertaining Knowledge*, with a salary of five hundred dollars; [Footnote: Conway, 45.]but he soon discovered that he had embarked on a ship with a rotten hulk. He started off heroically, writing the whole of the first number with the help of his sister Elizabeth; but by midsummer the concern was bankrupt, and he retired to his lonely cell, more gloomy and despondent than before. There are few sadder spectacles then that of a man seeking work without being able to obtain it; and this applies to the man of genius as well as to the day laborer.

Horatio Bridge now realized that the time had come for him to interfere. He recognized that Hawthorne was gradually lapsing into a hypochondria that might terminate fatally; that he was Goethe's oak planted in a flowerpot, and that unless the flower–pot could be broken, the oak would die. He also saw that Hawthorne would never receive the public recognition that was due to his ability, so long as he published magazine articles under an assumed name. He accordingly wrote to Goodrich—fortunately before his mill–dam gave way—suggesting the publication of a volume of Hawthorne's stories, and offered to guarantee the publisher against loss. This proposition was readily accepted, but Bridge might have made a much better bargain. What it amounted to was, the half–profit system without the half–profit. The necessary papers were exchanged and Hawthorne gladly acceded to Goodrich's terms. Bridge, however, had cautioned Goodrich not to inform Hawthorne of his share in the enterprise, and the consequence of this was that he shortly received a letter from Hawthorne, informing him of the good news—which he knew already—and praising Goodrich, to whom he proposed to dedicate his new volume. Bridge's generosity had come back to him, dried and salted,—as it has to many another.

What could Bridge do, in the premises? Goodrich had written to Hawthorne that the publisher, Mr. Howes, was confident of making a favorable arrangement *with a man of capital who would edit the book* ; but Bridge did not know this, and he suspected Goodrich of sailing into Hawthorne's favor under a false flag. He therefore wrote to Hawthorne, November 17, 1836:

The Life and Genius of Nathaniel Hawthorne

"I fear you will hurt yourself by puffing Goodrich *undeservedly*,—for there is no doubt in my mind of his selfishness in regard to your work and yourself. I am perfectly aware that he has taken a good deal of interest in you, but when did he ever do anything for you without a *quid pro quo*? The magazine was given to you for $100 less than it should have been. The *Token* was saved by your writing. Unless you are already committed, do not mar the prospects of your *first* book by hoisting Goodrich into favor."

This prevented the dedication, for which Hawthorne was afterward thankful enough. The book, which was the first volume of "Twice Told Tales" came from the press the following spring, and proved an immediate success, although not a highly lucrative one for its author. With the help of Longfellow's cordial review of it in the **North American** it established Hawthorne's reputation on a firm and irrefragable basis. All honor to Horatio.

As if Hawthorne had not seen a sufficiently long "winter of discontent" already, his friends now proposed to obtain the position of secretary and chronicler for him on Commodore Jones's exploring expedition to the South Pole! Franklin Pierce was the first to think of this, but Bridge interceded with Cilley to give it his support, and there can be no doubt that they would have succeeded in obtaining the position for Hawthorne, but the expedition itself failed, for lack of a Congressional appropriation. The following year, 1838, the project was again brought forward by the administration, and Congress being in a more amiable frame of mind granted the requisite funds; but Hawthorne had now contracted new ties in his native city, bound, as it were, by an inseparable cord stronger than a Manila hawser, and Doctor Nathaniel Peabody's hospitable parlors were more attractive to him than anything the Antarctic regions could offer.

We have now entered upon the period where Hawthorne's own diary commences, the autobiography of a pure–minded, closely observing man; an invaluable record, which began apparently in 1835, and was continued nearly until the close of his life; now published in a succession of American, English and Italian note–books. In it we find records of what he saw and thought; descriptive passages, afterward made serviceable in his works of fiction, and perhaps written with that object in view; fanciful notions, jotted down on the impulse of the moment; records of his social life; but little critical writing or personal confessions,— although the latter may have been reserved; from publication by his different editors. It is known that much of his diary has not yet been given to the public, and perhaps never will be.

The Life and Genius of Nathaniel Hawthorne

In July, 1837, Hawthorne went to Augusta, to spend a month with his friend Horatio Bridge; went fishing with him, for what they called white perch, probably the saibling; [Footnote: The American saibling, or golden trout, is only indigenous to Lake Sunapee, New Hampshire, and to a small lake near Augusta.] and was greatly entertained with the peculiarities of an idiomatic Frenchman, an itinerant teacher of that language, whom Bridge, in the kindness of his heart, had taken into his own house. The last of July, Cilley also made his appearance, but did not bring the Madeira with him, and Hawthorne has left this rather critical portrait of him in his diary:

"Friday, July 28th.—Saw my classmate and formerly intimate friend, ——, for the first time since we graduated. He has met with good success in life, in spite of circumstances, having struggled upward against bitter opposition, by the force of his abilities, to be a member of Congress, after having been for some time the leader of his party in the State Legislature. We met like old friends, and conversed almost as freely as we used to do in college days, twelve years ago and more. He is a singular person, shrewd, crafty, insinuating, with wonderful tact, seizing on each man by his manageable point, and using him for his own purpose, often without the man's suspecting that he is made a tool of; and yet, artificial as his character would seem to be, his conversation, at least to myself, was full of natural feeling, the expression of which can hardly be mistaken, and his revelations with regard to himself had really a great deal of frankness. A man of the most open nature might well have been more reserved to a friend, after twelve years separation, than ——was to me. Nevertheless, he is really a crafty man, concealing, like a murder–secret, anything that it is not good for him to have known. He by no means feigns the good feeling that he professes, nor is there anything affected in the frankness of his conversation; and it is this that makes him so fascinating. There is such a quantity of truth and kindliness and warm affections, that a man's heart opens to him, in spite of himself. He deceives by truth. And not only is he crafty, but, when occasion demands, bold and fierce like a tiger, determined, and even straightforward and undisguised in his measures,—a daring fellow as well as a sly one."

This can be no other than Jonathan Cilley; like many of his class, a man of great good humor but not over–scrupulous, so far as the means he might make use of were concerned. He did not, however, prove to be as skilful a diplomat as Hawthorne seems to have supposed him. The duel between Cilley and Graves, of Kentucky, has been so variously misrepresented that the present occasion would seem a fitting opportunity to tell the plain truth concerning it.

President Jackson was an honest man, in the customary sense of the term, and he would have scorned to take a dollar that was not his own; but he suffered greatly from parasites, who pilfered the nation's money,—the natural consequence of the spoils–of–office system. The exposure of these peculations gave the Whigs a decided advantage, and Cilley, who had quickly proved his ability in debate, attempted to set a back–fire by accusing Watson Webb, the editor of the *Courier and Enquirer*, of having been bribed to change the politics of his paper. The true facts of the case were, that the paper had been purchased by the Whigs, and Webb, of course, had a right to change his politics if he chose to; and the net result of Cilley's attack was a challenge to mortal combat, carried by Representative Graves, of Kentucky. Cilley, although a man of courage, declined this, on the ground that members of Congress ought not to be called to account outside of the Capitol, for words spoken in debate. "Then," said Graves, "you will at least admit that my friend is a gentleman."

This was a fair offer toward conciliation, and if Cilley had been peaceably inclined he would certainly have accepted it; but he obstinately refused to acknowledge that General Webb was a gentleman, and in consequence of this he received a second challenge the next day from Graves, brought by Henry A. Wise, afterward Governor of Virginia. Cilley still objected to fighting, but members of his party urged him into it: the duel took place, and Cilley was killed.

It may be said in favor of the "code of honor" that it discourages blackguardism and instructs a man to keep a civil tongue; but it is not always possible to prevent outbursts of temper, especially in hot climates, and a man's wife and children should also be considered. Andrew Jackson said at the close of his life, that there was nothing he regretted so much as having killed a human being in a duel. Man rises by humility, and angels fall from pride.

Hawthorne wrote a kindly and regretful notice of the death of his old acquaintance, which was published in the *Democratic Review*, and which closed with this significant passage:

"Alas, that over the grave of a dear friend, my sorrow for the bereavement must be mingled with another grief—that he threw away such a life in so miserable a cause! Why, as he was true to the Northern character in all things else, did he swerve from his Northern principles in this final scene?" [Footnote: Conway, 63.]

It will be well to bear this in mind in connection with a somewhat similar incident, which we have now to consider.

An anecdote has been repeated in all the books about Hawthorne published since 1880, which would do him little credit if it could be proved,—a story that he challenged one of his friends to a duel, at the instigation of a vulgar and unprincipled young woman. Horatio Bridge says in reference to it:

"This characteristic was notably displayed several years later, when a lady incited him to quarrel with one of his best friends on account of a groundless pique of hers. He went to Washington for the purpose of challenging the gentleman, and it was only after ample explanation had been made, showing that his friend had behaved with entire honor, that Pierce and Cilley, who were his advisers, could persuade him to be satisfied without a fight." [Footnote: Bridge, 5.]

How the good Horatio could have fallen into this pit is unimaginable, for a double contradiction is contained in his statement. "Some time after this," that is after leaving college, would give the impression that the affair took place about 1830, whereas Pierce and Cilley were not in Washington together till five or six years later—probably seven years later. Moreover, Hawthorne states in a letter to Pierce's friend O'Sullivan, on April 1, 1853, that he had never been in Washington up to that time. The Manning family and Mrs. Hawthorne's relatives never heard of the story previous to its publication.

The internal evidence is equally strong against it. What New England girl would behave in the manner that Hawthorne's son represents this one to have done? What young gentleman would have listened to such a communication as he supposes, and especially the reserved and modest Hawthorne? One can even imagine the aspect of horror on his face at such an unlady−like proceeding. The story would be an ignominious one for Hawthorne, if it were credible, but there is no occasion for our believing it until some tangible evidence is adduced in its support. There was no element of Quixotism in his composition, and it is quite as impossible to locate the identity of the person whom Hawthorne is supposed to have challenged.

CHAPTER V. EOS AND EROS: 1835–1839

It was fortunate for Hawthorne that there was at this time a periodical in the United States, the *North American Review*, which was generally looked upon as an authority in literature, and which in most instances deserved the confidence that was placed in it, for its reviews were written by men of distinguished ability. It was the *North American Review* which made the reputation of L. Maria Child, and which enrolled Hawthorne in the order of geniuses.

There is not much literary criticism in Longfellow's review, and he does not "rise to the level of the accomplished essayist" of our own time, [Footnote: Who writes so correctly and says so little to the purpose.] but he goes to the main point with the single–mindness of the true poet. "A new star," he says, "has appeared in the skies"—a veritable prediction. "Others will gaze at it with telescopes, and decide whether it is in the constellation of Orion or the Great Bear. It is enough for us to gaze at it, to admire it, and welcome it."

"Although Hawthorne writes in prose, he belongs among the poets. To every subject he touches he gives a poetic personality which emanates from the man himself. His sympathies extend to all things living, and even to the inanimates. Another characteristic is the exceeding beauty of his style. It is as clear as running waters are. Indeed he uses words as mere stepping–stones, upon which, with a free and youthful bound, his spirit crosses and re–crosses the bright and rushing stream of thought."

Again he says:

"A calm, thoughtful face seems to be looking at you from every page; with now a pleasant smile, and now a shade of sadness stealing over its features. Sometimes, though not often, it glares wildly at you, with a strange and painful expression, as, in the German romance, the bronze knocker of the Archivarius Lindhorst makes up faces at the Student Anselmus."

Here we have a portrait of Hawthorne, by one who knew him, in a few simple words; and behind a calm thoughtful face there is that mysterious unknown quantity which puzzles Longfellow here, and always perplexed Hawthorne's friends. It may have been the nucleus or tap–root of his genius.

Longfellow seems to have felt it as a dividing line between them. He probably felt so at college; and this brings us back to an old subject. Hawthorne's superiority to Longfellow as an artist consisted essentially in this, that he was never an optimist. Puritanism looked upon human nature with a hostile eye, and was inclined to see evil in it where none existed; and Doctor Channing, who inaugurated the great moral movement which swept Puritanism away in this country, tended, as all reformers do, to the opposite extreme,—to that scepticism of evil which, as George Brandes says, is greatly to the advantage of hypocrites and sharpers. This was justifiable in Doctor Channing, but among his followers it has often degenerated into an inverted or homoeopathic kind of Puritanism,—a habit of excusing the faults of others, or of themselves, on the score of good intentions—a habit of self–justification, and even to the perverse belief that, as everything is for the best, whatever we do in this world must be for good. To this class of sentimentalists the most serious evil is truth–seeing and truth–speaking. It is an excellent plan to look upon the bright side of things, but one should not do this to the extent of blinding oneself to facts. Doctor Johnson once said to Boswell, "Beware, my friend, of mixing up virtue and vice;" but there is something worse than that, and it is, to stigmatize a writer as a pessimist or a hypochondriac for refusing to take rainbow–colored views. This, however, would never apply to Longfellow.

Hawthorne, with his eye ever on the mark, pursued a middle course. He separated himself from the Puritans without joining their opponents, and thus attained the most independent stand–point of any American writer of his time; and if this alienated him from the various humanitarian movements that were going forward, it was nevertheless a decided advantage for the work he was intended to do. In this respect he resembled Scott, Thackeray and George Eliot.

What we call evil or sin is merely the negative of civilization,—a tendency to return to the original savage condition. In the light of history, there is always progress or improvement, but in individual cases there is often the reverse, and so far as the individual is concerned evil is no imaginary metaphor, but as real and absolute as what we call good. The Bulgarian massacres of 1877 were a historical necessity, and we console ourselves in thinking of them by the fact that they may have assisted the Bulgarians in obtaining their independence; but this was no consolation to the twenty or thirty thousand human beings who were ground to powder there. To them there was no comfort, no hope,—only the terrible reality. Neither can we cast the responsibility of such events on the mysterious ways of Providence. The ways of Providence are not so mysterious to those who have eyes to read with. Take for instance one of the most notable cases of depravity, that of Nero. If we consider the conditions under which he was born and brought up, the necessity of that form of government to hold a vast empire together, and the course of history for a hundred years previous, it is not difficult to trace the genesis of Nero's crimes to the greed of the Roman people (especially of its merchants) for conquest and plunder; and Nero was the price which they were finally called on to pay for this. Marcus Aurelius, a noble nature reared under favorable conditions for its development, became the Washington of his time.

It is the same in private life. In many families there are evil tendencies, which if they are permitted to increase will take permanent hold, like a bad demon, of some weak individual, and make of him a terror and a torment to his relatives—fortunate if he is not in a position of authority. He may serve as a warning to the general public, but in the domestic circle he is an unmitigated evil,—he or she, though it is not so likely to be a woman. When a crime is committed within the precincts of good society, we are greatly shocked; but we do not often notice the debasement of character which leads down to it, and still more rarely notice the instances in which fear or some other motive arrests demoralization before the final step, and leaves the delinquent as it were in a condition of moral suspense.

It was in such tragic situations that Hawthorne found the material which was best suited to the bent of his genius.

In the two volumes, however, of "Twice Told Tales,"—the second published two years later,—the tragical element only appears as an undercurrent of pathos in such stories as "The Gentle Boy," "Wakefield," "The Maypole of Merry–mount," and "The Haunted Mind," but reaches a climax in "The Ambitious Guest" and "Lady Eleanor's Mantle." There are others, like "Lights from a Steeple," and "Little Annie's Ramble," that are of a more cheerful cast, but are also much less serious in their composition. "The Minister's Black Veil," "The Great Carbuncle," and "The Ambitious Guest," are Dantean allegories. We notice that each volume begins with a highly patriotic tale, the "Gray Champion," and "Howe's Masquerade," but the patriotism is genuine and almost fervid.

The Life and Genius of Nathaniel Hawthorne

When I first looked upon the house in which Hawthorne lived at Sebago, I was immediately reminded of these earlier studies in human nature, which are of so simple and quiet a diction, so wholly devoid of rhetoric, that Elizabeth Peabody thought they must be the work of his sister, and others supposed them to have been written by a Quaker. They resemble Durer's wood–cuts,—gentle and tender in line, but unswerving in their fidelity. We sometimes wish that they were not so quiet and evenly composed, and then repent of our wish that anything so perfect should be different from what it is. His "Twice Told Tales" are a picture–gallery that may be owned in any house–hold. They stand alone in English, and there is not their like in any other language.

Yet Hawthorne is not a word–painter like Browning and Carlyle, but obtains his pictorial effect by simple accuracy of description, a more difficult process than the other, but also more satisfactory. His eyes penetrate the masks and wrappings which cover human nature, as the Rontgen rays penetrate the human body. He sees a man's heart through the flesh and bones, and knows what is concealed in it. He ascends a church–steeple, and looking down from the belfry the whole life of the town is spread out before him. Men and women come and go—Hawthorne knows the errands they are on. He sees a militia company parading below, and they remind him from that elevation of the toy soldiers in a shop–window,—which they turned out to be, pretty much, at Bull Run. A fashionable young man comes along the street escorting two young ladies, and suddenly at a crossing encounters their father, who takes them away from him; but one of them gives him a sweet parting look, which amply compensates him in its presage of future opportunities. How plainly that consolatory look appears between our eyes and the printed page! Then Hawthorne describes the grand march of a thunder–storm,—as in Rembrandt's "Three Trees,"—with its rolling masses of dark vapor, preceded by a skirmish–line of white feathery clouds. The militia company is defeated at the first onset of this, its meteoric enemy, and driven under cover. The artillery of the skies booms and flashes about Hawthorne himself, until finally: "A little speck of azure has widened in the western heavens; the sunbeams find a passage and go rejoicing through the tempest, and on yonder darkest cloud, born like hallowed hopes of the glory of another world and the trouble and tears of this, brightens forth the rainbow." All this may have happened just as it is set down.

"Lady Eleanor's Mantle" exemplifies the old proverb, "Pride goeth before destruction," in almost too severe a manner, but the tale is said to have a legendary foundation; and "The Minister's Black Veil" is an equally awful symbolism for that barrier between man and man, which we construct through suspicion and our lack of frankness in our dealings with one another. We all hide ourselves behind veils, and, as Emerson says, "Man crouches and blushes, absconds and conceals."

"The Ambitious Guest" allegorizes a vain imagination, and is the most important of these three. A young man suffers from a craving for distinction, which he believes will only come to him after this life is ended. He is walking through the White Mountains, and stops overnight at the house of the ill–fated Willey family. He talks freely on the subject of his vain expectations, when Destiny, in the shape of an avalanche, suddenly overtakes him, and buries him so deeply that neither his body nor his name has ever been recovered. Hawthorne might have drawn another allegory from the same source, for if the Willey family had trusted to Providence, and remained in their house, instead of rushing out into the dark, they would not have lost their lives.

In the *Democratic Review* for 1834, Hawthorne published the account of a visit to Niagara Falls, one of the fruits of his expedition thither in September, 1832, by way of the White Mountains and Burlington, the journey from Salem to Niagara in those days being fully equal to going from New York to the cataracts of the Nile in our own time. "The Ambitious Guest" was published in the same volume with it, and "The Ontario Steamboat" first appeared in the *American Magazine of Useful and Entertaining Knowledge*, in 1836. Hawthorne may have made other expeditions to the White Mountains, but we do not hear of them.

In addition to the three studies already mentioned, Hawthorne drew from this source the two finest of his allegories, "The Great Carbuncle" and "The Great Stone Face."

"The Great Carbuncle" is not only one of the most beautiful of Hawthorne's tales, but the most far–reaching in its significance. The idea of it must have originated in the Alpine glow, an effect of the rising or setting sun on the icy peaks of a mountain, which looks at a distance like a burning coal; an appearance only visible in the White Mountains during the winter, and there is no reason why Hawthorne should not have seen it at that season from Lake Sebago. At a distance of twenty miles or more it blazes wonderfully, but on a nearer approach it entirely disappears. Hawthorne could not have found a more fascinating subject, and he imagines it for us as a great carbuncle located in the upper recesses of the mountains.

The Life and Genius of Nathaniel Hawthorne

A number of explorers for this wonderful gem meet together at the foot of the mountain beyond the confines of civilization, and build a hut in which to pass the night. They are recognizable, from Hawthorne's description, as the man of one idea, who has spent his whole life seeking the gem; a scientific experimenter who wishes to grind it up for the benefit of his crucible; a cynical sceptic who has come to disprove the existence of the great gem; a greedy speculator who seeks the carbuncle as he would prospect for a silver-mine; an English lord who wishes to add it to his hereditary possessions; and finally a young married couple who want to obtain it for an ornament to their new cottage. The interest of the reader immediately centres on these last two, and we care much more concerning their fortunes and adventures than we do about the carbuncle.

The conversation that evening between these ill-assorted companions is in Hawthorne's most subtle vein of irony, and would have delighted old Socrates himself. Meanwhile the young bride weaves a screen of twigs and leaves, to protect herself and her husband from the gaze of the curious.

The following morning they all set out by different paths in search of the carbuncle; but our thoughts accompany the steps of the young bride, as she makes one toilsome ascent after another until she feels ready to sink to the ground with fatigue and discouragement. They have already decided to return, when the rosy light of the carbuncle bursts upon them from beneath the lifting clouds; but they now feel instinctively that it is too great a prize for their possession. The man of one idea also sees it, and his life goes out in the exultation over his final success. The skeptic appears, but cannot discover it, although his face is illumined by its light, until he takes off his large spectacles; whereupon, he instantly becomes blind. The English nobleman and the American speculator fail to discover it; the former returns to his ancestral halls, as wise as he was before; and the latter is captured by a party of Indians and obliged to pay a heavy ransom to regain freedom. The scientific pedant finds a rare specimen of primeval granite, which serves his purpose quite as well as the carbuncle; and the two young doves return to their cot, having learned the lesson of contentment.

How fortunate was Hawthorne at the age of thirty thus to anatomize the chief illusions of life, which so many others follow until old age!

It is an erroneous notion that Hawthorne found the chief material for his work in old New England traditions. There are some half-dozen sketches of this sort, but they are more formally written than the others, and remind one of those portraits by Titian which were painted from other portraits,—better than the originals, but not equal to those which he painted from Nature.

In the "Sights from a Steeple" Hawthorne exposes his methods of study and betrays the active principle of his existence. He says:

"The most desirable mode of existence might be that of a spiritualized Paul Pry hovering invisible round man and woman, witnessing their deeds, searching into their hearths, borrowing brightness from their felicity and shade from their sorrow, and retaining no emotion peculiar to himself."

There are those who would dislike this busybody occupation, and others, such as Emerson perhaps, might not consider it justifiable; but Hawthorne is not to be censured for it, for his motive was an elevated one, and without this close scrutiny of human nature we should have had neither a Hawthorne nor a Shakespeare. There is no quality more conspicuous in "Twice Told Tales" than the calm, evenly balanced mental condition of the author, who seems to look down on human life not so much from a church steeple as from the blue firmament itself.

Such was the *Eos* or dawn of Hawthorne's literary art.

Hawthorne returned thanks to Longfellow in a gracefully humorous letter, to which Longfellow replied with a cordial wish to see Hawthorne in Cambridge, and by advising him to dive into deeper water and write a history of the Acadians before and after their expulsion from Nova Scotia; but this was not practicable for minds like Hawthorne's, surcharged with poetic images, and the attempt might have proved a disturbing influence for him. He had already contributed the substance to Longfellow of "Evangeline," and he now wrote a eulogium on the poem for a Salem newspaper, which it must be confessed did not differ essentially from other reviews of the same order. He does not give us any clear idea of how the poem actually impressed him, which is after all the best that one can do in such cases. Poetry is not like a problem in mathematics, which can be marked right or wrong according to its solution.

When a young man obtains a substantial footing in his profession or business, he looks about him for a wife—unless he happens to be already pledged in that particular; and

The Life and Genius of Nathaniel Hawthorne

Hawthorne was not an exception to this rule. He was not obliged to look very far, and yet the chance came to him in such an exceptional manner that it seems as if some special providence were connected with it. His position in this respect was a peculiar one. He does not appear to have been much acquainted in Salem even now; and the only son of a widow with two unmarried sisters may be said to have rather a slim chance for escaping from those strong ties which have grown up between them from childhood. Many a mother has prevented her son from getting married until it has become too late for him to change his bachelor habits. His mother and his sisters realize that he ought to be married, and that he has a right to a home of his own; but in their heart of hearts they combat the idea, and their opposition takes the form of an unsparing criticism of any young lady whom he follows with his eyes. This frequently happens also in a family of girls: they all remain unmarried because, if one of them shows an inclination in that direction, the others unite in a conspiracy against her. On the other hand, a family of four or five boys will marry early, if they can obtain the means of doing so, simply from the need of feminine cheer and sympathy. A devoted female friend will sometimes prevent a young woman from being married. Love affairs are soft earth for an intriguing and unprincipled woman to work in, but, fortunately, Mrs. Hawthorne did not belong in that category.

It was stout, large-hearted Elizabeth Peabody who broke the spell of the enchanted castle in which Hawthorne was confined. The Peabodys were a cultivated family in Salem, who lived pretty much by themselves, as the Hawthornes and Mannings did. Doctor Nathaniel Peabody was a respectable practitioner, but he had not succeeded in curing the headaches of his daughter Sophia, which came upon her at the close of her girlhood and still continued intermittently until this time. The Graces had not been bountiful the Peabody family, so, to compensate for this, they all cultivated the Muses, in whose society they ascended no little distance on the way to Parnassus. Elizabeth Peabody was quite a feminine pundit. She learned French and German, and studied history and archaeology; she taught history on a large scale at Sanborn's Concord School and at many others; she had a method of painting dates on squares, which fixed them indelibly in the minds of her pupils; she talked at Margaret Fuller's transcendental club, and was an active member of the Radical or Chestnut Street Club, thirty years later; but her chief distinction was the introduction of Froebel's Kindergarten teaching, by which she well-nigh revolutionized primary instruction in America. She was a most self-forgetful person, and her scholars became devotedly attached to her.

Her sister Mary was as much like Elizabeth mentally as she differed from her in figure and general appearance, but soon after this she was married to Horace Mann and her public activity became merged in that of her husband, who was the first educator of his time. Sophia Peabody read poetry and other fine writings, and acquired a fair proficiency in drawing and painting. They lived what was then called the "higher life," and it certainly led them to excellent results.

Shortly before the publication of "Twice Told Tales," Elizabeth Peabody learned that the author of "The Gentle Boy," and other stories which she had enjoyed in the *Token*, lived in Salem, and that the name was Hawthorne. She immediately jumped to the conclusion that they were the work of Miss Elizabeth Hawthorne, whom she had known somewhat in earlier days, and she concluded to call upon her and offer her congratulations. When informed by Louisa Hawthorne, who came to her in the parlor, instead of the elder sister, that "The Gentle Boy" was written by Nathaniel, Miss Peabody made the significant remark, "If your brother can do work like that, he has no right to be idle" [Footnote: Lathrop, 168. Miss Peabody would seem to have narrated this to him.]—to which Miss Louisa retorted, it is to be hoped with some indignation, that her brother never was idle.

It is only too evident from this that public opinion in Salem had already decided that Hawthorne was an idle fellow, who was living on his female relatives. That is the way the world judges—from external facts without any consideration of internal causes or conditions. It gratifies the vanity of those who are fortunate and prosperous, to believe that all men have an equal chance in the race of life. Emerson once blamed two young men for idleness, who were struggling against obstacles such as he could have had no conception of. Those who have been fortunate from the cradle never learn what life is really like.

The spell, however, was broken and the friendliness of Elizabeth Peabody found a deeply sympathetic response in the Hawthorne household. Nathaniel at last found a person who expressed a genuine and heartfelt appreciation of his work, and it was like the return of the sun to the Arctic explorer after his long winter night. Rather to Miss Peabody's surprise he and his sisters soon returned her call, and visits between the two families thereafter became frequent.

Sophia Peabody belonged to the class of young women for whom Shakespeare's Ophelia serves as a typical example. She was gentle, affectionate, refined, and amiable to a fault,—much too tender–hearted for this rough world, if her sister Elizabeth had not always stood like a barrier between her and it.

How Hawthorne might have acted in Hamlet's place it is useless to surmise, but in his true nature he was quite the opposite of Hamlet,— slow and cautious, but driven onward by an inexorable will. If Hamlet had possessed half of Hawthorne's determination, he might have broken through the network of evil conditions which surrounded him, and lived to make Ophelia a happy woman. It was only necessary to come into Hawthorne's presence in order to recognize the force that was in him.

Sophia Amelia Peabody was born September 21, 1811, so that at the time of which we are now writing she was twenty–five years of age. Hawthorne was then thirty–two, when a man is more attractive to the fair sex than at any other time of life, for then he unites the freshness and vigor of youth with sufficient maturity of judgment to inspire confidence and trust. Yet her sister Elizabeth found it difficult to persuade her to come into the parlor and meet the handsomest man in Salem. When she did come she evidently attracted Nathaniel Hawthorne's attention, for, although she said little, he looked at her repeatedly while conversing with her sister. It may not have been an instance of love at first sight,—which may happen to any young man at a dancing party, and be forgotten two days later,—but it was something more than a casual interest. On his second or third call she showed him a sketch she had made of "the gentle boy," according to her idea of him, and the subdued tone with which he received it plainly indicated that he was already somewhat under her influence. Julian Hawthorne writes of this: [Footnote: J. Hawthorne, i. 179.]

"It may be remarked here, that Mrs. Hawthorne in telling her children, many years afterwards, of these first meetings with their father, used to say that his presence, from the very beginning, exercised so strong a magnetic attraction upon her, that instinctively, and in self–defence as it were, she drew back and repelled him. The power which she felt in him alarmed her; she did not understand what it meant, and was only able to feel that she must resist."

Every true woman feels this reluctance at first toward a suitor for her hand, but a sensitive young lady might well have a sense of awe on finding that she had attracted to herself such a mundane force as Hawthorne, and it is no wonder that this first impression was recollected throughout her life. There are many who would have refused

The Life and Genius of Nathaniel Hawthorne

Hawthorne's suit, because they felt that he was too great and strong for them, and it is to the honor of Sophia Peabody that she was not only attracted by the magnetism of Hawthorne, but finally had the courage to unite herself to such an enigmatical person.

We also obtain a glimpse of Hawthorne's side of this courtship from a letter which he wrote to Longfellow in June, 1837, and in which he says, "I have now, or shall soon have a sharper spur to exertion, which I lacked at an earlier period;" [Footnote: Conway, 75.] and this is all the information he has vouchsafed us on the subject. If there is anything more in his diary, it has not been given to the public, and probably never will be. A number of letters which he wrote to Miss Sophia from Boston, or Brook Farm, have been published by his son, but it would be neither right nor judicious to introduce them here.

It is, however, evident from the above that Hawthorne was already engaged in June, 1837, but his engagement long remained a secret, for three excellent reasons; viz., his slender means of support, the delicate health of his betrothed, and the disturbance which it might create in the Hawthorne family. The last did not prove so serious a difficulty as he seems to have imagined; but his apprehensiveness on that point many another could justify from personal experience. [Footnote: J. Hawthorne, i. 196.]

From this time also the health of Sophia Peabody steadily improved, nor is it necessary to account for it by any magical influence on the part of her lover. Her trouble was plainly some recondite difficulty of the circulation. The heart is supposed to be the seat of the affections because mental emotion stimulates the nervous system and acts upon the heart as the centre of all organic functions. A healthy natural excitement will cause the heart to vibrate more firmly and evenly; but an unhealthy excitement, like fear or anger, will cause it to beat in a rapid and uneven manner. Contrarily, despondency, or a lethargic state of mind, causes the movement of the blood to slacken. The happiness of love is thus the best of all stimulants and correctives for a torpid circulation, and it expands the whole being of a woman like the blossoming of a flower in the sunshine. From the time of her betrothal, Sophia Peabody's headaches became less and less frequent, until they ceased altogether. The true seat of the affections is in the mind. The first consideration proved to be a more serious matter. If Hawthorne had not succeeded in earning his own livelihood by literature so far, what prospect was there of supporting a wife and family in that manner? What should he do; whither should he turn? He continually turned the subject over in his mind, without, however, reaching any definite conclusion. Nor is this to be wondered at. If the ordinary avenues of human industry were not available to him as a college graduate, they were now permanently closed. A man in his predicament at the present time might obtain the position of librarian in one of our inland cities; but such places are few and the applications are many. Bronson Alcott once offered his services as teacher of a primary school, a position he might have filled better than most, for its one requisite is kindliness, but the Concord school committee would not hear of it. If Hawthorne had attempted to turn pedagogue he might have met with a similar experience.

Conway remarks very justly that an American author could not be expected to earn his own living in a country where foreign books could be pirated as they were in the United States until 1890, and this was especially true during the popularity of Dickens and George Eliot. Dickens was the great humanitarian writer of the nineteenth century, but he was also a caricaturist and a bohemian. He did not represent life as it is, but with a certain comical oddity. As an author he is to Hawthorne what a peony is to a rose, or a garnet is to a ruby; but ten, persons would purchase a novel of Dickens when one would select the "Twice Told Tales." Scott and Tennyson are exceptional instances of a high order of literary work which also proved fairly remunerative; but they do not equal Hawthorne in grace of diction and in the rare quality of his thought,—whatever advantages they may possess in other respects. Thackeray earned his living by his pen, but it was only in England that he could have done this.

CHAPTER VI. PEGASUS AT THE CART: 1839–1841

Horatio Bridge's dam was washed away in the spring of 1837, by a sudden and unprecedented rising of the Androscoggin River. Bridge was financially ruined, but like a brave and generous young man he did not permit this stroke of evil fortune, severe as it was, to oppress him heavily, and Hawthorne seems to have felt no shadow of it during his visit to Augusta the following summer. He returned to Salem in August with pleasanter anticipations than ever before,—to enjoy the society of his *fiancee*, and to prepare the second volume of "Twice Told Tales."

The course of Hawthorne's life during the next twenty months is mostly a blank to us. He would seem to have exerted himself to escape from the monotone in which he had been living so long, but of his efforts, disappointments, and struggles against the giant coils of Fate, there is no report. He wrote the four Province House tales as a send–off to his second volume, as well as "The Toll–Gatherer's Day," "Footprints on the Seashore," "Snow–Flakes," and "Chippings with a Chisel," which are to be found in it. [Footnote: J. Hawthorne, 176.] There is a long blank in Hawthorne's diary during the winter of 1837–38 which may be owing to his indifference to the outer world at that time, but more likely because its contents have not yet been revealed to us. It was the period of Cilley's duel, and what Hawthorne's reflections were on that subject, aside from the account which he wrote for the *Democratic Review*, would be highly interesting now, but the absence of any reference to it is significant, and there is no published entry in his diary between December 6, 1837, and May 11, 1838.

Horatio Bridge obtained the position of paymaster on the United States warship "Cyane," which arrived at Boston early in June, and on the 16th of the month Hawthorne went to call on his friend in his new quarters, which he found to be pleasant enough in their narrow and limited way. Bridge returned with him to Boston, and they dined together at the Tremont House, drinking iced champagne and claret in pitchers,—which latter would seem to have been a fashion of the place. Hawthorne's description of the day is purely external, and he tells us nothing of his friend,—concerning whom we were anxious to hear,—or of the new life on which he had entered.

On July 4, his thirty–fifth birthday, he wrote a microscopic account of the proceedings on Salem Common, which is interesting now, but will become more valuable as time goes on and the customs of the American people change with it. The object of these detailed pictorial studies, which not only remind one of Durer's drawings but of Carlyle's local descriptions (when he uses simple English and does not fly off into recondite comparisons), is not clearly apparent; but the artist has instincts of his own, like a vine which swings in the wind and seizes upon the first tree that its tendrils come into contact with. We sometimes wish that, as in the case of Bridge and his warship, they were not so objective and external, and that, like Carlyle, he would throw more of himself into them.

On July 27, Hawthorne started on an expedition to the Berkshire Hills, by way of Worcester, remaining there nearly till the first of September, and describing the scenery, the people he met by the way, and the commencement at Williams College, which then took place in the middle of August, in his customary accurate manner. He has given a full and connected account of his travels; so full that we wonder how he found time to write to Miss Sophia Peabody. He would seem to have been entirely alone, and to have travelled mainly by stage. On the route from Pittsfield to North Adams he notices the sunset, and describes it in these simple terms: [Footnote: American Note–book, 130.]

"After or about sunset there was a heavy shower, the thunder rumbling round and round the mountain wall, and the clouds stretching from rampart to rampart. When it abated the clouds in all parts of the visible heavens were tinged with glory from the west; some that hung low being purple and gold, while the higher ones were gray. The slender curve of the new moon was also visible, brightening amidst the fading brightness of the sunny part of the sky."

At North Adams he takes notice of one of the Select–men, and gives this account of him: [Footnote: American Note–book, 153.]

"One of the most sensible men in this village is a plain, tall, elderly person, who is overseeing the mending of a road,—humorous, intelligent, with much thought about matters and things; and while at work he had a sort of dignity in handling the hoe or crow–bar, which shows him to be the chief. In the evening he sits under the stoop, silent and observant from under the brim of his hat; but, occasion suiting, he holds an argument about the benefit or otherwise of manufactories or other things. A simplicity characterizes him more than appertains to most Yankees."

He did not return to Salem until September 24. A month later he was at the Tremont House in Boston, looking out of the windows toward Beacon Street, which may have served him for an idea in "The Blithedale Romance." After this there are no entries published from his diary till the following spring, so that the manner in which he occupied himself during the winter of 1838–39 will have to be left to the imagination. On April 27, 1839, he wrote a letter to Miss Sophia Peabody from Boston, in which he says:

"I feel pretty secure against intruders, for the bad weather will defend me from foreign invasion; and as to Cousin Haley, he and I had a bitter political dispute last evening, at the close of which he went to bed in high dudgeon, and probably will not speak to me these three days. Thus you perceive that strife and wrangling, as well as east winds and rain, are the methods of a kind Providence to promote my comfort,—which would not have been so well secured in any other way. Six or seven hours of cheerful solitude! But I will not be alone. I invite your spirit to be with me,—at any hour and as many hours as you please, but especially at the twilight hour before I light my lamp. I bid you at that particular time, because I can see visions more vividly in the dusky glow of firelight than either by daylight or lamplight. Come, and let me renew my spell against headache and other direful effects of the east wind. How I wish I could give you a portion of my insensibility! and yet I should be almost afraid of some radical transformation, were I to produce a change in that respect. If you cannot grow plump and rosy and tough and vigorous without being changed into another nature, then I do think, for this short life, you had better remain just what you are. Yes; but you will be the same to me, because we have met in eternity, and there our intimacy was formed. So get well as soon as you possibly can."

This statement deserves consideration under two headings; and the last shall be first, and the first shall be last.

It will be noticed that the accounts in Hawthorne's diary are for the most part of a dispassionate objective character, as if he had come down from the moon to take an observation of mundane affairs. His letters to Miss Peabody were also dispassionate, but strongly subjective, and, like the one just quoted, mainly evolved from his imagination, like orchids living in the air. It was also about this time that Carlyle wrote to Emerson concerning the *Dial* that it seemed "like an unborn human soul." The orchid imagination was an influence of the time, penetrating everywhere like an ether.

In the opening sentences in this letter, Hawthorne comes within an inch of disclosing his political opinions, and yet provokingly fails to do so. There is nothing about the man concerning which we are so much in the dark, and which we should so much like to know, as this; and it is certain from this letter that he held very decided opinions on political subjects and could defend them with a good deal of energy. On one occasion when Hawthorne was asked why he was a Democrat, he replied, "Because I live in a democratic country," which was, of course, simply an evasion; and such were the answers which he commonly gave to all interrogatories. His proclivities were certainly not democratic; but the greater the tenacity with which a man holds his opinions, the less inclined he feels to discuss them with others. The Boston aristocracy now vote the Democratic ticket out of opposition to the dominant party in Massachusetts, and Hawthorne may have done so for a similar reason.

Hawthorne was now a weigher and gauger in the Boston Custom House, one of the most laborious positions in the government service. The defalcation of Swartwout with over a million dollars from the New York customs' receipts had forced upon President Van

The Life and Genius of Nathaniel Hawthorne

Buren the importance of filling such posts with honorable men, instead of political shysters, and Bancroft, though a rather narrow historian, was a gentleman and a scholar. He was the right man to appreciate Hawthorne, but whether he bestowed this place upon him of his own accord, or through the ulterior agency of Franklin Pierce, we are not informed. It is quite possible that Elizabeth Peabody had a hand in the case, for she was always an indefatigable petitioner for the benefit of the needy, and had opportunities for meeting Bancroft in Boston society. His kindness to Hawthorne was at least some compensation for having originated the most ill-favored looking public building in the city. [Footnote: The present Boston Custom House. George S. Hillard called it an architectural monstrosity.]

Hawthorne's salary was twelve hundred dollars a year,—fully equal to eighteen hundred at the present time,—and his position appears to have been what is now called a store-keeper. He fully earned his salary. He had charge and oversight of all the dutiable imports that came to Long Wharf, the most important in the city, and was obliged to keep an account of all dutiable articles which were received there. He had to superintend personally the unloading of vessels, and although in some instances this was not unpleasant, he was constantly receiving shiploads of soft coal,—Sidney or Pictou coal,—which is the dirtiest stuff in the world; it cannot be touched without raising a dusty vapor which settles in the eyes, nose, and mouth, and inside the shirt-collar. He counted every basketful that was brought ashore, and his position on such occasions was to be envied only by the sooty laborers who handled that commodity. We wonder what the frequenters of Long Wharf thought of this handsome, poetic-looking man occupied in such a business.

Yet he appreciated the value of this Spartan discipline,—the inestimable value of being for once in his life brought down to hard-pan and the plain necessities of life. The juice of wormwood is bitter, but it is also strengthening. On July 3, 1839, he wrote: [Footnote: American Note-book.]

"I do not mean to imply that I am unhappy or discontented, for this is not the case. My life only is a burden in the same way that it is to every toilsome man, and mine is a healthy weariness, such as needs only a night's sleep to remove it. But from henceforth forever I shall be entitled to call the sons of toil my brethren, and shall know how to sympathize with them, seeing that I likewise have risen at the dawn, and borne the fervor of the midday sun, nor turned my heavy footsteps homeward till eventide. Years hence, perhaps, the experience that my heart is acquiring now will flow out in truth and wisdom."

This is one of the noblest passages in his writings.

On August 27 he notices the intense heat in the centre of the city, although it is somewhat cooler on the wharves. At this time Emerson may have been composing his "Wood Notes" or "Threnody" in the cool pine groves of Concord. Such is the difference between inheriting twenty thousand dollars and two thousand. Hawthorne lived in Boston at such a boarding–place as Doctor Holmes describes in the "Autocrat of the Breakfast Table," and for all we know it may have been the same one. He lived economically, reading and writing to Miss Peabody in the evening, and rarely going to the theatre or other entertainments,—a life like that of a store clerk whose salary only suffices for his board and clothing. George Bancroft was kindly disposed toward him, and would have introduced Hawthorne into any society that he could have wished to enter; but Hawthorne, then and always, declined to be lionized. Hawthorne made but one friend in Boston during this time, and that one, George S. Hillard, a most faithful and serviceable friend,—not only to Hawthorne during his life, but afterwards as a trustee for his family, and equally kind and helpful to them in their bereavement, which is more than could be said of all his friends,—especially of Pierce. Hillard belonged to the brilliant coterie of Cambridge literary men, which included Longfellow, Sumner and Felton. He was a lawyer, politician, editor, orator and author; at this time, or shortly afterward, Sumner's law partner; one of the most kindly sympathetic men, with a keen appreciation of all that is finest in art and literature, but somewhat lacking in firmness and independence of character. His "Six Months in Italy," written in the purest English, long served as a standard work for American travellers in that ideal land, and his rather unsymmetrical figure only made the graces of his oratory more conspicuous.

Hawthorne kept at his work through summer's heat and winter's cold. On February 11, 1840, he wrote to his fiancee:

"I have been measuring coal all day, on board of a black little British schooner, in a dismal dock at the north end of the city. Most of the time I paced the deck to keep myself warm....

"... Sometimes I descended into the dirty little cabin of the schooner, and warmed myself by a red–hot stove among biscuit barrels, pots and kettles, sea chests, and innumerable lumber of all sorts,—my olfactories, meanwhile, being greatly refreshed by the odor of a pipe, which the captain or some of his crew was smoking."

[Illustration: HAWTHORNE. FROM THE PORTRAIT BY CHARLES OSGOOD IN 1840. IN THE POSSESSION OF MRS. RICHARD C. MANNING, SALEM, MASS. FROM NEGATIVE IN POSSESSION OF AND OWNED BY FRANK COUSIN, SALEM]

One would have to go to Dante's "Inferno" to realize a situation more thoroughly disagreeable; yet the very pathos of Hawthorne's employment served to inspire him with elevated thoughts and beautiful reflections. His letters are full of aerial fancies. He notices what a beautiful day it was on April 18, 1840, and regrets that he cannot "fling himself on a gentle breeze and be blown away into the country." April 30 is another beautiful day,—"a real happiness to live; if he had been a mere vegetable, a hawthorn bush, he would have felt its influence." He goes to a picture gallery in the Athenaeum, but only mentions seeing two paintings by Sarah Clarke. He returns to Salem in October, and writes in his own chamber the passage already quoted, in which he mourns the lonely years of his youth, and the long, long waiting for appreciation, "while he felt the life chilling in his veins and sometimes it seemed as if he were already in the grave;" but an early return to his post gives him brighter thoughts. He takes notice of the magnificent black and yellow butterflies that have strangely come to Long Wharf, as if seeking to sail to other climes since the last flower had faded. Mr. Bancroft has appointed him to suppress an insurrection among the government laborers, and he writes to Miss Sophia Peabody:

"I was not at the end of Long Wharf to–day, but in a distant region,— my authority having been put in requisition to quell a rebellion of the captain and 'gang' of shovellers aboard a coal–vessel. I would you could have beheld the awful sternness of my visage and demeanor in the execution of this momentous duty. Well,—I have conquered the rebels, and proclaimed an amnesty; so to–morrow I shall return to that paradise of measurers, the end of Long Wharf,—not to my former salt–ship, she being now discharged, but to another, which will probably employ me well–nigh a fortnight longer."

A month later we meet with this ominous remark in his diary:

The Life and Genius of Nathaniel Hawthorne

"I was invited to dine at Mr. Bancroft's yesterday with Miss Margaret Fuller; but Providence had given me some business to do, for which I was very thankful."

Had Hawthorne already encountered this remarkable woman with the feminine heart and masculine mind, and had he already conceived that aversion for her which is almost painfully apparent in his Italian diary? Certainly in many respects they were antipodes.

The Whig party came into power on March 4, 1841, with "Tippecanoe" for a figure–head and Daniel Webster as its conductor of the "grand orchestra." A month later Bancroft was removed, and Hawthorne went with him, not at all regretful to depart. In fact, he had come to feel that he could not endure the Custom House, or at least his particular share of it, any longer. One object he had in view in accepting the position was, to obtain practical experience, and this he certainly did in a rough and unpleasant manner. The experience of a routine office, however, is not like that of a broker who has goods to sell and who must dispose of them to the best advantage, in order to keep his reputation at high–water mark; nor is it like the experience of a young doctor or a lawyer struggling to obtain a practice. Those are the men who know what life actually is; and it is this thoroughness of experience which makes the chief difference between a Dante and a Tennyson.

These reflections lead directly to Hawthorne's casual and oft–repeated commentary on American politicians. He wrote March 15:

"I do detest all offices—all, at least, that are held on a political tenure. And I want nothing to do with politicians. Their hearts wither away, and die out of their bodies. Their consciences are turned to india–rubber, or to some substance as black as that, and which will stretch as much. One thing, if no more, I have gained by my custom– house experience,—to know a politician." [Footnote: American Notebook, i. 220.]

This seems rather severe, but at the time when Hawthorne wrote it, American politics were on the lowest plane of demagogism. It was the inevitable result of the spoils–of–office system, and the meanest species of the class were the ward politicians who received small government offices in return for services in canvassing ignorant foreign voters. They were naturally coarse, hardened adventurers, and it was such that Hawthorne chiefly came in contact with in his official business. Cleon, the brawling tanner of Athens, has reappeared in every representative government since his time, and plays his clownish part with multifarious variations; but it is to little purpose that we deride the men who govern us, for they are what we and our institutions have made them. If we want better representatives, we must mend our own ways and especially purge ourselves of political cant and national vanity,—which is the food that ward politicians grow fat on. The profession of a politician is based on instability, and he cannot acquire, as matters now stand, the solidity of character that we look for in other professions.

So far, however, was Hawthorne at this juncture from considering men and things critically, that he closes the account of his first government experience in this rather optimistic manner:

"Old Father Time has gone onward somewhat less heavily than is his wont when I am imprisoned within the walls of the Custom–house. My breath had never belonged to anybody but me. It came fresh from the ocean....

"... It was exhilarating to see the vessels, how they bounded over the waves, while a sheet of foam broke out around them. I found a good deal of enjoyment, too, in the busy scene around me. It pleased me to think that I also had a part to act in the material and tangible business of this life, and that a portion of all this industry could not have gone on without my presence." [Footnote: American Note–book, i. 230.]

When Hawthorne philosophizes it is not in old threadbare proverbs or Orphic generalities, but always specifically and to the point.

CHAPTER VII. HAWTHORNE AS A SOCIALIST: 1841–1842

Who can compute the amount of mischief that Fourier has done, and those well–meaning but inexperienced dreamers who have followed after him? A Fourth–of–July firecracker once consumed the half of a large city. The boy who exploded it had no evil intentions; neither did Fourier and other speculators in philanthropy contemplate what might be the effect of their doctrines on minds actuated by the lowest and most inevitable wants. Wendell Phillips, in the most brilliant of his orations, said: "The track of God's lightning is a straight line from justice to iniquity," and one might have said to Phillips, in his later years, that there is in the affairs of men a straight line from infatuation to destruction. In what degree Fourier was responsible for the effusion of blood in Paris in the spring of 1871 it is not possible to determine; but the relation of Rousseau to the first French revolution is not more certain. *Fate* is the spoken word which cannot be recalled, and who can tell the good and evil consequences that lie hidden in it? The proper cure for socialism, in educated minds, would be a study of the law. There we discover what a wonderful mechanism is the present organization of society, and how difficult it would be to reconstruct this, if it once were overturned.

As society is constituted at present, the honest and industrious are always more or less at the mercy of the vicious and indolent, and the only protection against this lies in the right of individual ownership. In a general community of goods, there might be some means of preventing or punishing flagrant misdemeanors, but what protection could there be against indolence? Those who were ready and willing to work would have to bear all the burdens of society.

In order that an idea should take external or concrete form it has to be married, as it were, to some desire or tendency in the individual. Reverend George Ripley had become imbued with Fourierism through his studies of French philosophy, but he had also been brought up on a farm, and preferred the fresh air and vigorous exercise of that mode of life to city preaching. He was endowed with a strong constitution and possessed of an independent fortune, and his aristocratic wife, more devoted than women of that class are usually, sympathized with his plans, and was prepared to follow him to the ends of the earth. He not only felt great enthusiasm for the project but was capable of inspiring others with it. There were many socialistic experiments undertaken about that time, but George Ripley's was the only one that has acquired a historical value. It is much to his credit that he gave the scheme a thorough trial, and by carrying it out to a logical conclusion proved its radical impracticability.

Such a failure is more valuable than the successes of a hundred men who merely make their own fortunes and leave no legacy of experience that can benefit the human race.

It must have been Elizabeth Peabody who persuaded Hawthorne to enlist in the Brook Farm enterprise. She wrote a paper for the *Dial* [Footnote: *Dial*, ii. 361.] on the subject, explaining the object of the West Roxbury community and holding forth the prospect of the "higher life" which could be enjoyed there. Hawthorne was in himself the very antipodes of socialism, and it was part of the irony of his life that he should have embarked in such an experiment; but he invested a thousand dollars in it, which he had saved from his Custom House salary, and was one of the first on the ground. What he really hoped for from it—as we learn by his letters to Miss Sophia Peabody— was a means of gaining his daily bread, with leisure to accomplish a fair amount of writing, and at the same time to enter into such society as might be congenial to his future consort. It seemed reasonable to presume this, and yet the result did not correspond to it. He went to West Roxbury on April 12, 1841, and as it happened in a driving northeast snowstorm,—an unpropitious beginning, of which he has given a graphic account in "The Blithedale Romance."

At first he liked his work at the Farm. The novelty of it proved attractive to him. On May 3 he wrote a letter to his sister Louisa, which reflects the practical nature of his new surroundings; and it must be confessed that this is a refreshing change from the sublunary considerations at his Boston boarding–house. He has already "learned to plant potatoes, to milk cows, and to cut straw and hay for the cattle, and does various other mighty works." He has gained strength wonderfully, and can do a day's work without the slightest inconvenience; wears a tremendous pair of cowhide boots. He goes to bed at nine, and gets up at half–past four to sound the rising–horn,—much too early for a socialistic paradise, where human nature is supposed to find a pleasant as well as a salutary existence. George Ripley would seem to be driving the wedge in by the larger end. Hawthorne is delighted with the topographical aspect, and writes:

"This is one of the most beautiful places I ever saw in my life, and as secluded as if it were a hundred miles from any city or village. There are woods, in which we can ramble all day without meeting anybody or scarcely seeing a house. Our house stands apart from the main road, so that we are not troubled even with passengers looking at us. Once in a while we have a transcendental visitor, such as Mr. Alcott; but generally we pass whole days without seeing a single face save those of the brethren. The whole fraternity eat together; and such a delectable way of life has never been seen on earth since the days of the early Christians." [Footnote: J. Hawthorne, i. 228.]

From Louisa Hawthorne's reply, it may be surmised that his family did not altogether approve of the Brook Farm venture, perhaps because it withdrew him from his own home at a time when they had looked with fond expectation for his return; and here we have a glimpse into the beautiful soul of this younger sister, otherwise so little known to us. Elizabeth is skeptical of its ultimate success, but Louisa is fearful that he may work too hard and wants him to take good care of himself. She is delighted with the miniature of him, which they have lately received: "It has one advantage over the original,—I can make it go with me where I choose!"

Louisa wrote another warm and beautiful letter on June 11, recalling the days when they used to go fishing together on Lake Sebago, and adds:

"Elizabeth Cleveland says she saw Mr. George Bradford in Lowell last winter, and he told her he was going to be associated with you; but they say his mind misgave him terribly when the time came for him to go to Roxbury, and whether to make such a desperate step or not he could not tell." [Footnote: J. Hawthorne, i. 232.]

George P. Bradford was the masculine complement to Elizabeth Peabody— flitting across the paths of Emerson and Hawthorne throughout their lives. His name appears continually in the biographies of that time, but future generations would never know the sort of man he was, but for Louisa's amiable commentary. He appeared at Brook Farm a few days later, and became one of George Ripley's strongest and most faithful adherents. He is the historian of the West Roxbury community, and late in life the editor of the *Century* asked him to write a special account of it for that periodical. Bradford did so, and received one hundred dollars in return for his manuscript; but it never was published, presumably because it was too original for the editor's purpose.

Is it possible that Hawthorne put on a good face for this letter to his sister, in order to keep up appearances; or was it like the common experience of music and drawing teachers that the first lessons are the best performed; or did he really have some disagreement with Ripley, like that which he represents in "The Blithedale Romance"? The last is the more probable, although we do not hear of it otherwise. Spring is the least agreeable season for farming, with its muddy soil, its dressing the ground, its weeds to be kept down and its insects to be kept off. After the first week of June, the work becomes much pleasanter; and the harvesting is delightful,—stacking the grain, picking the fruit,—with the cheery wood fires, so restful to mind and body. Yet we find on August 12 that Hawthorne had become thoroughly disenchanted with his Arcadian life, although he admits that the labors of the farm were not so pressing as they had been. Ten days later, he refers to having spent the better part of a night with one of his co-workers, "who was quite out of his wits" and left the community next day. He then continues in his diary: [Footnote: American Notebook, ii. 15.]

"It is extremely doubtful whether Mr. Ripley will succeed in locating his community on the farm. He can bring Mr. E——to no terms, and the more they talk about the matter, the further they appear to be from a settlement. We must form other plans for ourselves; for I can see few or no signs that Providence purposes to give us a home here. I am weary, weary, thrice weary, of waiting so many ages. Whatever may be my gifts, I have not hitherto shown a single one that may avail to gather gold."

Here are already three disaffected personages, desirous of escaping from an earthly paradise. Mr. Ripley has by no means an easy row to hoe. Yet he keeps on ploughing steadily through his difficulties, as he did through the soil of his meadows. In September we find Hawthorne at Salem, and on the third he writes: [Footnote: American Notebook, ii. 16.]

"But really I should judge it to be twenty years since I left Brook Farm; and I take this to be one proof that my life there was unnatural and unsuitable, and therefore an unreal one. It already looks like a dream behind me. The real Me was never an associate of the community: there has been a spectral appearance there, sounding the horn at daybreak, and milking the cows, and hoeing potatoes, and raking hay, toiling in the sun, and doing me the honor to assume my name. But this spectre was not myself."

This idea of himself as a spectre seems to have accompanied him much in the way that the daemon did Socrates, and to have served in a similar manner as a warning to him. He left Brook Farm almost exactly as he describes himself doing, in "The Blithedale Romance," and he returned again on the twenty–second, but the brilliant woodland carnival which he describes, both in his "Note–book" and in "The Blithedale Romance," did not take place there until September 28. It was a masquerade in which Margaret Fuller and Emerson appeared as invited guests, and held a meeting of the Transcendental club "*sub tegmine fagi.*" As Hawthorne remarks, "Much conversation followed,"—in which he evidently found little to interest him. Margaret Fuller also made a present of a heifer to the live–stock of the Farm, of whose unruly gambols Hawthorne seems to have taken more particular notice. He would seem in fact to have attributed the same characteristics to the animal and its owner.

Having more time at his own disposal, he now attempted to write another volume of history for Peter Parley's library, but, although this was rather a childish affair, he found himself unequal to it. "I have not," he said, "the sense of perfect seclusion here, which has always been essential to my power of producing anything. It is true, nobody intrudes into my room; but still I cannot be quiet. Nothing here is settled; and my mind will not be abstracted." During the whole of October he went on long woodland walks, sometimes alone and at others with a single companion. He tried, like Emerson, courting Nature in her solitudes, and made the acquaintance of her denizens as if he were the original Adam taking an account of his animal kingdom. He picks up a terrapin, the *Emys picta*, which attempts to hide itself from him in a stone wall, and carries it considerately to a pond of water; but there is not much to be found in the woods, and one can travel a whole day in the forest primeval without coming across anything better than a few squirrels and small birds. In fact, two young sportsmen once rode on horseback with their guns from the Missouri River to the Pacific Ocean without meeting any larger game than prairie–chickens.

It was all in vain. Hawthorne's nature was not like Emerson's, and what stimulated the latter mentally made comparatively little impression on the former. Hawthorne found, then as always, that in order to practice his art, he must devote himself to it, wholly and completely, leaving side issues to go astern. In order to create an ideal world of his own, he was obliged to separate himself from all existing conditions, as Beethoven did when composing his symphonies. Composition for Hawthorne meant a severe mental strain. Those sentences, pellucid as a mountain spring, were not clarified without an effort. The faculty on which Hawthorne depended for this, as every artist does, was his imagination, and imagination is as easily disturbed as the electric needle. There is no fine art without sensitiveness. We see it in the portrait of Leonardo da Vinci, a man who could bend horseshoes in his hands; and Bismarck, who was also an artist in his way, confessed to the same mental disturbance from noise and general conversation, which Hawthorne felt at Brook Farm. It was the mental sensitiveness of Carlyle and Bismarck which caused their insomnia, and much other suffering besides.

George Ripley published an essay in the *Dial*, in which he heralded Fourier as the great man who was destined to regenerate society; but Fourier has passed away, and society continues in its old course. What he left out of his calculations, or perhaps did not understand, was the principle of population. If food and raiment were as common as air and water, mankind would double its numbers every twelve or fifteen years, and the tendency to do so produces a pressure on poor human nature, which is almost like the scourge of a whip, driving it into all kinds of ways and means in order to obtain sufficient sustenance. Most notable among the methods thus employed is, and always has been, the division of labor, and it will be readily seen that a community like Brook Farm, where skilled labor, properly speaking, was unknown, and all men were all things by turns, could never sustain so large a population relatively as a community where a strict division of industries existed. If a nation like France, for instance, where the population is nearly stationary, were to adopt Fourier's plan of social organization, it would prove a more severe restriction on human life than the wars of Napoleon. This is the reason why the attempt to plant a colony of Englishmen in Tennessee failed so badly. There was a kind of division of labor among them, but it was purely a local and a foreign division and not adapted to the region about them. Ripley's method of allowing work to be counted by the hour instead of by the day or half–day, was of itself sufficient to prevent the enterprise from being a financial success. Farming everywhere except on the Western prairies requires the closest thrift and economy, and all hands have to work hard.

Neither could such an experiment prove a success from a moral point of view. Emerson said of it: "The women did not object so much to a common table as they did to a common nursery." In truth one might expect that a common nursery would finally result in a free fight. The tendency of all such institutions would be to destroy the sanctity of family life; and it would also include a tendency to the deterioration of manliness. One of the professed objects of the Brook Farm association was, to escape from the evils of the great world,—from the trickery of trade, the pedantry of colleges, the flunkyism of office, and the arrogant pretensions of wealth. Every honest man must feel a sympathy with this; there are times when we all feel that the struggle of life is an unequal conflict, from which it would be a permanent blessing to escape; yet he who turns his back upon it, is like a soldier who runs away from the battle–field. It is the conflict with evil in the great world, and in ourselves, that constitutes virtue and develops character. It is *good* to learn the trickery of knaves and to expose it, to contend against pedantry and set a better example, to administer offices with a modest impartiality, and to treat the gilded fool with a dignified contempt. But if the wings of the archangel are torn and soiled in his conflict with sin, does it not add to the honor of the victory? The man who left his wife and children, because he found that he could not live with them without occasionally losing his temper, committed a grievous wrong; and it is equally true that hypocrisy, the meanest of vices, may sometimes become a virtue.

George P. Bradford, and a few others, enjoyed the life at Brook Farm, and would have liked to remain there longer. John S. Dwight, the translator of Goethe's and Schiller's ballads, [Footnote: One of the most musical translations in any language.] said in his old age that if he were a young man, he would be only too glad to return there; and it is undeniable that such a place is suited to a certain class of persons, both men and women. It cannot be repeated too often, however, that the true object of life is not happiness, but development. It is our special business on this planet, to improve the human race as our progenitors improved it, and developed it out of we know not what. By doing this, we also improve ourselves and happiness comes to us incidentally; but if we pursue happiness directly, we soon become pleasure–seekers, and, like Faust, join company with Mephistopheles. Happiness comes to a philosopher, perhaps while he is picking berries; to a judge, watching the approach of a thunder–storm; to a merchant, teaching his boy to skate. It came to Napoleon listening to a prayer–bell, and to Hawthorne playing games with his children. [Footnote: Perhaps also in his kindliness to the terrapin.] Happiness flies when we seek it, and steals upon us unawares.

George P. Bradford's account of Brook Farm in the "Memorial History of Boston" [Footnote: Vol. iv. 330.] is not so satisfactory as it might have been if he had given more specific details in regard to its management. The general supposition has been that there was an annual deficit in the accounts of the association, which could only be met by Mr. Ripley himself, who ultimately lost the larger portion of his investment. It is difficult to imagine how such an experiment could end otherwise, and the final conflagration of the principal building, or "The Hive," as it was called, served as a fitting consummation of the whole enterprise,—a truly dramatic climax. George Ripley went to New York to become literary editor of the *Tribune*, and was as distinguished there for the excellence of his reviews, and the elegance of his turnout in Central Park as he had been for the use of the spade and pitchfork at West Roxbury.

Mr. Bradford returned to the instruction of young ladies in French and Latin; and John S. Dwight became one of the civilizing forces of his time, by editing the Boston *Journal of Music*. None of them were the worse for their agrarian experiment.

Even if the West Roxbury *commune* had proved a success for two or three generations, it would not have sufficed for a test of Fourier's theory for it would have been a republic within a republic, protected by the laws and government of the United States, without being subjected to the inconvenience of its own political machinery. The only fair trial for such a system would be to introduce it in some tract of country especially set apart and made independent for the purpose; but the chances are ten to one that a community organized in this manner would soon be driven into the same process of formation that other colonies have passed through under similar conditions. The true socialism is the present organization of society, and although it might be improved in detail, to revolutionize it would be dangerous. Yet the interest that has been aroused at various times by discussions of the Brook Farm project, shows how strong the undercurrent is setting against the present order of things; and this is my chief excuse for making such a long digression on the subject.

During these last months of his bachelorhood, Hawthorne appears to us somewhat in the light of a hibernating bear; for we hear nothing of him at that season at all. Between the last of October, 1841, and July, 1842, there are a large number of odd fancies, themes for romances, and the like, published from his diary, but no entries of a personal character. We hear incidentally that he was at Brook Farm during a portion of the spring, which is not surprising in view of the fact that Doctor Nathaniel Peabody had removed from Salem to Boston in the mean time. One conclusion Hawthorne had evidently arrived at during the winter months, and it was that his engagement to Miss Sophia Peabody ought to be terminated in the way all such affairs should be; viz., by matrimony. Their prospects in life were not brilliant, but it was difficult to foresee any advantage in waiting longer, and there were decided disadvantages in doing so. It was accordingly agreed that they should be married at, or near, the summer solstice, the most suitable of all times for weddings—or engagements. On June 20, he wrote to his *fiancee* from Salem, reminding her that within ten days they were to become man and wife, and added this significant reflection: "Nothing can part us now; for God himself hath ordained that we shall be one. So nothing remains but to reconcile yourself to your destiny. Year by year we shall grow closer to each other; and a thousand years hence, we shall be only in the honeymoon of our marriage."

Yet we find him writing again the tenderest and most graceful of love– letters on June 30. [Footnote: J. Hawthorne, i. 241.] The wedding has evidently been postponed; but two days later he is in Boston, and finds a pleasant recreation watching the boys sail their toy boats on the Frog Pond. The ceremony finally was performed on July 9, and it was only the day previous that Hawthorne wrote the following letter, which is dated from 54 Pinckney Street:

"MY DEAR SIR:

"Though personally a stranger to you, I am about to request of you the greatest favor which I can receive from any man. I am to be married to Miss Sophia Peabody to–morrow, and it is our mutual desire that you should perform the ceremony. Unless it should be decidedly a rainy day, a carriage will call for you at half–past eleven o'clock in the forenoon.

> "Very respectfully yours,
> "NATH. HAWTHORNE.

"REV. JAMES F. CLARKE,
   "Chestnut St."

George S. Hillard lived on Pinckney Street, and Hawthorne may have been visiting him at the moment. The Peabodys attended service at Mr. Clarke's church in Indiana Place, where Hawthorne may also have gone with them. He could not have made a more judicious choice; but, singularly enough, although Mr. Clarke became Elizabeth Peabody's life–long friend, and even went to Concord to lecture, he and Hawthorne never met again after this occasion.

The ceremony was performed at the house of Sophia Peabody's father, No. 13 West Street, a building of which not one stone now rests upon another. It was a quiet family wedding (such as oftenest leads to future happiness), and most deeply impressive to those concerned in it. What must it have been to Hawthorne, who had known so much loneliness, and had waited so long for the comfort and sympathy which only a devoted wife can give?

Time has drawn a veil over Hawthorne's honeymoon, but exactly four weeks after the wedding, we find him and his wife installed in the house at Concord, owned by the descendants of Reverend Dr. Ripley. It will be remembered that Hawthorne had invested his only thousand dollars in the West Roxbury Utopia, whence it was no longer possible to recover it. He had, however, an unsubstantial Utopian sort of claim for it, against the Association, which he placed in the hands of George S. Hillard, and subsequent negotiation would seem to have resulted in giving Hawthorne a lease of the Ripley house, or "Old Manse," in return for it. It was already classic ground, for Emerson had occupied the house for a time and had written his first book there; and thither Hawthorne went to locate himself, determined to try once more if he could earn his living by his pen.

[Illustration: THE OLD MANSE, RESIDENCE OF DR. RIPLEY]

CHAPTER VIII. CONCORD AND THE OLD MANSE: 1842–1845

The Ripley house dates back to the times of Captain Daniel Hathorne, or even before him, and at Concord Fight the British left wing must have extended close to it. Old and unpainted as it is, it gives a distinct impression of refinement and good taste. Alone, I believe, among the Concord houses of former times, it is set back far enough from the country–road to have an avenue leading to it, lined with balm of Gilead trees, and guarded at the entrance by two tall granite posts somewhat like obelisks. On the further side of the house, Dr. Ripley had planted an apple orchard, which included some rare varieties, especially the blue pearmain, a dark–red autumn apple with a purple bloom upon it like the bloom upon the rye. A high rounded hill on the northeast partially shelters the house from the storms in that direction; and on the opposite side the river sweeps by in a magnificent curve, with broad meadows and rugged hills, leading up to the pale–blue outline of Mount Wachusett on the western horizon. The Musketequid or Concord River has not been praised too highly. Its clear, gently flowing current, margined by bulrushes and grassy banks, produces an effect of mental peacefulness, very different from the rushing turbulent waters and rocky banks of Maine and New Hampshire rivers. From whatever point you approach the Old Manse, it becomes the central object in a charming country scene, and it does not require the peculiar effect of mouldering walls to make it picturesque. It has stood there long, and may it long remain.

There was formerly an Indian encampment on the same ground,—a well–chosen position both strategically and for its southern exposure. Old Mrs. Ripley had a large collection of stone arrow–heads, corn–mortars, and other relics of the aborigines, which she used to show to the young people who came to call on her grandchildren; and there were among them pieces of a dark–bluish porphyry which she said was not to be found in Massachusetts, but must have been brought from northern New England. There was no reason why they should not have been. The Indians could go from Concord in their canoes to the White Mountains or the Maine lakes, and shoot the deer that came down to drink from the banks of the river; but the deer disappeared before the advance of the American farmer, and the Indians went with them. Now a grandson of Madam Ripley, in the bronze likeness of a minuteman of 1775, stands sentinel at "The Old North Bridge."

The Life and Genius of Nathaniel Hawthorne

Hawthorne ascended the hill opposite his house and wrote of the view from it:

"The scenery of Concord, as I beheld it from the summit of the hill, has no very marked characteristics, but has a great deal of quiet beauty, in keeping with the river. There are broad and peaceful meadows, which, I think, are among the most satisfying objects in natural scenery. The heart reposes on them with a feeling that few things else can give, because almost all other objects are abrupt and clearly defined; but a meadow stretches out like a small infinity, yet with a secure homeliness which we do not find either in an expanse of water or air."

The great cranberry meadows below the north bridge are sometimes a wonderful place in winter, when the river overflows its banks and they become a broad sheet of ice extending for miles. There one can have a little skating, an exercise of which Hawthorne was always fond.

It was now, and not at Brook Farm, that he found his true Arcadia, and we have his wife's testimony that for the first eighteen months or more at the Old Manse, they were supremely happy. Every morning after breakfast he donned the blue frock, which he had worn at West Roxbury, and went to the woodshed to saw and split wood for the daily consumption. After that he ascended to his study in the second story, where he wrote and pondered until dinner–time. It appears also that he sometimes assisted in washing the dishes—like a helpful mate. After dinner he usually walked to the post–office and to a reading–room in the centre of the town, where he looked over the Boston *Post* for half an hour. Later in the afternoon, he went rowing or fishing on the river, but his wife does not seem to have accompanied him in these excursions, for Judge Keyes, who often met him in his boat, does not mention seeing her with him. In the evenings he read Shakespeare with Mrs. Hawthorne, commencing with the first volume, and going straight through to the end, "Titus Andronicus" and all,—and this must have occupied them a large portion of the winter. How can a man fail to be happy in such a mode of life!

Hawthorne also went swimming in the river when the weather suited— rather exceptional in Concord for a middle–aged gentleman; but there were two very attractive bathing places near the Old Manse, one, a little above on the opposite side of the river, and the other, afterwards known as Simmons's Landing, where there was a row of tall elms a short distance below the bridge. It is probable that Hawthorne frequented the latter place, as being more remote from human habitations. He did not take to his gun again, although he could see the wild ducks in autumn, flying past his house. There were grouse and quail in the woods, and woodcock were to be found along the brook which ran through Emerson's pasture; but perhaps Hawthorne had become too tenderhearted for field-sports.

If Boston is the hub of the universe, Concord might be considered as the linchpin which holds it on. Its population was originally derived from Boston, and it must be admitted that it retains more Bostonian peculiarities than most other New England towns. It does not assimilate readily to the outside world. Nor is it surprising that few local visitors called upon the Hawthornes at the Old Manse. Emerson, always hospitable and public-spirited, went to call on them at once; and John Keyes, also a liberal-minded man, introduced Hawthorne at the reading-club. Margaret Fuller came and left a book for Hawthorne to read, which may have annoyed him more than anything she could have said. Elizabeth Hoar, a woman of exalted character, to whose judgment Emerson sometimes applied for a criticism of his verses, also came sometimes; but the Old Manse was nearly a mile away from Emerson's house, and also from what might be called the "court end" of the town. Hawthorne's nearest neighbor was a milk-farmer named George L. Prescott, afterward Colonel of the Thirty-second Massachusetts Volunteers. He not only brought them milk, but also occasionally a bouquet culled out of his own fine nature, as a tribute to genius. A slightly educated man, he was nevertheless one of Nature's gentlemen, and his death in Grant's advance on Richmond was a universal cause of mourning at a time when so many brave lives were lost.

Hawthorne, as usual, was on the lookout for ghosts, and there could not have been a more suitable abode for those airy nothings, than the Old Manse. Mysterious sounds were heard in it repeatedly, especially in the nighttime, when the change of temperature produces a kind of settlement in the affairs of old woodwork. Under date of August 8 he writes in his diary:

"We have seen no apparitions as yet,—but we hear strange noises, especially in the kitchen, and last night, while sitting in the parlor, we heard a thumping and pounding as of somebody at work in my study. Nay, if I mistake not (for I was half asleep), there was a sound as of some person crumpling paper in his hand in our very bedchamber. This must have been old Dr. Ripley with one of his sermons."

The Life and Genius of Nathaniel Hawthorne

Evidently he would have preferred seeing a ghost to receiving an honorary degree from Bowdoin College, and if the shade of Doctor Ripley had appeared to him in a dissolving light, like the Rontgen rays, Hawthorne would certainly have welcomed him as a kindred spirit and have expressed his pleasure at the manifestation.

Another idiosyncrasy of his, which seems like the idiom in a language, was his total indifference to distinguished persons, simply as such. It was not that he considered all men on a level, for no one recognized more clearly the profound inequalities of human nature; but he was quite as likely to take an interest in a store clerk as in a famous writer. It is not necessary to suppose that a man is a parasite of fame because he goes to a President's reception, or wishes to meet a celebrated English lecturer. It is natural that we should desire to know how such people appear—their expression, their tone of voice, their general behavior; but Hawthorne did not care for this. At the time of which we write, Doctor Samuel G. Howe, the hero of Greek independence and the mental liberator of Laura Bridgman, was a more famous man than Emerson or Longfellow. He came to Concord with his brilliant wife, and they called at the Old Manse, where Mrs. Hawthorne received them very cordially, but they saw nothing of her husband, except a dark figure gliding through the entry with his hat over his eyes. One can only explain this by one of those fits of exceeding bashfulness that sometimes overtake supersensitive natures. School–girls just budding into womanhood often behave in a similar manner; and they are no more to be censured for it than Hawthorne,—to whom it may have caused moments of poignant self–reproach in his daily reflections. But Doctor Howe was the man of all men whom Hawthorne ought to have known, and half an hour's conversation might have made them friends for life.

George William Curtis was a remarkably brilliant young man, and gave even better promise for the future than he afterwards fulfilled,—as the editor of a weekly newspaper. He was at Brook Farm with Hawthorne, and afterward followed him to Concord, but is only referred to by Hawthorne once, and then in the briefest manner. Neither has Hawthorne much to say of Emerson; but Thoreau and Ellery Channing evidently attracted his attention, for he refers to them repeatedly in his diary, and he has left the one life–like portrait of Thoreau—better than a photograph—that now exists. He surveys them both in rather a critical manner, and takes note that Thoreau is the more substantial and original of the two; and he is also rather sceptical as to Channing's poetry, which Emerson valued at a high rate; yet he narrowly missed making a friend of Channing, with whom he afterward corresponded in a desultory way.

The Life and Genius of Nathaniel Hawthorne

We should not have known of Hawthorne's skating at Concord, but for Mrs. Hawthorne's "Memoirs," from which we learn that he frequently skated on the overflowed meadows, where the Lowell railway station now stands. She writes: "Wrapped in his cloak, he moved like a self–impelled Greek statue, stately and grave." This is the manner in which we should imagine Hawthorne to have skated; but all others were a foil to her husband in the eyes of his wife. [Footnote: "Memories of Hawthorne," 52.] He was evidently a fine skater, gliding over the ice in long sweeping curves. Emerson was also a dignified skater, but with a shorter stroke, and stopping occasionally to take breath, or look about him, as he did in his lectures. Thoreau came sometimes and performed rare glacial exploits, interesting to watch, but rather in the line of the professional acrobat. What a transfiguration of Hawthorne, to think of him skating alone amid the reflections of a brilliant winter sunset!

When winter came Emerson arranged a course of evening receptions at his house for the intellectual people of Concord, with apples and gingerbread for refreshments. Curtis attended these, and has told us how Hawthorne always sat apart with an expression on his face like a distant thunder–cloud, saying little, and not only listening to but watching the others. Curtis noticed a certain external and internal resemblance in him to Webster, who was at times a thunderous–looking person—denoting, I suppose, the electric concentration in his cranium. Emerson also watched Hawthorne, and the whole company felt his silent presence, and missed him greatly once or twice when he failed to come. Miss Elizabeth Hoar said:

"The people about Emerson, Channing, Thoreau and the rest, echo his manner so much that it is a relief to him to meet a man like Hawthorne, on whom his own personality makes no impression." Neither did Mrs. Emerson echo her husband.

The greater a man is, intellectually, the more distinct his difference from a general type and also from other men of genius. No two personalities could be more unlike than Hawthorne and Emerson.

It would seem to be part of the irony of Fate that they should have lived on the same street, and, have been obliged to meet and speak with each other. One was like sunshine, the other shadow. Emerson was transparent, and wished to be so; he had nothing to conceal from friend or enemy. Hawthorne was simply impenetrable. Emerson was cordial and moderately sympathetic. Hawthorne was reserved, but his sympathies were as profound as the human soul itself. To study human nature as Hawthorne and Shakespeare did, and to make models of their acquaintances for works of fiction, Emerson would have considered a sin; while the evolution of sin and its effect on character was the principal study of Hawthorne's life. One was an optimist, and the other what is sometimes unjustly called a pessimist; that is, one who looks facts in the face and sees people as they are.

[Footnote: "Sketches from Concord and Appledore."]

While Emerson's mind was essentially analytic, Hawthorne's was synthetic, and, as Conway says, he did not receive the world into his intellect, but into his heart, or soul, where it was mirrored in a magical completeness. The notion that the artist requires merely an observing eye is a superficial delusion. Observation is worth little without reflection, and everything depends on the manner in which the observer deals with his facts. Emerson looked at life in order to penetrate it; Hawthorne, in order to comprehend it, and assimilate it to his own nature. The one talked heroism and the other lived it. Not but that Emerson's life was a stoical one, but Hawthorne's was still more so, and only his wife and children knew what a heart there was in him.

The world will never know what these two great men thought of one another. Hawthorne has left some fragmentary sentences concerning Emerson, such as, "that everlasting rejecter of all that is, and seeker for he knows not what," and "Emerson the mystic, stretching his hand out of cloud–land in vain search for something real;" but he likes Emerson's ingenuous way of interrogating people, "as if every man had something to give him." However, he makes no attempt at a general estimate; although this expression should also be remembered: "Clergymen, whose creed had become like an iron band about their brows, came to Emerson to obtain relief,"—a sincere recognition of his spiritual influence.

Several witnesses have testified that Emerson had no high opinion of Hawthorne's writing,—that he preferred Reade's "Christie Johnstone" to "The Scarlet Letter," but Emerson never manifested much interest in art, simply for its own sake. Like Bismarck, whom he also resembled in his enormous self–confidence, he cared little for anything that had not a practical value. He read Shakespeare and Goethe, not so much for the poetry as for the "fine thoughts" he found in them. George Bradford stated more than once that Emerson showed little interest in the pictorial art; and after walking through the sculpture–gallery of the Vatican, he remarked that the statues seemed to him like toys.

The Life and Genius of Nathaniel Hawthorne

His essay on Michel Angelo is little more than a catalogue of great achievements; he recognizes the moral impressiveness of the man, but not the value of his sublime conceptions. Music, neither he nor Hawthorne cared for, for it belongs to emotional natures.

In his "Society and Solitude" Emerson has drawn a picture of Hawthorne as the lover of a hermitical life; a picture only representing that side of his character, and developed after Emerson's fashion to an artistic extreme. "Whilst he suffered at being seen where he was, he consoled himself with the delicious thought of the inconceivable number of places where he was not," and "He had a remorse running to despair, of his social *gaucheries*, and walked miles and miles to get the twitching out of his face, the starts and shrugs out of his shoulders."

[Footnote: "Society and Solitude," 4, 5.]

There is a touch of arrogance in this, and it merely marks the difference between the modest author of the "Essays," and the proud, censorious Emerson of 1870; but his love of absolute statements ofttimes led him into strange contradictions, and the injustice which results from judging our fellow–mortals by an inflexible standard was the final outcome of his optimism. Hawthorne was more charitable when he remarked that without Byron's faults we should not have had his virtues; but the truth lies between the two.

There have been many instances of genius as sensitive as Hawthorne's in various branches of art: Shelley and Southey, Schubert and Chopin, Correggio and Corot. Southey not only blushed red but blushed blue—as if the life were going out of him; and in Chopin and Correggio at least we feel that they could not have been what they were without it. Napoleon, whose nerves were like steel wires, suffered nevertheless from a peculiar kind of physical sensitiveness. He could not take medicines like other men,—a small dose had a terrible effect on him,— and it was much the same with respect to changes of food, climate, and the like.

What Hawthorne required was sympathetic company. Do not we all require it? The hypercritical morality of the Emersonians, especially in Concord, could not have been favorable to his mental ease and comfort. How could a man in a happily married condition feel anything but repugnance to Thoreau's idea of marriage as a necessary evil; or Alcott's theory that eating animal food tended directly to the commission of crime?

On the first anniversary of Hawthorne's wedding, a tragical drama was enacted in Concord, in which he was called upon to perform a subordinate part. One Miss Hunt, a school–teacher and the daughter of a Concord farmer, drowned herself in the river nearly opposite the place where Hawthorne was accustomed to bathe. The cause of her suicide has never been adequately explained, but as she was a transcendentalist, or considered herself so, there were those who believed that in some occult way that was the occasion of it. However, as one of her sisters afterward followed her example, it would seem more likely to have come from the development of some family trait. She was seen walking upon the bank for a long time, before she took the final plunge; but the catastrophe was not discovered until near evening.

Ellery Channing came with a man named Buttrick to borrow Hawthorne's boat for the search, and Hawthorne went with them. As it happened, they were the ones who found the corpse, and Hawthorne's account in his diary of its recovery is a terribly accurate description,—softened down and poetized in the rewritten statement of "The Blithedale Romance." There is in fact no description of a death in Homer or Shakespeare so appalling as this literal transcript of the veritable fact.

[Footnote: J. Hawthorne, i. 300.]

What concerns us here, however, are the comments he set down on the dolorous event. Concerning her appearance, he says:

"If she could have foreseen while she stood, at five o'clock that morning on the bank of the river, how her maiden corpse would have looked eighteen hours afterwards, and how coarse men would strive with hand and foot to reduce it to a decent aspect, and all in vain,—it would surely have saved her from the deed."

And again:

"I suppose one friend would have saved her; but she died for want of sympathy—a severe penalty for having cultivated and refined herself out of the sphere of her natural connections."

The first remark has often been misunderstood. It is not the vanity of women, which is after all only a reflection (or the reflective consequence) of the admiration of man, which

The Life and Genius of Nathaniel Hawthorne

Hawthorne intends, but that delicacy of feeling which Nature requires of woman for her own protection; and he may not have been far wrong in supposing that if Miss Hunt had foreseen the exact consequences of her fatal act she would not have committed it. Hawthorne's remark that her death was a consequence of having refined and cultivated herself beyond the reach of her relatives, seems a rather hard judgment. The latter often happens in American life, and although it commonly results in more or less family discord, are we to condemn it for that reason? If she died as Hawthorne imagines, from the lack of intellectual sympathy, we may well inquire if there was no one in Concord who might have given aid and encouragement to this young aspiring soul.

> "Take her up tenderly;
> Lift her with care,
> Fashioned so slenderly,
> Young and so fair."

And one is also tempted to add:

> "Alas! for the rarity
> Of Christian charity."

Hawthorne's earthly paradise only endured until the autumn of 1843. When cool weather arrived, want and care came also. On November 26 he wrote to George S. Hillard:

"I wish at some leisure moment you would give yourself the trouble to call into Munroe's book–store and inquire about the state of my 'Twice– told Tales.' At the last accounts (now about a year since) the sales had not been enough to pay expenses; but it may be otherwise now—else I shall be forced to consider myself a writer for posterity; or at all events not for the present generation. Surely the book was puffed enough to meet with a sale."

[Footnote: London Athenaum, August 10, 1889.]

The interpretation of this is that Longfellow, Hillard and Bridge could appreciate Hawthorne's art, but the solid men of Boston (with some rare exceptions) could not. Even Webster preferred the grotesque art of Dickens to Hawthorne's "wells of English undefiled." Recently, one of the few surviving original copies of "Fanshawe" was sold at auction for six hundred dollars. Such is the difference between genius and celebrity.

The trouble then and now is that wealthy Americans as a class feel no genuine interest in art or literature. They do not form a true aristocracy, but a plutocracy, and are for the most part very poorly educated. It was formerly the brag of the Winthrops and Otises that they could go through college and learn their lessons in the recitation–room. Now they go to row, and play foot–ball, and after they graduate, they leave the best portion of their lives behind them. Then if they have a talent for business they become absorbed in commercial affairs; or if not, they travel from one country to another, picking up a smattering of everything, but not resting long enough in any one place for their impressions to develop and bear good fruit. They are not like the aristocratic classes of England, France and Germany, who become cultivated men and women, and serve to maintain a high standard of art and literature in those countries.

The captain of a Cunard steamship, who owned quite a library, said in 1869: "I have bought some very interesting books in New York, especially by a writer named Hawthorne, but the type and paper are so poor that they are not worth binding." The reason why American publishers do not bring out books in such good form as foreign publishers—is that there is no demand for a first–rate article. Thus do the fine arts languish. When rich young Americans take as much interest in painting and sculpture as they do in foot–ball and yachting, we shall have our Vandycks and Murillos,—if nothing better.

Discouraged with the ill success of "Fanshawe," Hawthorne had limited himself since then to the writing of short sketches, such as would be acceptable to the magazine editors, and now that he had formed this habit, he found it difficult to escape from it. He informs us in the preface to "Mosses from an Old Manse" that he had hoped a more serious and extended plot would come to him on the banks of Concord River, but his imagination did not prove equal to the occasion. Most of the stories in "Mosses" must have been composed at Concord, but "Mrs. Bull–Frog'" and "Monsieur du Miroir" must have been written previously, for he refers to them in a letter at Brook Farm. A few were published in the *Democratic Review*, and others may have been elsewhere; but the proceeds he derived from them would not have supported a day–laborer, and toward the close of his second year at the Manse, Hawthorne found himself running in debt for the necessaries of life. He endured this with his usual stoical reticence, although there is nothing like debt to sicken a man's heart,—unless he be a decidedly light–minded man. Better fortune, however, was on its way to him in the shape of a political revolution.

On March 3, 1844, a daughter was born to the Hawthornes, whom they named Una, in spite of Hillard's objection that the name was too poetic or too fanciful for the prosaic practicalities of real life. The name was an excellent one for a poet's daughter, and did not seem out of place in Arcadian Concord. Miss Una grew up into a graceful, fair and poetic young lady,—in all respects worthy of her name. She had an uncommonly fine figure, and, as often happens with first-born children, resembled her father much more than her mother. Her name also suggests the early influence of Spenser in her father's style and mode of thought.

Soon after this fortunate event Hawthorne wrote a letter to Hillard, in which he said:

"I find it a very sober and serious kind of happiness that springs from the birth of a child. It ought not come too early in a man's life—not till he has fully enjoyed his youth—for methinks the spirit can never be thoroughly gay and careless again, after this great event. We gain infinitely by the exchange; but we do give up something nevertheless. As for myself who have been a trifler preposterously long, I find it necessary to come out of my cloud-region, and allow myself to be woven into the sombre texture of humanity."

It seems then that his conscience sometimes reproached him, but this only proves that his moral nature was in a healthy normal condition. There was a certain kind of indolence in him, a love of the *dolce far niente*, and an inclination to general inactivity which he may have inherited from his seafaring ancestors. Much better so, than to suffer from the nervous restlessness, which is the rule rather than the exception in New England life.

In the same letter he mentions having forwarded a story to *Graham's Magazine*, which was accepted but not yet published after many months. He also anticipates an amelioration of his affairs from a Democratic victory in the fall elections.

Meanwhile, Horatio Bridge had been traversing the high seas in the "Cyane," which was finally detailed to watch for slavers and to protect American commerce on the African coast. He had kept a journal of his various experiences and observations, which he sent to Hawthorne with a rather diffident interrogation as to whether it might be worth publishing. Hawthorne was decidedly of the opinion that it ought to be published,—in which we cordially agree with him,—and was well pleased to edit it for his friend; and, although it has now shared the fate of most of the books of its class, it is excellent reading for those who chance to find a copy of it. Bridge was a good observer, and a candid writer.

The election of 1844 was the most momentous that had yet taken place in American history. It decided the annexation of Texas, and the acquisition of California, with a coast–line on the Pacific Ocean nearly equal to that on the Atlantic; but it also brought with it an unjust war of greed and spoliation, and other evil consequences of which we are only now begining to reach the end. The slaveholders and the Democratic leaders desired Texas in order to perpetuate their control of the government, and it was precisely through this measure that they lost it,—as happens so often in human affairs. It was the gold discoveries in California that upset their calculations. California would *not* come into the Union as a slave state. Enraged at this failure, the Southern politicians made a desperate attempt to recover lost ground, by seizing on the fertile prairies in the Northwest; but there they came into conflict with the industrial classes of the North, who fought them on their own ground and abolished slavery. Never had public injustice been followed by so swift and terrible a retribution.

In regard to the candidates of 1844, it was hardly possible to compare them. Polk possessed the ability to preside over the House of Representatives, but he did not rise above this; while Clay could be fairly compared on some points with Washington himself, and united with this a persuasive eloquence second only to Webster's. He was practically defeated by fifteen or twenty thousand abolitionists who preferred to throw away their votes rather than to cast them for a slave–holder.

Hawthorne, in the quiet seclusion of his country home, did not realize this danger to the Republic. He only knew that his friends were victorious, and was happy in the expectation of escaping from his debts, and of providing more favorably for his little family.

CHAPTER IX. "MOSSES PROM AN OLD MANSE": 1845

There is no evidence in the Hawthorne documents or publications to show exactly when the first edition of "Mosses from an Old Manse" made its appearance, and copies of it are now exceedingly rare, but we find the Hawthorne family in Salem reading the book in the autumn of 1845, so that it was probably brought out at that time and helped to maintain its author during his last days at Concord.

There must have been some magical influence in the Old Manse or in its surrounding scenery, to have stimulated both Emerson's and Hawthorne's love of Nature to such a degree. Emerson's eye dilates as he looks upon the sunshine gilding the trunks of the balm of Gilead trees on his avenue; and Hawthorne dwells with equal delight on the luxuriant squash vines which spread over his vegetable garden. Discoursing on this he says:

"Speaking of summer squashes, I must say a word of their beautiful and varied forms. They presented an endless diversity of urns and vases, shallow or deep, scalloped or plain, molded in patterns which a sculptor would do well to copy, since art has never invented anything more graceful."

And again:

"A cabbage, too—especially the early Dutch cabbage, which swells to a monstrous circumference, until its ambitious heart often bursts asunder—is a matter to be proud of when we can claim a share with the earth and sky in producing it."

It would seem as if no one before Hawthorne had rightly observed these common vegetables, whose external appearance is always before our eyes. He not only humanizes whatever attracts his attention, but he looks through a refining medium of his own personality. He has the gift of Midas to bring back the Golden Age for us. Who besides Homer has been able to describe a chariot-race, and who but Hawthorne could extract such poetry from a farmer's garden?

If we compare this introductory chapter with such earlier sketches as "The Vision at the Fountain" and "The Toll-Gatherer's Day," we recognize the progress that Hawthorne has made since the first volume of "Twice Told Tales." We are no longer reminded of the plain unpainted house on Lake Sebago. His style is not only more graceful, but has acquired greater fulness of expression, and he is evidently working in a deeper and richer vein of thought. Purity of expression is still his polar star, and his writing is nowhere overloaded, but it has a warmer tone, a deeper perspective, and an atmospheric quality which painters call *chi-aroscuro*. He charms with pleasing fancies, while he penetrates to the soul.

Hawthorne rarely repeats himself in details, and never in designs. Two of Dickens's most interesting novels, "Oliver Twist" and "David Copperfield," are constructed on the same theme, but each of the studies in this collection has a distinct individuality which appeals to the reader after a fashion of its own. Each has its moral, or rather central, idea to which all its component parts are related, and teaches a lesson of its own, so unobtrusively that we become possessed of it almost unawares. Some are intensely, even tragically, serious; others so light and airy that they seem as if woven out of gossamer.

There are a few, however, that do not harmonize with the general tone and character of the rest,—especially "Mrs. Bull–Frog," which Hawthorne himself confessed to having been an experiment, and which strangely enough is much more in the style of his son Julian. "Monsieur du Miroir" and "Sketches from Memory" are relics of his earlier writings; perhaps also "Feather–Top" and "The Procession of Life." It would have been better perhaps if "Young Goodman Brown" had been used to light a fire at the Old Manse.

"Monsieur du Miroir" is chiefly interesting as an example of Hawthorne's faculty for elaborating the most simple subject until every possible phase of it has been exhausted. It may also throw some light scientifically on the origin of consciousness. We see ourselves reflected not only in the mirror, but on the blade of a knife, or a puddle in the road; and, if we look sharply enough, in the eyes of other men—even in the expression of their faces. In such manner does Nature force upon us a recognition of our various personalities—the nucleus of self–knowledge, and self–respect.

Whittier once spoke of "Young Goodman Brown" as indicating a mental peculiarity in Hawthorne, which like the cuttle–fish rarely rises to the surface. The plot is cynical, and largely enigmatical. The very name of it (in the way Hawthorne develops the story) is a fearful satire on human nature. He may have intended this for an exposure of the inconsistency, and consequent hypocrisy, of Puritanism; but the name of Goodman Brown's wife is Faith, and this suggests that Brown may have been himself intended for an incarnation of *doubt*, or *disbelief* carried to a logical extreme. Whatever may have been Hawthorne's design, the effect is decidedly unpleasant.

The Life and Genius of Nathaniel Hawthorne

Emerson talked in proverbs, and Hawthorne in parables. The finest sketches in this collection are parables. "The Birth Mark," "Rappacini's Daughter," "A Select Party," "Egotism," and "The Artist of the Beautiful." "The Celestial Railroad" is an allegory, a variation on "Pilgrim's Progress."

"The Birth Mark" and "Rappacini's Daughter" are like divergent lines, which originate at an single point; and that point is the radical viciousness of trying experiments on human beings. It is bad enough, although excusable, to vivisect dogs and rabbits; but why should we attempt the same course of procedure with those that are nearest and dearest to us? Such parables were not required in the time of Tiberius Casar and men and women grew up in a natural, vigorous manner; but now we have become so scientific that we continually attempt to improve on Nature,—like the artist who left the rainbow out of his picture of Niagara because its colors did not harmonize with the background.

The line of divergence in "The Birth Mark" is indicated by its name. We all have our birth–marks,—traits of character, which may be temporarily suppressed, or relegated to the background, but which cannot be eradicated and are certain to reappear at unguarded moments, or on exceptional occasions. Education and culture can do much to soften and temper the disposition, but the original material remains the same. The father who attempts to force his son into a mode of life for which Nature did not intend him, or the mother who quarrels with her daughter's friends, commits an error similar to that of Hawthorne's alchemist, who endeavors to remove the birthmark from the otherwise beautiful face of his wife, but only succeeds in effecting this together with her death. The tragical termination of the alchemist's experiments, the pathetic yielding up of life by his sweet "Clytie," is described with an impressive tenderness. She sinks to her last sleep without a murmur of reproach.

"Rappacini's Daughter" might serve as a protest against bringing up children in an exceptional and abnormal manner. I once knew an excellent lady, who, with the best possible intentions, brought up her daughter to be different from all other girls. As a consequence, she *was* different,—could not assimilate herself to others. She had no admirers, or young friends of her own sex, for there were few points of contact between herself and general society. Her mother was her only friend. She aged rapidly and died early. Similarly, a boy brought up in a secluded condition of purity and ignorance, finally developed into one of the most vicious of men.

Hawthorne has prefigured this by a bright colored flower which sparkles like a gem, very attractive at a distance, but exhaling a deadly perfume. He may not have been aware that the opium poppy has so brilliant a flower that it can be seen at a distance from which all other flowers are invisible. The scene of his story is placed in Italy,—the land of beauty, but also the country of poisoners. Rappacini, an old botanist and necromancer, has trained up his daughter in the solitary companionship of this flower, from which she has acquired its peculiar properties. A handsome young student is induced to enter the garden, partly from curiosity and partly through the legerdemain of Rappacini. The student soon falls under the daughter's influence and finds himself being gradually poisoned. A watchful apothecary, who has penetrated the necromancer's secret, provides the young man with an antidote which saves him, but deprives the maiden of life. She crosses the barrier which separated her from a healthy existence, and the poison reacts upon her system and kills her. The old apothecary looks out from his window, and cries, "O Rappacini! Is this the consummation of your experiment?"

The underlying agreement between this story and "The Birth Mark" becomes apparent when we observe that the termination of one is simply a variation upon the last scene of the other. In one instance a beautiful daughter is sacrificed by her father, and in the other a lovely wife is victimized by her husband. There have been thousands, if not millions, of such cases.

There is no other writer but Shakespeare who has portrayed the absolute devotion of a woman's love with such delicacy of feeling and depth of sympathy as Hawthorne. In the two stories we have just considered, and also in "The Bosom Serpent," this element serves, like the refrain of a Greek chorus, to give a sweet, penetrating undertone which reconciles us to much that would otherwise seem intolerable. The heroines in these pieces have such a close spiritual relationship that one suspects them of having been studied from the same model, and who could this have been so likely as Hawthorne's own wife. [Footnote: Notice also the similar character of Sophia in J. Hawthorne's "Bressant."]

The theme of "The Bosom Serpent" is a husband's jealousy; and it is the self–forgetful devotion of his wife that finally cures his malady and relieves him of his unpleasant companion. The tale ends with one of those mystifying passages which Hawthorne weaves so skilfully, so that it is difficult to determine from the text whether there was a real serpent secreted under the man's clothing, or only an imaginary one,— although we presume the latter. Francis of Verulam says, "the best fortune for a husband is for his wife to consider him wise, which she will never do if she find him jealous"; and with good reason, for if he is unreasonably jealous, it shows a lack of confidence in her; but mutal confidence is the well—spring from which love flows, and if the well dries up, there is an end of it.

"The Select Party" is quite a relief, after this tragical trilogy. It is easy to believe that Hawthorne imagined this dream of a summer evening, while watching the great cumulus clouds, tinted with rose and lavender like aerial snow—mountains, floating toward the horizon. Here were true castles in the air, which he could people with shapes according to his fancy; but he chose the most common abstract conceptions, such as, the Clerk of the Weather, the Beau Ideal, Mr. So—they—say, the Coming Man, and other ubiquitous personages, whom we continually hear of, but never see. The Man of Fancy invites these and many others to a banquet in his cloud—castle, where they all converse and behave according to their special characters. A ripple of delicate humor, like the ripple made by a light summer breeze upon the calm surface of a lake, runs through the piece from the first sentence to the last; and the scene is brought to a close by the approach of a thunder—storm, which spreads consternation among these unsubstantial guests, much like that which takes place at a picnic under similar circumstances; and Hawthorne, with his customary mystification, leaves us in doubt as to whether they ever reached *terra firma* again.

There is one proverbial character, however, whom Hawthorne has omitted from this account; namely, Mr. Everybody. "What Everybody says, must be true;" but unfortunately Everybody's information is none of the best, and his judgment does not rise above his information. His self—confidence, however, is enormous. He understands law better than the lawyer, and medicine better than the physicians. He is never tired of settling the affairs of the country, and of proposing constitutional amendments. Is it not perfectly natural that Everybody should understand Everybody's business as well as or better than his own? He is continually predicting future events, and if they fail to take place he predicts them again. He is omnipresent, but if you seek him he is nowhere to be found,—which we may presume to be the reason why he did not appear at the entertainment given by the Man of Fancy.

That which gives the elevated character to Raphael's faces—as in the "Sistine Madonna" and other paintings—is not their drawing, though that is always refined, but the expression of the eyes, which are truly the windows of the soul. It was the same in

Hawthorne's face, and may be observed in all good portraits of him. An immutable calmness overspread his features, but in and about his eyes there was a spring–like mirthfulness; while down in the shadowy depth of those luminous orbs was concealed the pathos that formed the undercurrent of his life. So it is that high comedy, as Plato long ago observed, lies very close to tragedy.

A well–known French writer compares English humor, in a general way, to beer–drinking, and this is more particularly applicable to Dickens's characters. The very name of Mark Tapley suggests ale bottles. Thackeray's humor is of a more refined quality, but a trifle sharp and satirical. It is, however, pure and healthful and might be compared to Rhine–wine. Hawthorne's humor at its best is more refined than Thackeray's, as well as of a more amiable quality, and reminds one (on Taine's principle) of those delicate Italian wines which have very little body, but a delightful bouquet. As a humorist, however, Hawthorne varies in different times and places more than in any other respect. He adapts himself to his subject; is light and playful in "The Select Party"; takes on a more serious vein in "The Celestial Railroad"; in his resuscitation of Byron, in the letter from a lunatic called "P's Correspondence" he is simply sardonic; and "The Virtuoso's Collection" has all the effect, although he does not anywhere descend to low comedy, of a roaring farce. In "Mrs. Bull–Frog," as the title intimates, he approaches closely to the grotesque.

In "The Virtuoso's Collection" we have the humor of impossibility. Nothing is more common than this, but Hawthorne gives it a peculiar value of his own. A procession of mythological objects, strange historical relics, and the odd creations of fiction passes before our eyes. The abruptness of their juxtaposition excites continuous laughter in us. It would be an extremely phlegmatic person who could read it with a serious face. Don Quixote's Rosinante, Doctor Johnson's cat, Shelley's skylark, a live phonix, Prospero's magic wand, the hard–ridden Pegasus, the dove which brought the olive branch, and many others appear in such rapid succession that the reader has no time to take breath, or to consider what will turn up next. Like an accomplished showman, Hawthorne enlivens the performance here and there with original reflections on life, which are perfectly dignified, but become humorous from contrast with their surroundings. In spite of its comical effect, the piece has a very genteel air, for its material is taken from that general stock of information that passes current in cultivated families. The young man of fashion who had never heard of Elijah, or of Poe's "Raven," would not have understood it.

The Life and Genius of Nathaniel Hawthorne

In "The Hall of Fantasy," we catch some glimpses of Hawthorne's favorite authors:

"The grand old countenance of Homer, the shrunken and decrepit form, but vivid face, of Asop, the dark presence of Dante, the wild Ariosto, Rabelais's smile of deep–wrought mirth, the profound, pathetic humor of Cervantes, the all glorious Shakespeare, Spenser, meet guest for an allegoric structure, the severe divinity of Milton and Bunyan, molded of the homeliest clay, but instinct with celestial fire—were those that chiefly attracted my eye. Fielding, Richardson, and Scott occupied conspicuous pedestals."

He also adds Goethe and Swedenborg, and remarks of them:

"Were ever two men of transcendent imagination more unlike?"

It is evident that Byron was not a favorite with Hawthorne. In addition to his severe treatment of that poet, in "P's Correspondence," he says in "Earth's Holocaust," where he imagines the works of various authors to be consumed in a bonfire:

"Speaking of the properties of flame, me–thought Shelley's poetry emitted a purer light than almost any other productions of his day, contrasting beautifully with the fitful and lurid gleams and gushes of black vapor that flashed and eddied from the volumes of Lord Byron."

This seems like rather puritanical treatment. If there are false lines in Byron, there are quite as many weak lines in Shelley. If sincerity were to give out a pure flame, Byron would stand that test equal to any. His real fault is to be found in his somewhat glaring diction, like the *voix blanc* in singing, and in an occasional stroke of *persiflage*. This increases his attractiveness to youthful minds, but to a nature like Hawthorne's anything of an exhibitory character must always be unpleasant.

Emerson and Hawthorne only knew Goethe through the translations of Dwight, Carlyle and Margaret Fuller, and yet his poetry made a deeper impression on them than on Lowell and Longfellow, who read it in the original. Hawthorne appears to have taken lessons in German while at Brook Farm, for we find him studying a German book at the Old Manse, with a grammar and lexicon; but, as he confesses in his diary, without making satisfactory progress.

"The Artist of the Beautiful" is a Dantean allegory, and a poetic gem. A young watchmaker, imbued with a spirit above his calling, neglects the profits of his business in order to construct an artificial butterfly,—at once the type of useless beauty and the symbol of immortality, and he perseveres in spite of the difficulties of the undertaking and the contemptuous opposition of his acquaintances. He finally succeeds in making one which seems to be almost endowed with life, but only to be informed that it is no better than a toy, and that he has wasted his time on a thing which has no practical value. A child (who represents the thoughtlessness of the great world) crushes the exquisite piece of workmanship in his little hand; but the watch–maker does not repine at this, for he realizes that after having achieved the beautiful, in his own spirit, the outward symbol of it has comparatively little value. The Artist of the Beautiful is Hawthorne himself; and in this exquisite fable he has not only unfolded the secret of all high art, but his own life–secret as well.

HAWTHORNE AND TRANSCENDENTALISM

The French and English scepticism of the eighteenth century, produced a reaction in the more contemplative German nature, which took the form of a strong assertion of spirit or mind as an entity in itself, and distinct from matter. This movement was more like a national impulse than the proselytism of a sect, but the individual in whom this spiritual impulse of the German people manifested itself at that time was Immanuel Kant. Without discrediting the revelations of Hebrew tradition, he taught the doctrine that instead of looking for evidence of a Supreme Being in the external world, we should seek him in our own hearts; that every man could find a revelation in his own conscience,— in the consciousness of good and evil, by which man improves his condition on earth; that the ideas of a Supreme Being, or of immortality and freedom of will, are inherent in the human mind, and are not to be acquired from experience; but that, as the finite mind cannot comprehend the infinite, we cannot know God in the same sense that we know our own earthly fathers, or as Goethe afterwards expressed it,——

> "Who can say I know Him;
> Who can say, I know Him not;"

and that it is in this aspiration for the unattainable, in this reverence for absolute purity, wisdom and love, that the spirit of true religion consists.

The Life and Genius of Nathaniel Hawthorne

The new philosophy was named "Transcendentalism" by Kant's followers, because it included ideas which were beyond the range of experience. It became popular in Germany, as Platonism, to which it is closely related, became popular in ancient Greece. It has never been accepted in France, where scepticism still predominates, though we hear of it in Taine and a few other writers; but in Great Britain, although the English universities repudiated it, Transcendentalism became so influential that Gladstone has spoken of it, in his Romanes lecture, as the dominant philosophy of the nineteenth century. Every notable English writer of that period, with the exception of Macaulay, Mill, and Spencer, became largely imbued with it. In America its influence did not extend much beyond New England, but in that section at least its proselytes were numbered by thousands, and it effected an intellectual revolution which has since influenced the whole country.

The Concord group of transcendentalists did not accept the teaching of Kant in its original purity; but mixed with it a number of other imported products, that in no way appertain to it. Thoreau was an American *sansculotte*, a believer in the natural man; Ripley was mainly a socialist; Margaret Fuller was one of the earliest leaders in woman's rights; Alcott was a Neo–Platonist, a vegetarian, and a non–resistant; while Emerson sympathized largely with Thoreau, and from his poetic exaltation of Nature was looked upon as a pantheist by those who were not accustomed to nice discriminations. Thus it happened that Transcendentalism came to be associated in the public mind with any exceptional mode or theory of life. Its best representatives in America, like Professor Hedge of Harvard, Reverend David A. Wasson and Doctor William T. Harris (so long Chief of the National Bureau of Education), were much abler men than Emerson's followers, but did not attract so much attention, simply because they lived according to the customs of good society.

Sleepy Hollow, before it was converted into a cemetery, was one of the most attractive sylvan resorts in the environs of Concord. It was a sort of natural amphitheatre, a small oval plane, more than half surrounded by a low wooded ridge; a sheltered and sequestered spot, cool in summer, but also warm and sunny in spring, where the wild flowers bloomed and the birds sang earlier than in other places.

There, on August 22, 1842, a notable meeting took place, between Hawthorne, Emerson, and Margaret Fuller, who came that afternoon to enjoy the inspiration of the place, without preconcerted agreement. Margaret Fuller was first on the ground, and Hawthorne found her seated on the hill–side—his gravestone now overlooks the spot—reading a book with a peculiar name, which he "did not understand, and could not afterward recollect." Such a description could only apply to Kant's "Critique of Pure Reason," the original fountain–head and gospel of Transcendentalism.

It does not appear that Nathaniel Hawthorne ever studied "The Critique of Pure Reason." His mind was wholly of the artistic order,—the most perfect type of an artist, one might say, living at that time,—and a scientific analysis of the mental faculties would have been as distasteful to him as the dissection of a human body. History, biography, fiction, did not appear to him as a logical chain of cause and effect, but as a succession of pictures illustrating an ideal determination of the human race. He could not even look at a group of turkeys without seeing a dramatic situation in them. In addition to this, as a true artist, he was possessed of a strong dislike for everything eccentric and abnormal; he wished for symmetry in all things, and above all in human actions; and those restless, unbalanced spirits, who attached themselves to the transcendental movement and the anti–slavery cause, were particularly objectionable to him. It has been rightly affirmed that no revolutionary movement could be carried through without the support of that ill–regulated class of persons who are always seeking they know not what, and they have their value in the community, like the rest of us; but Hawthorne was not a revolutionary character, and to his mind they appeared like so many obstacles to the peaceable enjoyment of life. His motto was, "Live and let live." There are passages in his Concord diary in which he refers to the itinerant transcendentalist in no very sympathetic manner.

His experience at Brook Farm may have helped to deepen this feeling. There is no necessary connection between such an idyllic–socialistic experiment and a belief in the direct perception of a great First Clause; but Brook Farm was popularly supposed at that time to be an emanation of Transcendentalism, and is still largely so considered. He was wearied at Brook Farm by the philosophical discussions of George Ripley and his friends, and took to walking in the country lanes, where he could contemplate and philosophize in his own fashion,—which after all proved to be more fruitful than theirs. Having exchanged his interest in the West Roxbury Association for the Old Manse at Concord (truly a poetic bargain), he wrote the most keenly humorous of his shorter sketches, his "The Celestial Railroad," and in it represented the dismal cavern where Bunyan located the two great enemies of true religion, the Pope and the Pagan, as now occupied by a German giant, the Transcendentalist, who "makes it his business to seize upon honest travellers and fat them for his table with plentiful meals of smoke, mist, moonshine, raw potatoes, and sawdust."

That Transcendentalism was largely associated in Hawthorne's mind with the unnecessary discomforts and hardships of his West Roxbury life is evident from a remark which he lets fall in "The Virtuoso's Collection." The Virtuoso calls his attention to the seven–league boots of childhood mythology, and Hawthorne replies, "I could show you quite as curious a pair of cowhide boots at the transcendental community of Brook Farm." Yet there could have been no malice in his satire, for Mrs. Hawthorne's two sisters, Mrs. Mann and Miss Peabody, were both transcendentalists; and so was Horace Mann himself, so far as we know definitely in regard to his metaphysical creed. Do not we all feel at times that the search for abstract truth is like a diet of sawdust or Scotch mist,—a "chimera buzzing in a vacuum"?

James Russell Lowell similarly attacked Emerson in his Class Day poem, and afterward became converted to Emerson's views through the influence of Maria White. It is possible that a similar change took place in Hawthorne's consciousness; although his consciousness was so profound and his nature so reticent that what happened in the depths of it was never indicated by more than a few bubbles at the surface. He was emphatically an idealist, as every truly great artist must be, and Transcendentalism was the local costume which ideality wore in Hawthorne's time. He was a philosopher after a way of his own, and his reflections on life and manners often have the highest value. It was inevitable that he should feel and assimilate something from the wave of German thought which was sweeping over England and America, and if he did this unconsciously it was so much the better for the quality of his art.

There are evidences of this even among his earliest sketches. In his account of "Sunday at Home" he says: "Time—where a man lives not—what is it but Eternity?" Does he not recognize in this condensed statement Kant's theorem that time is a mental condition, which only exists in man, and for man, and has no place in the external world? In fact, it only exists by divisions of time, and it is *man* who makes the divisions. The rising of the sun does not constitute time; for the sun is always rising—somewhere. The positivists and Herbert Spencer deny this, and argue to prove that time is an external entity—independent of man—like electricity; but Hawthorne did not agree with them. He evidently trusted the validity of his consciousness. In that exquisite pastoral, "The Vision at the Fountain," he says:

"We were aware of each other's presence, not by sight or sound or touch, but by an inward consciousness. Would it not be so among the dead?"

You have probably heard of the German who attempted to evolve a camel out of his inner consciousness. That and similar jibes are common among those persons of whom the Scriptures tell us that they are in the habit of straining at gnats; but Hawthorne believed consciousness to be a trustworthy guide. Why should he not? It was the consciousness of *self* that raised man above the level of the brute. This was the rock from which Moses struck forth the fountain of everlasting life.

Again, in "Fancy's Show-Box" we meet with the following:

"Or, while none but crimes perpetrated are cognizable before an earthly tribunal, will guilty thoughts,—of which guilty deeds are no more than shadows,—will these draw down the full weight of a condemning sentence in the supreme court of eternity?"

Is this not an induction from or corollary to the preceding? If it is not Kantian philosophy, it is certainly Goethean. Margaret Fuller was the first American critic, if not the first of all critics, to point out that Goethe in writing "Elective Affinities" designed to show that an evil thought may have consequences as serious and irremediable as an evil action—in addition to the well-known homily that evil thoughts lead to evil actions. In his "Hall of Fantasy" Hawthorne mentions Goethe and Swedenborg as two literary idols of the present time who may be expected to endure through all time. Emerson makes the same prediction in one of his poems.

In "Rappacini's Daughter" Hawthorne says: "There is something truer and more real than what we can see with the eyes and touch with the finger."

And in "The Select Party" he remarks: "To such beholders it was unreal because they lacked the imaginative faith. Had they been worthy to pass within its portals, they would have recognized the truth that the dominions which the spirit conquers for itself among unrealities become a thousand times more real than the earth whereon they stamp their feet, saying, 'This is solid and substantial! This may be called a fact!'"

The essence of Transcendentalism is the assertion of the indestructibility of spirit, that mind is more real than matter, and the unseen than the seen. "The visible has value only," says Carlyle, "when it is based on the invisible." No writer of the nineteenth century affirms this more persistently than Hawthorne, and in none of his romances is the principle so conspicuous as in "The House of the Seven Gables." It is a sister's love which, like a cord stronger than steel, binds together the various incidents of the story, while the avaricious Judge Pyncheon, "with his landed estate, public honors, offices of trust and other solid *un_realities," has after all only succeeded in building a card castle for himself, which may be dissipated by a single breath. Holgrave, the daguerreotypist, who serves as a contrast to the factitious judge, is a genuine character, and may stand for a type of the young New England liberal of 1850: a freethinker, and so much of a transcendentalist that we suspect Hawthorne's model for him to have been one of the younger associates of the Brook Farm experiment. He is evidently studied from life, and Hawthorne says of him:*

"Altogether, in his culture and want of culture, in his crude, wild, and misty philosophy, and the practical experience that counteracted some of its tendencies; in his magnanimous zeal for man's welfare, and his recklessness of whatever the ages had established in man's behalf; in his faith, and in his infidelity; in what he had, and in what he lacked, the artist might fitly enough stand forth as the representative of many compeers in his native land."

This is a fairly sympathetic portrait, and it largely represents the class of young men who went to hear Emerson and supported Charles Sumner. In the story, Holgrave achieves the reward of a veracious nature by winning the heart of the purest and loveliest young woman in American fiction.

If Hawthorne were still living he might object to the foregoing argument as a misrepresentation; nor could he be blamed for this, for Ripley, Thoreau, Alcott and other like visionary spirits have so vitiated the significance of Transcendentalism that it ought now to be classed among words of doubtful and uncertain meaning.

Students of German philosophy are now chiefly known as Kantists or Hegelians, and outside of the universities they are commonly classed as Emersonians.

CHAPTER X. FROM CONCORD TO LENOX: 1845–1849

In May, 1845, Paymaster Bridge found himself again on the American coast. Meeting with Franklin Pierce in Boston, they agreed to go to Concord together, and look into Hawthorne's affairs. Soon after breakfast, Mrs. Hawthorne espied them coming through the gateway. She had never met Pierce, but she recognized Bridge's tall, elegant figure, when he waved his hat to her in the distance. Hawthorne himself was sawing and splitting in the wood–shed, and thither she directed his friends—to his no slight astonishment when they appeared before him. Pierce had his arm across Hawthorne's broad shoulders when they reappeared. There is one pleasure, indeed, which young people cannot know, and that is, the meeting of old friends. Mrs. Hawthorne was favorably impressed with Franklin Pierce's personality; while Horatio Bridge danced about and acted an impromptu pantomime, making up faces like an owl. They assured Hawthorne that something should be done to relieve his financial embarrassment.[Footnote: J. Hawthorne, 281.]

All those whose attention Hawthorne attracted out of the rush and hurry of the world were sure to become interested in his welfare. O'Sullivan, the editor of the *Democratic Review*, had already exerted himself in Hawthorne's behalf; but President Polk evidently did not know who Hawthorne was, so that O'Sullivan was obliged to have a puff inserted in his review for the President's better information. George Bancroft was now in the Cabinet, and could easily have obtained a lucrative post for Hawthorne, but it is plain that Bancroft was not over–friendly to him and that Hawthorne was fully aware of this. Hawthorne had suggested the Salem postmastership, but when O'Sullivan mentioned this, Bancroft objected on the ground that the present incumbent was too good a man to be displaced, and proposed the consulates of Genoa and Marseilles, two deplorable positions and quite out of the question for Hawthorne, in the condition of his family at that time. Perhaps it would have been better for him in a material sense, if he had accepted the invitation to dine with Margaret Fuller.

The summer wore away, but nothing was acomplished; and late in the autumn Hawthorne left the Old Manse to return to his Uncle Robert Manning's house in Salem, where he could always count on a warm welcome. There he spent the winter with his wife and child, until suddenly, in March, 1846, he was appointed Surveyor of the Port, or, as it is now more properly called, Collector of Customs.

This was, in truth, worth waiting for. The salary was not large, but it was a dignified position and allowed Hawthorne sufficient leisure for other pursuits,—the leisure of the merchant or banker. Salem had already begun to lose its foreign trade, and for days together it sometimes happened that there was nothing to do. Hawthorne's chief business was to prevent the government from being cheated, either by the importers or by his own subordinates; and it required a pretty sharp eye to do this. All the appointments, even to his own clerks, were made by outside politicians, and when a reduction of employees was necessary, Hawthorne consulted with the local Democratic Committee, and followed their advice. Such a method was not to the advantage of the public service, but it saved Hawthorne from an annoying responsibility. His strictness and impartiality, however, soon brought him into conflict with his more self-important subordinates, who were by no means accustomed to exactness in their dealings, and this finally produced a good deal of official unpleasantness; and the unfavorable reports which were afterward circulated concerning Hawthorne's life during this period, probably originated in that quarter.

[Illustration: THE CUSTOM HOUSE, SALEM, MASS., WHERE HAWTHORNE WAS EMPLOYED AS SURVEYOR OF THE FORT OF SALEM, AT THE TIME OF HIS WRITING "THE SCARLET LETTER"]

All the poetry that Hawthorne could extract from his occupation at the Custom House is to be found in his preface to "The Scarlet Letter," but he withholds from us the prosaic side of it,—as he well might. At times he comes close to caricature, especially in his descriptions of "those venerable incumbents who hibernated during the winter season, and then crawled out during the warm days of spring to draw their pay and perform those pretended duties, for which they were engaged." There were formerly large numbers of moss-grown loafers in the government service, with whiskey-reddened noses and greasy old clothing, who would sun themselves on the door-steps, and tell anecdotes of General Jackson, Senator Benton, and other popular heroes, with whom they would intimate a good acquaintance at some remote period of their lives. If removed from office, they were quite as likely to turn up in a neighboring jail as in any other location. This is no satire, but serious truth; and instances of it can be given.

Hawthorne's life during the next three years was essentially domestic. In June, 1846, his son Julian was born—a remarkably vigorous baby—at Doctor Peabody's house in West Street, Boston; Mrs. Hawthorne wisely preferring to be with her own mother during her confinement. [Footnote: At the age of thirty-five, Julian resembled his father so closely that Nathaniel Hawthorne's old friends were sometimes startled by him, as if they had seen an apparition. He was, however, of a stouter build, and his eyes were different.] With two small children on her hands, Mrs. Hawthorne had slight opportunity to enjoy general society, fashionable or otherwise. Rebecca Manning says, however:

The Life and Genius of Nathaniel Hawthorne

"Neither Hawthorne nor his wife could be said to be 'in society' in the technical sense. When the Peabody family lived in Salem, they were, I have been told, somewhat straitened pecuniarily. After Hawthorne's marriage, I think I remember hearing of his wife going to parties and dinners occasionally. Dr. Loring's wife was her cousin. Other friends were the Misses Howes, one of whom is now Mrs. Cabot of Boston. Mrs. Foote, who was a daughter of Judge White, was a friend, and I remember some Silsbees who were also her friends. Hawthorne's wife knew how to cultivate her friends and make the most of them far better than either Hawthorne or his sisters did. I have been told that when Hawthorne was a young man, before his marriage, if he had chosen to enter Salem's 'first circle' he would have been welcome there."

During this last sojourn in his native city Hawthorne was chosen on the committee for the lyceum lecture course, and proved instrumental in bringing Webster to Salem,—where he had not been popular since the trial of the two Knapps,—to deliver an oration on the Constitution; of which Mrs. Hawthorne has given a graphic description in a letter to her mother on November 19, 1848:

"The old Lion walked the stage with a sort of repressed rage, when he referred to those persons who cried out, 'Down with the Constitution!' 'Madmen! Or most wicked if not mad!' said he with a glare of fire."

A pure piece of acting. The national Constitution was not even endangered by the Southern rebellion,—much less by the small band of original abolitionists; and Webster was too sensible not to be aware of this.

While Hawthorne was at the Salem Custom House, he made at least two valuable friends: Doctor George B. Loring, who had married a cousin of Mrs. Hawthorne, and William B. Pike, who occupied a subordinate position in the Custom House, but whom Hawthorne valued for moral and intellectual qualities of which he would seem to have been the first discoverer. They were not friends who would be likely to affect Hawthorne's political views, except to encourage him in the direction to which he had always tended. Four years earlier, Doctor Loring had been on cordial terms with Longfellow and Sumner, being a refined and intellectual sort of man, but like Hillard, had withdrawn from them on account of political differences. He was an able public speaker, and became a Democratic politician, until 1862, when he went over to the Republicans; but after that he was looked upon with a good deal of suspicion by both parties. The governorship was supposed to have been the object of his ambition, but he never could obtain the nomination. Late in life he was appointed Commissioner of Agriculture, a post for which he was eminently fitted, and finally went to Portugal as United States Minister.

William B. Pike either lacked the opportunity or the necessary concentration to develop his genius in the larger world, but Hawthorne continued to communicate with him irregularly until the close of his life. He invited him to Lenox when he resided there, and Mrs. Lathrop recollects seeing him at the Wayside in Concord, after Hawthorne's return from Europe. She discribes him as a "short, sturdy, phlegmatic and plebeian looking man," but with a gentle step and a finely modulated voice. It may have been as well for him that he never became distinguished. [Footnote: Mrs. Lathrop, "Memories of Hawthorne," 154.]

The war with Mexico was now fairly afield, and Franklin Pierce, who left the United States Senate on account of his wife's health, was organizing a regiment of New Hampshire volunteers, as a "patriotic duty." Salem people thought differently, and party feeling there soon rose to the boiling–point. There is no other community where political excitement is so likely to become virulent as in a small city. In a country town, like Concord, every man feels the necessity for conciliating his neighbor, but the moneyed class in Salem was sufficient for its own purposes, and was opposed to the war in a solid body. The Whigs looked upon the invasion of Mexico as a piratical attempt of the Democratic leaders to secure the permanent ascendency of their party, and this was probably the true reason for Franklin Pierce's joining it. In their eyes, Hawthorne was the representative of a corrupt administration, and they would have been more than human if they had not wished him to feel this. The Salem gentry could not draw him into an argument very well, but they could look daggers at him on the street and exhibit their coldness toward him when they went on business to the Custom House. It is evident that he was made to suffer in some such manner, and to a tenderhearted man with a clear conscience, it must have seemed unkind and unjust. [Footnote: When the engagement between the "Chesapeake" and the "Shannon" took place off Salem harbor in August, 1813, and Captain Lawrence was killed in the action, the anti–war sentiment ran so high that it was difficult to find a respectable mansion where his funeral would be permitted.] In his Custom House preface, Hawthorne compares the Whigs rather unfavorably with the Democrats, and this is not to be wondered at; but he should have remembered that it was his own party which first introduced the spoils–of–office system.

The Life and Genius of Nathaniel Hawthorne

The first use that Hawthorne made of his government salary was to cancel his obligations to the Concord tradespeople, and the next was to provide a home for his wife and mother. They first moved to 18 Chestnut Street, in June, 1846; and thence to a larger house, 14 Mall Street, in September, 1847, in which "The Snow Image" was prepared for publication, and "The Scarlet Letter" was written. Hawthorne's study or workshop was the front room in the third story, an apartment of some width but with a ceiling in direct contradiction to the elevated thoughts of the writer. There is an ominous silence in the American Note–book between 1846 and 1850, which is rather increased than diminished by the publication from his diary of a number of extracts concerning the children. The babies of geniuses do not differ essentially from those of other people, and it is not supposable that Hawthorne's reflections during this period were wholly confined to his own family. It is to be hoped that fuller information will yet be given to the public concerning their affairs in Salem; for the truth deserves to be told.

In January, 1846, Mrs. Hawthorne wrote to her mother:

"No one, I think, has a right to break the will of a child, but God; and if the child is taught to submit to Him through love, all other submission will follow with heavenly effect upon the character. God never drives even the most desperate sinner, but only invites or suggests through the events of His providence."

Nothing is more unfortunate than to break the will of a child, for all manliness and womanliness is grounded in the will; but it is often necessary to control the desires and humors of children for their self–preservation. Hawthorne himself was not troubled with such fancies. Alcott, who was his nearest neighbor at the Wayside, once remarked that there was only one will in the Hawthorne family, and that was Nathaniel's. His will was law and no one thought of disputing it. Yet what he writes concerning children is always sweet, tender, and beautiful, with the single exception of a criticism of his own daughter, which was published long after his death and could not have been intended for the public eye.

The war with Mexico was wonderfully successful from a military point of view, but its political effects were equally confounding to the politicians who projected it. The American people resemble the French, quite as much perhaps as they do the English, and the admiration of military glory is one of their Gallic traits. It happened that the two highest positions in the army were both held by Whig generals, and the victory of Buena

The Life and Genius of Nathaniel Hawthorne

Vista carried Zachary Taylor into the White House, in spite of the opposition of Webster and Clay, as well as that of the Democrats and the Free Soilers. Polk, Bancroft, and Pierce had all contributed to the defeat of their own party. The war proved their political terminus to the two former; but, *mirabile dictu*, it became the cap of Fortunatus to Pierce and Hawthorne.

This, however, could not have been foreseen at the time, and the election of Taylor in November, 1848, had a sufficiently chilling effect on the little family in Mall Street. Hawthorne entertained the hope that he might be spared in the general out-turning, as a distinguished writer and an inoffensive partisan, and this indicates how loath he was to relinquish his comfortable position. Let us place ourselves in his situation and we shall not wonder at it. He was now forty-five, with a wife and two children, and destitution was staring him in the face. For ten years he had struggled bravely, and this was the net result of all his endeavors. Never had the future looked so gloomy to him.

The railroad had superseded his Uncle Manning's business, as it had that of half the mercantile class in the city, and his father-in-law was in a somewhat similar predicament. At this time Elizabeth Peabody was keeping a small foreign book-store in a room of her father's house on West Street. One has to realize these conditions, in order to appreciate the mood in which Hawthorne's Custom House preface was written.

There is one passage in it, however, that is always likely to be misunderstood. It is where he says:

"I thought my own prospects of retaining office, to be better than those of my Democratic brethren; but who can see an inch into futurity, beyond his nose? My own head was the first that fell!"

It is clear that some kind of an effort was made to prevent his removal, presumably by George S. Hillard, who was a Whig in good favor; but the conclusion which one would naturally draw from the above, that Hawthorne was turned out of office in a summary and ungracious manner, is not justified by the evidence. He was not relieved from duty until June 14, 1849; that is, he was given a hundred days of grace, which is much more than officeholders commonly are favored with, in such cases. We may consider it morally certain that Hillard did what he could in Hawthorne's behalf. He was well acquainted with Webster, but unfortunately Webster had opposed the nomination of General Taylor, and was so imprudent as to characterize it as a nomination not fit to be made. This was echoed all over the country, and left Webster without influence at Washington. For the time being Seward was everything, and Webster was nothing.

In a letter to Horace Mann, shortly after his removal, Hawthorne refers to two distinct calumnies which had been circulated concerning him in Salem, and only too widely credited. The most important of these—for it has seriously compromised a number of Salem gentlemen—was never explained until the publication of Mrs. Lathrop's "Memories of Hawthorne" in 1897; where we find a letter from Mrs. Hawthorne to her mother, dated June 10, 1849, and containing the following passage:

"Here is a pretty business, discovered in an unexpected manner to Mr. Hawthorne by a friendly and honorable Whig. Perhaps you know that the President said before he took the chair that he should make no removals except for dishonesty and unfaithfulness. It is very plain that neither of these charges could be brought against Mr. Hawthorne. Therefore a most base and incredible falsehood has been told—written down and signed and sent to the Cabinet in secret. This infamous paper certifies among other things (of which we have not heard)—that Mr. Hawthorne has been in the habit of writing political articles in magazines and newspapers!" So it appears that the gutta–percha formula [Footnote: By which eighty–eight per cent, of the classified service were removed.] of President Cleveland in regard to "offensive partisanship" was really invented forty years before his time, and had as much value in one case as in the other. It is possible that such a document as Mrs. Hawthorne describes was circulated, signed, and sent to Washington, to make the way easy for President Taylor's advisers, and if so it was a highly contemptible proceeding; but the statement rests wholly on the affirmation of a single witness, whose name has always been withheld, and even if it were true that Hawthorne had written political articles for Democratic papers the fact would have in no wise been injurious to his reputation. The result must have been the same in any case. General Taylor was an honorable man, and no doubt intended to keep his word, as other Presidents have intended since; but what could even a brave general effect against the army of hungry office–seekers who were besieging the White House,—a more formidable army than the Mexicans whom he had defeated at Buena Vista? In all probability he knew nothing of Hawthorne and never heard of his case.

The second calumny which Hawthorne refers to was decidedly second–rate, and closely resembles a servant's intrigue. The Department at Washington, in a temporary fit of

116

economy, had requested him to discharge two of his supervisors. He did not like to take the men's bread away from them, and made a mild protest against the order. At the same time he consulted his chief clerk as to what it might be best to do, and they agreed upon suspending two of the supervisors who might suffer less from it than some others. As it happened, the Department considered Hawthorne's report favorably, and no suspension took place; but his clerk betrayed the secret to the two men concerned, who hated Hawthorne in consequence, and afterward circulated a report that he had threatened to discharge them unless they contributed to the Democratic campaign fund. This return of evil for good appears to have been a new experience for Hawthorne, but those who are much concerned in the affairs of the world soon become accustomed to it, and pay little attention to either the malice or the mendacity of mankind.

Twenty years later one of Hawthorne's clerks, who had prudently shifted from the Democratic to the Republican ranks, held a small office in the Boston Navy Yard, and was much given to bragging of his intimacy with "Nat," and of the sprees they went on together; but the style and description of the man were sufficient to discredit his statements without further evidence. There were, however, several old shipmasters in the Salem Custom House who had seen Calcutta, Canton, and even a hurricane or two; men who had lived close to reality, with a vein of true heroism in them, moreover; and if Hawthorne preferred their conversation to that of the shipowners, who had spent their lives in calculating the profits of commercial adventures, there are many among the well educated who would agree with him. He refers particularly to one aged inspector of imports, whose remarkable adventures by flood and field were an almost daily recreation to him; and if the narratives of this ancient mariner were somewhat mixed with romance, assuredly Hawthorne should have been the last person to complain of them on that account.

At first he was wholly unnerved by his dismissal. He returned to Mall Street and said to his wife: "I have lost my place. What shall we now do for bread?" But Mrs. Hawthorne replied: "Never fear. You will now have leisure to finish your novel. Meanwhile, I will earn bread for us with my pencil and paint–brush." [Footnote: Mrs. George S. Hillard.] Besides this, she brought forward two or three hundred dollars, which she had saved from his salary unbeknown to him; but who would not have been encouraged by such a brave wife? Fortunately her pencil and paint–brush were not put to the test; at least so far as we know. Already on June 8, her husband had written a long letter to Hillard, explaining the state of his affairs and containing this pathetic appeal:

"If you could do anything in the way of procuring me some stated literary employment, in connection with a newspaper, or as corrector of the press to some printing establishment, etc., it could not come at a better time. Perhaps Epes Sargent, who is a friend of mine, would know of something. I shall not stand upon my dignity; that must take care of itself. Perhaps there may be some subordinate office connected with the Boston Athenaum (Literary). Do not think anything too humble to be mentioned to me." [Footnote: Conway, 113.]

There have been many tragical episodes in the history of literature, but since "Paradise Lost" was sold for five pounds and a contingent interest, there has been nothing more simply pathetic than this,—that an immortal writer should feel obliged to apply for a subordinate position in a counting–room, a description of work which nobody likes too well, and which to Hawthorne would have been little less than a death in life. "Do not think anything too humble to be mentioned to me"!

What Hillard attempted to do at this time is uncertain, but he was not the man to allow the shrine of genius to be converted into a gas–burner, if he could possibly prevent it. We may presume that he went to Salem and encouraged Hawthorne in his amiable, half–eloquent manner. But we do not hear of him again until the new year. Meanwhile Madam Hawthorne fell into her last illness and departed this life on July 31; a solemn event even to a hard–hearted son—how much more to such a man as she had brought into the world. Three days before her death, he writes in his diary of "her heart beating its funeral march," and diverts his mind from the awful *finale* by an accurate description of his two children playing a serio–comic game of doctor and patient, in the adjoining room.

It was under such tragical conditions, well suited to the subject, that he continued his work on "The Scarlet Letter," and his painfully contracted brow seemed to indicate that he suffered as much in imagination, as the characters in that romance are represented to have suffered. In addition he wrote "The Great Stone Pace," one of the most impressive of his shorter pieces (published, alas! in a Washington newspaper), and the sketch called "Main Street," both afterward included in the volume of "The Snow Image." On January 17, 1850, he was greatly surprised to receive a letter from George S. Hillard with a large check in it,—more than half–way to a thousand dollars,—which the writer with all possible delicacy begged him to accept from a few of his Boston admirers. It was only from such a good friend as Hillard that Hawthorne would have accepted assistance in this form; but he always considered it in the character of a loan, and afterward insisted on repaying it to the original subscribers,—Professor Ticknor, Judge Curtis, and others. Hillard also persuaded James T. Fields, the younger partner of Ticknor &Company, to take an interest in Hawthorne as an author who required to be encouraged, and perhaps coaxed a little, in order to bring out the best that was in him. Fields accordingly went to Salem soon afterward, and has given an account of his first interview with Hawthorne in "Yesterdays with Authors," which seems rather melodramatic: "found him cowering over a stove," and altogether in a woe–begone condition. The main point of discussion between them, however, was whether "The Scarlet Letter" should be published separately or in conjunction with other subjects. Hawthorne feared that such a serious plot, continued with so little diversity of motive, would not be likely to produce a favorable impression unless it were leavened with material of a different kind. Fields, on the contrary, thought it better that the work should stand by itself, in solitary grandeur, and feared that it would only be dwarfed by any additions of a different kind. He predicted a good sale for the book, and succeeded in disillusionizing Hawthorne from the notions he had acquired from the failure of "Fanshawe."

As it was late in the season, Fields would not even wait for the romance to be finished, but sent it to the press at once; and on February 4, Hawthorne wrote to Horatio Bridge:

"I finished my book only yesterday; one end being in the press at Boston, while the other was in my head here at Salem; so that, as you see, the story is at least fourteen miles long."

The time of publication was a propitious one: the gold was flowing in from California, and every man and woman had a dollar to spend. The first edition of five thousand copies was taken up within a month, and after this Hawthorne suffered no more financial embarrassments. The succeeding twelve years of his life were as prosperous and cheerful as his friends and readers could desire for him; although the sombre past still seemed to cast a ghostly shadow across his way, which even the sunshine of Italy could not entirely dissipate.

"THE SCARLET LETTER"

The germ of this romance is to be found in the tale of "Endicott and the Red Cross," published in the *Token* in 1838, so that it must have been at least ten years sprouting and developing in Hawthorne's mind. In that story he gives a tragically comic description of the Puritan penitentiary,—in the public square,—where, among others, a good–looking young woman was exposed with a red letter A on her breast, which she had embroidered herself, so elegantly that it seemed as if it was rather intended for a badge of distinction than as a mark of infamy. Hawthorne did not conjure this up wholly out of his imagination, for in 1704 the General Court of Massachusetts Bay passed the following law, which he was no doubt aware of:

"Convicted before the Justice of Assize,—both Man and Woman to be set on the Gallows an Hour with a Rope about their Necks and the other end cast over the Gallowses. And in the way from thence to the common Gaol, to he Scourged not exceeding Forty Stripes. And forever after to wear a Capital A of two inches long, of a contrary colour to their cloathes, sewed on their upper Garments, on the Back or Arm, in open view. And as often as they appear without it, openly to be Scourged, not exceeding Fifteen Stripes." [Footnote: Boston, Timothy Green, 1704.]

The most diligent investigation, however, has failed to discover an instance in which punishment was inflicted under this law, so that we must conclude that Hawthorne invented that portion of his statement. In fact, nothing that Hawthorne published himself is to be considered of historical or biographical value. It is all fiction. He sported with historical facts and traditions, as poets and painters always have done, and the manuscript which he pretends to have discovered in his office at the Custom House, written by one of his predecessors there, is a piece of pure imagination, which serves to give additional credibility to his narrative. He knew well enough how large a portion of what is called history is fiction after all, and the extent to which professed historians deal in romance. He felt that he was justified so long as he did not depart from the truth of human nature. We may thank him that he did not dispel the illusion of his poetic imagery by the introduction of well–known historical characters. This is permissible in a certain class of novels, but its effect is always more or less prosaic.

Our Puritan ancestors evidently did not realize the evil effects of their law against faithless wives,—its glaring indelicacy, and brutalizing influence on the minds of the young; but it was of a piece with their exclusion of church–music and other amenities of civilization. Was it through a natural attraction for the primeval granite that they landed on the New England coast? Their severe self–discipline was certainly well adapted to their situation, but, while it built up their social edifice on an enduring foundation, its tendency was to crush out the gentler and more sympathetic qualities in human nature. In no other community would the story of Hester Prynne acquire an equal cogency and significance. A German might, perhaps, understand it; but a Frenchman or an Italian not at all.

The same subject has been treated in its most venial form by Shakespeare in "Measure for Measure," and in its most condemnable form in Goethe's "Faust." "The Scarlet Letter" lies midway between these two. Hester Prynne has married a man of morose, vindictive disposition, such as no woman could be happy with. He is, moreover, much older than herself, and has gone off on a wild expedition in pursuit of objects which he evidently cares for, more than for his wife. She has not heard from him for over a year, and knows not whether he has deserted her, or if he is no longer living. She is alone in a strange wild country, and it is natural that she should seek counsel and encouragement from the young clergyman, who is worthy of her love, but, unfortunately, not a strong character. Lightning is not swifter than the transition in our minds from good to evil, and in an unguarded moment he brings ruin upon himself, and a life–long penance on Hester Prynne. Hawthorne tells this story with such purity and delicacy of feeling that a maiden of sixteen can read it without offence.

"The Scarlet Letter" is at once the most poetic and the most powerful of Hawthorne's larger works, much more powerful than "The Vicar of Wakefield," which has been accepted as the type of a romance in all languages. Goldsmith's tale will always be more popular than "The Scarlet Letter," owing to its blithesome spirit, its amusing incidents and bright effects of light and shade; but "The Scarlet Letter" strikes a more penetrating chord in the human breast, and adheres more closely to the truth of life. There are certain highly improbable circumstances woven in the tissue of "The Vicar of Wakefield," which a prudent, reflective reader finds it difficult to surmount. It is rather surprising that the Vicar should not have discovered the true social position of his friend Mr. Burchell, which must have been known to every farmer in the vicinity; and still more so that Mr. Burchell should have permitted the father of a young woman in whom he was deeply interested, to be carried to prison for debt without making an inquiry into his case. "The Scarlet Letter" is, as Hawthorne noticed, a continual variation on a single theme, and that a decidedly solemn one; but its different incidents form a dynamic sequence, leading onward to the final catastrophe, and if its progress is slow—the narrative extends over a period of seven years—this is as inevitable as the march of Fate. From the first scene in the drama, we are lifted above ourselves, and sustained so by Hawthorne's genius, until the close.

This sense of power arises from dealing with a subject which demanded the whole force and intensity of Hawthorne's nature. Hester Prynne herself is a strong character, and her errors are those of strength and independence rather than of weakness. She says to Mr. Dimmesdale that what they did "had a consecration of its own," and it is this belief which supports her under a weight of obloquy that would have crushed a more fragile spirit. She does not collapse into a pitiful nonentity, like Scott's Effie Deans, nor is she maddened to crime like George Eliot's "Hetty Sorrel"; [Footnote: A name apparently compounded from Hester Prynne and Schiller's Agnes Sorrel.] but from the outset she forms definite resolutions,—first to rehabilitate her own character, and next to protect the partner of her shame. This last may seem to be a mistaken devotion, and contrary to his true interest, for the first step in the regeneration from sin is to acknowledge manfully the responsibility of it; but to give the repentance even the appearance of sincerity, the confession must be a voluntary one, and not be forced upon the delinquent person by external pressure. We cannot withhold our admiration for Hester's unswerving fidelity to this twofold purpose. We may condemn her in our minds, but we cannot refuse her a measure of sympathy in our hearts.

I believe this to be the explanation of her apparent inconsistency at the close of the book. Many of Hawthorne's commentators have been puzzled by the fact that Hester, after so many years of contrition, should advise Dimmesdale to fly to England, and even offered to accompany him. Women have not the same idea of law that men have. In their ideas of right and wrong they depend chiefly on their sense of purity; and it is very difficult to persuade a woman that she could be wrong in obeying the dictates of her heart. Hester perceives that her former lover is being tortured to death by the silent tyranny of Chillingworth; the tide of affection so long restrained flows back into her soul; and her own reputation is as nothing compared with the life of the man she hopes to save. There is no other passage in American fiction so pathetic as that woodland meeting, at which their mutual hopes of happiness blaze up like the momentary brightness of a dying flame. Hester's innocent child, however, representing the spirit of truthfulness, is suddenly seized with an aversion to her father and refuses to join their company,—an unfavorable omen and dark presage of the minister's doom.

Pearl's behavior, on this occasion, may be supposed to represent the author's own judgment. How far shall we agree with him? The past generation witnessed one of the noblest of women uniting herself, for life and death, to a man whom she could not marry on account of purely legal objections. Whether Hester's position in the last act of this drama is comparable with that of Marian Evans every one must decide according to his or her conscience.

Hawthorne certainly proves himself a good Puritan when he says, "And be the stern and sad truth spoken that the breach which guilt has once made into the human soul, is never in this mortal state repaired." The magnitude of the evil of course makes a difference; but do we not all live in a continual state of sinning, and self–correction? That is the road to self–improvement, and those who adhere most closely to inflexible rules of conduct discover at length that the rules themselves have become an evil. Mankind has not yet fully decided as to what things are evil, and what are good; and neither Hawthorne nor the Puritan lawmakers would seem to have remembered Christ's admonition on a similar occasion: "Let him who is without sin among you, cast the first stone."

A writer in the *Andover Review*, some twenty years ago, criticised the impersonation of Pearl as a fable—"a golden wreck." He quoted Emerson to the effect that in all the ages that man has been upon the earth, no communication has been established between him and the lower animals, and he affirmed that we know quite as little of the thoughts and motives of our own children. Both conclusions are wide of the mark. There is much more communication between man and the domestic animals than between animals of the same species. The understanding between an Arab and his horse is almost perfect, and so is that between a sportsman and his setters. Even the sluggish ox knows the word of command. Then what shall we say of the sympathetic relation between a mother and her child? Who can describe it—that clairvoyant sensibility, intangible, too swift for words? Who has depicted it, except Hawthorne and Raphael? Pearl is like a pure spirit in "The Scarlet Letter," reconciling us to its gloomy scenes. She is like the sunshine in a dark forest, breaking through the tree–tops and dancing in our pathway. It is true that Hawthorne has carried her clairvoyant insight to its furthest limits, but this is in accordance with the ideal character of his work. She has no rival except Goethe's Mignon.

Hawthorne's method of developing his stories resembled closely that of the historical painter; and it was only in this way that he could produce such vivid effects. He selected models for his principal characters and studied them as his work progressed. The original of Reverend Mr. Dimmesdale was quickly recognized in Salem as an amiable inoffensive person, of whom no one suspected any evil,—and that was, no doubt, the reason why Hawthorne selected him for his purpose. It was no discredit to the man himself, although tongues were not wanting to blame Hawthorne for it. Who Hester may have been still remains a mystery; but it was evidently some one with whom the author was well acquainted,—perhaps his younger sister. So Rubens painted his own wife at one time an angel, and at another in the likeness of Herodias. It is still more probable that Pearl is a picture of Hawthorne's own daughter, who was of the right age for such a study, and whose sprightly, fitful, and impulsive actions correspond to those of Hester's child. This would also explain why her father gave Una so much space in his Note–book. He may have noticed the antagonism between her and the Whig children of the neighborhood and have applied it to Pearl's case. It was also his custom, as appears from his last unfinished work, to leave blank spaces in his manuscript while in the heat of composition, which, like a painter's background, were afterwards filled in with descriptions of scenery or some subsidiary narrative.

The models of the novelist cannot be hired for the purpose, like those used by the painter or sculptor, but have to be studied when and where they can be found, for the least self–consciousness spoils the effect. Hawthorne in this only followed the example of the best authors and dramatists; and those who think that good fiction or dramatic poetry can be written wholly out of a man's or a woman's imagination, would do well to make the experiment themselves.

CHAPTER XI. PEGASUS IS FREE: 1850–1852

Frederick W. Loring, that bright young poet who was so soon lost to us, once remarked: "Appreciation is to the artist what sunshine is to flowers. He cannot expand without it." The success of "The Scarlet Letter" proved that all Hawthorne's genius required was a little moderate encouragement,—not industry but opportunity. His pen, no longer slow and hesitating, moved freer and easier; the long pent–up flood of thoughts, emotions, and experiences had at length found an outlet; and the next three years were the most productive of his life.

His first impulse, however, was to escape from Salem. Although his removal from office had been a foregone conclusion, Hawthorne felt a certain degree of chagrin connected with it, and also imagined a certain amount of animosity toward himself which made the place uncomfortable to him. He was informed that the old Sparhawk mansion, close to the Portsmouth Navy Yard, was for sale or to rent, and the first of May, Hawthorne went thither to consider whether it would serve him for a home. [Footnote: Lathrop, 225.] One would suppose that sedate old Portsmouth, with its courteous society and its dash of military life, would have suited Hawthorne even better than Concord; but he decided differently, and he returned to meet his family in Boston, where he made the acquaintance of Professor Ticknor, who introduced him at the Athenaeum Library. He saw Hildreth at the Athenaum working on his history of the United States; sat for his portrait to C. E. Thompson; went to the theatre; studied human nature in the smoking-room at Parker's; and relaxed himself generally. He must have stayed with his family at Doctor Peabody's on West Street, for he speaks of the incessant noise from Washington Street, and of looking out from the back windows on Temple Place. This locates the house very nearly.

Two months later, July 5, 1850, he was at Lenox, in the Berkshire Mountains. Mrs. Caroline Sturgis Tappan, a brilliant Boston lady, equally poetic and sensible, owned a small red cottage there, which she was ready to lease to Hawthorne for a nominal rent. Lowell was going there on account of his wife, a delicate flower-like nature already beginning to droop. Doctor Holmes was going on account of Lowell, and perhaps with the expectation of seeing a rattlesnake; Fields was going on account of Lowell and Holmes. Mrs. Frances Kemble, already the most distinguished of Shakespearian readers, had a summer cottage there; and it was hoped that in such company Hawthorne would at last find the element to which he properly belonged.

Unfortunately Hawthorne took to raising chickens, and that seems to have interested him more than anything else at Lenox. He fell in cordially with the plans of his friends; ascended Monument Mountain, and went on other excursions with them; but it may be more than suspected that Lowell and Holmes did most of the talking. He assimilated himself more to Holmes perhaps than to any of the others. His meeting with Mrs. Kemble must have been like a collision of the centrifugal and centripetal forces; and for once, Hawthorne may be said to have met his antipodes. They could sincerely admire one another as we all do, in their respective spheres; but such a chasm as yawned between them in difference of temperament, character, and mode of living, could not have been bridged over by Captain Eads.

Fannie Kemble, as she was universally called, had by long and sympathetic reading of Shakespeare transformed herself into a woman of the Elizabethan era, and could barely be said to belong to the nineteenth century. Among other Elizabethan traits she had acquired an unconsciousness of self, together with an enormous self–confidence, and no idea of what people thought of her in polite society ever seems to have occurred to her. She had the heart of a woman, but mentally she was like a composite picture of Shakespeare's *dramatis personae*, and that Emerson should have spoken of her as "a great exaggerated creature" is not to be wondered at. In her own department she was marvellous.

The severity of a mountain winter and the disagreeableness of its thawing out in spring, is atoned for by its summer,—that fine exhilarating ether, which seems to bring elevated thoughts, by virtue of its own nature. Hawthorne enjoyed this with his children and his chickens; and his wife enjoyed it with him. It is evident from her letters that she had not been so happy since their first year at the Old Manse. She had now an opportunity to indulge her love of artistic decoration, in adorning the walls of their little red cottage, which has since unfortunately been destroyed by fire. She even began to give her daughter, who was only six years old, some instruction in drawing. The following extract concerning her husband, from a letter written to her mother, is charmingly significant of her state of mind at this time.

"Beauty and the love of it, in him, are the true culmination of the good and true, and there is no beauty to him without these bases. He has perfect dominion over himself in every respect, so that to do the highest, wisest, loveliest thing is not the least effort to him, any more than it is to a baby to be innocent. It is his spontaneous act, and a baby is not more unconscious in its innocence. I never knew such loftiness, so simply borne. I have never known him to stoop from it in the most trivial household matter, any more than in a larger or more public one." [Footnote: J. Hawthorne, i. 373.]

Truly this gives us a beautiful insight into their home–life, and Hawthorne himself could not have written a more accurate eulogium. As intimated in the last chapter, we all make our way through life by correcting our daily trespasses, and Hawthorne was no exception to it; but as a mental analysis of this man at his best Mrs. Hawthorne's statement deserves a lasting recognition.

"THE HOUSE OF THE SEVEN GABLES"

It was not until early frosts and shortening days drove Hawthorne within doors that he again took up his writing, but who can tell how long he had been dreaming over his

126

subject? Within five months, or by the last week of January, "The House of the Seven Gables" was ready for the press. There is no such house in Salem, exactly as he describes it; but an odd, antiquated–looking structure at No. 54 Turner Street is supposed to have served him for the suggestion of it. The name is picturesque and well suited to introduce the reader to a homely suburban romance.

The subject of the story goes back to the witchcraft period, and its active principle is a wizard's curse, which descends from one generation to another, until it is finally removed by the marriage of a descendant of the injured party to a descendant of the guilty one. Woven together with this, there is an exposition of mesmerism, or, as it is now called, Christian Science, with its good and evil features.

Each of Hawthorne's larger romances has a distinct style and quality of its own, apart from the fine individualized style of the author. Lathrop makes an excellent remark in regard to "The House of the Seven Gables," that the perfection of its art seems to stand between the reader and his subject. It resembles in this respect those Dutch paintings whose enamelled surface seems like a barrier to prevent the spectator from entering the scenes which they represent. It would be a mistake to consider this a fault, but one cannot help noticing the accuracy with which the subordinate details of the plot are elaborated. Is it possible that this is connected in a way with the rarefied atmosphere of Lenox, in which distant objects appear so sharply defined?

"The House of the Seven Gables" might be symbolized by two paintings, in the first of which Hepzibah Pyncheon stands as the central figure, her face turned upward in a silent prayer for justice, her brother Clifford, with his head bowed helplessly, at one side, and the judge, with his chronic smile of satisfaction, behind Clifford; on the other side the keen–eyed Holgrave would appear, sympathetically watching the progress of events, with Phoebe Pyncheon at his left hand. Old Uncle Banner and little Ned Higgins might fill in the background. In the second picture the stricken judge would be found in a large old–fashioned arm–chair, with Clifford and Hepzibah flying through a doorway to the right, while Phoebe and Holgrave, the one happy and the other startled, enter on the left.

Hepzibah, not Phoebe, is the true heroine of the romance,—or at least its central figure. Nowhere do we look more deeply into Hawthorne's nature than through this sympathetic portrait of the cross–looking old maid, whose only inheritance is the House of the Seven Gables, in which she has lived many years, poor, solitary, friendless, with a disgrace upon her family, only sustained by the hope that she may yet be a help and comfort to her unfortunate brother. The jury before whom Clifford was tried believed him to be guilty, but his sister never would believe it. She lives for him and suffers with him. Hawthorne does not mitigate the unpleasantness of her appearance, but he instructs us that there is a divine spark glowing within. Very pitiful is her attempt to support the enfeebled brother by keeping a candy store; but noble and heroic is her resistance to the designs of her tyrannical cousin. It is her intrepidity that effects the crisis of the drama.

Both Hepzibah and Clifford Pyncheon are examples of what fine portraiture Hawthorne could accomplish in exceptional or abnormal personalities, without ever descending to caricature. Judge Pyncheon has been criticised as being too much of a stage villain, but the same might be alleged of Shakespeare's (or Fletcher's) Richard III. What is he, in effect, but a Richard III. reduced to private life? Moreover, his habit of smiling is an individual trait which gives him a certain distinction of his own. Usually,

> Faces ever blandly smiling
> Are victims of their own beguiling.

But Judge Pyncheon is a candidate for the governorship, and among the more mercenary class of politicians smiling often becomes a habit for the sake of popularity. Hawthorne might have added something to the judge's *personale* by representing him with a droll wit, like James Fiske, Jr., or some others that we have known, and he might have exposed more of his internal reflections; but he serves as a fair example of the hard, grasping, hypocritical type of Yankee. We see only one side of him, but there are men, and women too, who only have one side to their characters.

It has been affirmed that Hawthorne made use of the Honorable Mr. Upham, the excellent historian of Salem witchcraft, as a model for Judge Pyncheon, and that this was done in revenge for Mr. Upham's inimical influence in regard to the Salem surveyorship. It is impossible, at this date, to disentangle the snarl of Hawthorne's political relations in regard to that office, but Upham had been a member of Congress and was perhaps as influential a Whig as any in the city. If Hawthorne was removed through his instrumentality, he performed our author a service, which neither of them could have realized at the time. Hawthorne, however, had a strong precedent in his favor in this instance; namely, Shakespeare's caricature of Sir Thomas Luce, as Justice Shallow in "The Merry Wives of Windsor"; but there is no reason why we should think better or worse of Mr. Upham on this account.

Phoebe Pyncheon is an ideal character, the type of youthful New England womanhood, and the most charming of all Hawthorne's feminine creations. Protected by the shield of her own innocence, she leaves her country home from the same undefined impulse by which birds fly north in spring, and accomplishes her destiny where she might have least expected to meet with it. She fills the whole book with her sunny brightness, and like many a young woman at her age she seems more like a spirit than a character. Her maidenly dignity repels analysis, and Hawthorne himself extends a wise deference to his own creation.

The future of a great nation depends more on its young women than upon its laws or its statesmen.

In regard to Holgrave, we have already said somewhat; but he is so lifelike that it seems as if he must have been studied from one of the younger members of the Brook Farm association; perhaps the one of whom Emerson tells us, [Footnote: Lecture on Brook Farm.] that he spent his leisure hours in playing with the children, but had "so subtle a mind" that he was always consulted whenever important business was on foot. He is visible to our mental perspective as a rather slender man, above medium height, with keen hazel eyes, a long nose, and long legs, and quick and lively in his movements. Phoebe has a more symmetrical figure, bluish–gray eyes, a complexion slightly browned from going without her hat, luxuriant chestnut–brown hair, always quiet and graceful. We have no doubt that Holgrave made a worthy husband for her, and that he occasionally took a hand in public affairs.

Judge Pyncheon's duplicity is revealed to Holgrave by the medium of a daguerreotype. Men or women who are actors in real life should avoid being photographed, for the camera is pretty sure to penetrate their hypocrisy, and expose them to the world as they actually are. Every photograph album is to a certain extent a rogues' gallery, in which our faults, peculiarities, and perhaps vices are ruthlessly portrayed for the student of human nature. If a merchant were to have all his customers photographed, he would soon learn to distinguish those who were not much to be trusted.

Notice also Hawthorne's eye for color. When Clifford, Hepzibah, and Phoebe are about to leave the seven–gabled house for the last time, "A plain, but handsome dark–green barouche" is drawn to the door. This is evidently his idea of a fine equipage; and it happens that the background of Raphael's "Pope Julius" is of this same half–invisible green, and harmonizes so well with the Pope's figure that few realize its coloring.

The plot of this picturesque story is the most ingenious of Hawthorne's life, but sufficiently probable throughout to answer the purpose of a romance, and it is the only one of Hawthorne's larger works which ends happily. It was brought out by Ticknor &Company at Easter 1850,—less than ten weeks after it was finished; but we think of the House of the Seven Gables as standing empty, deserted and forlorn.

In December Emerson had written to Hawthorne concerning a new magazine in which he and Lowell were interested, and if Hawthorne would only give it his support its success could not be questioned. What Hawthorne replied to this invitation has never been discovered, but he had seen too many such periodicals go to wreck to feel much confidence in this enterprise. [Footnote: J. Hawthorne, i. 381.] It is of more importance now that Emerson should have addressed him as "My dear Hawthorne," for such cordial friendliness was rare in "the poet of the pines." Mrs. Alcott once remarked that Emerson never spoke to her husband otherwise than as "Mr. Alcott," and it is far from likely that he ever spoke to Hawthorne differently from this. The conventionalities of letter– writing run back to a period when gentlemen addressed one another—and perhaps felt so too—in a more friendly manner than they do at present.

Works of fiction and sentimental poetry stir up a class of readers which no other literature seems to reach, and Hawthorne was soon inundated with letters from unknown, and perhaps unknowable, admirers; but the most remarkable came from a man named Pyncheon, who asserted that his grandfather had been a judge in Salem, and who was highly indignant at the use which Hawthorne had made of his name. [Footnote: Conway, 135.] This shows how difficult it is for a writer of fiction or a biographer to escape giving offence. The lightning is sure to strike somewhere.

"THE SNOW IMAGE"

The question now was, what next? As it happened, the next important event in the Hawthorne family was the advent of their younger daughter, born like Agassiz, "in the lovely month of May," and amid scenery as beautiful as the Pays de Vaud. Her father named her Rose, in defiance of Hillard's objection to idyllic nomenclature; and as a child she seemed much like the spirit of that almost fabulous flower, the wild orange–rose. Ten years later, she was the most graceful girl in the Concord dancing–school, and resembled her elder sister so closely that they could not have been mistaken for anything but sisters. As she grew older she came more and more to resemble her mother.

It was said that Hawthorne's "Wonder Book" originated in his telling free versions of the Greek myths to his children on winter evenings; and also that Horace Mann's boys, who were almost exactly of the same age as Una and Julian, participated in the entertainment. This may have happened the following winter at Newton, but could hardly have taken place at Lenox; and otherwise it is quite impossible to identify all the children with botanical names in Hawthorne's introduction. Julian once remarked, at school, that he believed that he was the original of Squash–blossom, and that is as near as we can get to it. Some of them may have been as imaginary as the ingenious Mr. Eustace Bright, and might serve as well to represent one group of children as another.

The book was written very rapidly, at an average of ten pages a day, and it has Hawthorne's grace and purity of style, but it does not belong to the legitimate series of his works. It is an excellent book for the young, for they learn from it much that every one ought to know; but to mature minds the original fables, even in a translation, are more satisfactory than these Anglo–Saxon versions in the "Wonder Book."

The collection of tales which passes by the name of "The Snow Image" is a much more serious work. "The Great Stone Face" and one or two others in the collection were prepared at Salem for the same volume as "The Scarlet Letter," but judiciously excluded by Mr. Fields. "The Snow Image" itself, however, is plainly derived from Hawthorne's own experience during the winter at Lenox. The common–sensible farmer and his poetic wife could not be mistaken for Mr. and Mrs. Hawthorne, but the two sportive children are easily identified as Una and Julian. They are not only of the same age, but the "slight graceful girl" and "chubby red–cheeked boy" describes them exactly. The idea has been derived from the fable of the Greek sculptor Pygmalion whose statue came to life. That seems far enough off to be pleasantly credible, but to have such a transubstantiation take place in the front yard of a white–fenced American residence, is rather startling. Yet Hawthorne, with the help of the twilight, carries us through on the broad wings of his imagination, even to the melting of the little snow–sister before an airtight stove in a close New England parlor. The moral that Hawthorne draws from this fable might be summed up in the old adage, "What is one man's meat is another man's poison"; but it has a deeper significance, which the author does not seem to have perceived. The key–note of the fable is the same as that in Goethe's celebrated ballad, "The Erl King"; namely, that those things which children imagine, are as real to them as the facts of the external world. Nor do we altogether escape from this so long as we live.

The origin of "The Great Stone Face" is readily traced to the profile face in the Franconia Mountains,—which has not only a strangely human appearance, but a grave dignified expression, and, as a natural phenomenon, ranks next to Niagara Falls. The value of the fable, however, has perhaps been over–estimated. It is an old story in a modern garb, the saying so often repeated in the Book of Isaiah: "The last shall be first, and the first shall be last." The man Ernest, who is much in his ways like Hawthorne himself, spends his leisure in contemplating the Great Stone Face, and thus acquires a similar expression in his own. The wealthy merchant, the famous general, the great party leader, and the popular poet, all come upon the scene; but not one of them appears to advantage before the tranquil countenance of the Great Stone Face. Finally, Ernest in his old age carries off the laurel; and in this Hawthorne hits the mark, for it is only through earnestness that man becomes immortal. Yet, one would suppose that constantly gazing at a face of stone, would give one a rather stony expression; as sculptors are liable to become statuesque from their occupation.

Another Dantean allegory, and fully equal in power to any Canto in Dante's "Inferno," is the story of "Ethan Brandt," or "The Unpardonable Sin." We have a clew to its origin in the statement that it was part of an unfinished romance; presumably commenced at Concord, but afterward discarded, owing to the author's dissatisfaction with his work—an illustration of Hawthorne's severe criticism of his own writing. The scene is laid at a limekiln in a dark and gloomy wood, where a lime–burner, far from human habitations, is watching his fires at night. To him Ethan Brandt appears, a strange personage, long known for his quest after the unpardonable sin, and the solitude echoes back the gloominess of their conversation. Finally, the lime–burner fixes his fires for the night, rolls himself up in his blanket, and goes to sleep. When he awakes in the morning, the stranger is gone, but, on ascending the kiln to look at his caldron, he finds there the skeleton of a man, and between its ribs a heart of white marble. This is the unpardonable sin, for which there is neither dispensation nor repentance. Ethan Brandt has committed suicide because life had become intolerable on such conditions.

The Life and Genius of Nathaniel Hawthorne

The summer of 1851 in Lenox was by no means brilliant. It had not yet become the tip end of fashion, and Hawthorne's chief entertainment seems to have been the congratulatory letters he received from distinguished people. Mrs. Frances Kemble wrote to him from England, announcing the success of his book there, and offering him the use of her cottage, a more palatial affair than Mrs. Tappan's, for the ensuing winter. Mrs. Hawthorne, however, felt the distance between herself and her relatives, and perhaps they both felt it. Mrs. Hawthorne's sister Mary, now Mrs. Horace Mann, was living in West Newton, and the last of June Mrs. Hawthorne went to her for a long summer visit, taking her two daughters with her and leaving Julian in charge of his father, with whom it may be affirmed he was sufficiently safe. It rarely happens that a father and son are so much together as these two were, and they must have become very strongly attached.

For older company he had Hermann Melville, and G. P. R. James, whose society he may have found as interesting as that of more distinguished writers, and also Mr. Tappan, whom Hawthorne had learned to respect for his good sense and conciliatory disposition—a true peace-maker among men and women. Burill Curtis, the amateur brother of George W. Curtis, came to sketch the lake from Hawthorne's porch, and Doctor Holmes turned up once or twice. On July 24 Hawthorne wrote to his friend Pike at Salem: [Footnote: Mrs. Lathrop, 151.]

"By the way, if I continue to prosper as heretofore in the literary line, I shall soon be in a condition to buy a place; and if you should hear of one, say worth from $1500 to $2000, I wish you would keep your eye on it for me. I should wish it to be on the seacoast, or at all events with easy access to the sea."

The evident meaning of this is that the Hawthornes had no desire to spend a second winter in the Berkshire hills. The world was large, but he knew not where to rest his head. Mrs. Hawthorne solved the problem on her return to Lenox, and it was decided to remove to West Newton when cold weather came. Thither they went November 21 in a driving storm of snow and sleet,—a parting salute from old Berkshire,—and reached Horace Mann's house the same evening.

Nobody knows where the Hawthornes lived in Newton. The oldest survivors of both families were only five years of age at that time. Mrs. Hawthorne's father also resided in Newton that winter, and it is more than likely that they made their residence with him. Julian Hawthorne has a distinct recollection of the long freight-trains with their clouds of black smoke blowing across his father's ground during the winter; so they could not have lived very far from the Worcester railroad. Horace Mann's house is still standing, opposite a school-house on the road from the station, where a by-way meets it at an acute angle. The freight-trains and their anthracite smoke must have had a disturbing influence on Hawthorne's sensibility.

The long-extended town of Newton, which is now a populous city, has much the best situation of any of the Boston suburbs—on a moderately high range of hills, skirted by the Charles River, both healthful and picturesque. It is not as hot in summer nor so chilly at other seasons as Concord, and enjoys the advantage of a closer proximity to the city. Its society is, and always has been, more liberal and progressive than Salem society in Hawthorne's time. Its citizens, mainly professional and mercantile men, are active, intelligent, and sensible, without being too fastidious. It was a healthful change for Hawthorne, and we are not surprised to find that his literary work was affected by it. Mrs. L. Maria Child lived there at the time, and so did Celia Thaxter, although not yet known to fame. The sound, penetrating intelligence of Horace Mann may have also had its salutary effect.

"THE BLITHEDALE ROMANCE"

Hawthorne's "Wonder Book" and "The Snow Image" were expressed to Ticknor &Company before leaving Lenox, and "The Blithedale Romance" may also have been commenced before that change of base. We only know, from his diary, that it was finished on the last day of April, 1852, and that he received the first proof-sheets of it two weeks later— which shows what expedition publishers can make, when they feel inclined.

The name itself is somewhat satirical, for Hawthorne did not find the life at Brook Farm very blithesome, and in the story, with the exception of the sylvan masquerade, there is much more rue than heart's-ease, as commonly happens in his stories. The tale ends tragically, and without the gleam of distant happiness which lights up the last scenes of "The Scarlet Letter." It commences with a severe April snowstorm, an unfavorable omen; the same in which Hawthorne set out to join the West Roxbury community.

And yet the name is not without a serious meaning—a stern, sad moral significance. The earth is not naturally beautiful, for rank Nature ever runs to an excess. It is only beautiful when man controls and remodels it; but what man makes physically, he can unmake spiritually. We pass by a handsome estate, a grand arcade of elms over its avenue, spacious lawns, an elegant mansion, a luxurious flower–garden; but we are informed that happiness does not dwell there, that its owner is a misanthropic person, whose nature has been perverted by the selfishness of luxury; that there are no pleasant parties on the lawn, no happy wooing in that garden, no marriage festivals in those halls; and those possessions, which might have proved a blessing to generations yet unborn, are no better than a curse and a whited sepulchre. How many such instances could be named.

It may have occurred to Hawthorne, that, if George Ripley, instead of following after a will–o'–the–wisp notion, which could only lead him into a bog, had used the means at his disposal to cultivate Brook Farm in a rational manner, and had made it a hospitable rendezvous for intellectual and progressive people,—an oasis of culture amid the wide waste of commercialism,—the place might well have been called Blithedale, and Mr. Ripley would have inaugurated a movement as rare as it was beneficial. It was only at a city like Boston, whose suburbs were pleasant and easily accessible, that such a plan could be carried out; and it was only a man of Mr. Ripley's scholarship and intellectual acumen who could have drawn together the requisite elements for it. It looks as if he missed an opportunity.

We should avoid, however, confounding George Ripley with Hawthorne's Hollingsworth. It is quite possible that Hawthorne made use of certain traits in Ripley's character for this purpose, and also that he may have had some slight collision with him, such as he represents in "The Blithedale Romance;" but Ripley was an essentially veracious nature, who, as already remarked, carried out his experiment to its logical conclusion. Hollingsworth, on the contrary, proposes to pervert the trust confided to him, in order to establish at Blithedale an institution for the reformation of criminals, by which proceeding he would, after a fashion, become a criminal himself. At the same time, he plays fast and loose with the affections of Zenobia and Priscilla, who are both in love with him, designing to marry the one who would make the most favorable match for his purpose. It is through the junction of these two streams of evil that the catastrophe is brought about.

Priscilla is evidently taken from the little seamstress whom Hawthorne mentions in his diary for October 9, 1841, and if she ever discovered this, she could hardly have been displeased, for she is one of his most lovable creations; not so much of an ideal as Phoebe

Pyncheon, for she is older and has already seen hard fortune. Her quiet, almost submissive ways at first excite pity rather than admiration, but at length we discover that there is a spirit within her, which shines through its earthly envelope, like the twinkling of a star.

Zenobia has a larger nature and a more gifted mind than Priscilla, but also a more mixed character. Her name suggests a queenly presence and she is fully conscious of this. She does not acquire an equal influence over the other sex, for she is evidently in love with herself. She is described as handsome and attractive, but no sooner had "Blithedale" been published than people said, "Margaret Fuller" [Footnote: the name of Zenobia is not very remotely significant of Margaret Fuller. Palmyra was the centre of Greek philosophy in Zenobia's time, and she also resembled Margaret in her tragical fate.]—although Margaret Fuller was rather plain looking, and never joined the Brook Farm association.

If this surmise be correct, it leads to a curious consideration. After painting a portrait of Zenobia in Chapter VI of "Blithedale," quite worthy of Rubens or Titian, he remarks, through the incognito of Miles Coverdale, in the first part of Chapter VII, that Priscilla reminds him of Margaret Fuller, and says this to Priscilla herself. Now it proves in the sequel that Priscilla and Zenobia are half–sisters, but it would be as difficult to imagine this from anything that is said in the story about them, as it is to understand how the shy, undemonstrative Priscilla could have reminded Coverdale of the brilliant and aggressive leader of the Transcendentalists.

The introduction of Margaret Fuller's name in that place comes abruptly on the reader, and momentarily dispels the illusion of the tale. Was Hawthorne conscious of the undercurrent of relationship, which he had already formulated in his mind, between Priscilla and Zenobia; or what is more likely, did he make the comparison in order to lead his readers away from any conceptions they might have formed in regard to the original of his heroine? If the latter supposition be true, he certainly was not very successful, for in either case it is evident that Margaret Fuller was prominent in his thoughts at the time he wrote those two chapters.

Hawthorne's idea of her, however, should not be accepted as a finality. What Emerson and other friends have said concerning her should also be considered in order to obtain a just impression of a woman who combined more varied qualities than perhaps any other person of that time. Hawthorne says of Zenobia, that she was naturally a stump oratoress,— rather an awkward expression for him—and that "her mind was full of weeds." Margaret Fuller was a natural orator, and her mind was full of many subjects in which Hawthorne could take little interest. She was a revolutionary character, a sort of female Garibaldi, who attacked old Puritan traditions with a two–edged sword; she won victories for liberalism, but left confusion behind her. Like all such characters, she made friends and enemies wherever she went. She sometimes gave offence by hasty impulsive utterances, but more frequently by keenly penetrating arguments for the various causes which she espoused. Only a woman could deliver such telling shots.

Lowell, who was fond of an argument himself, did not like her better than Hawthorne did. There may be some truth in what he says in "The Fable for Critics," that the expression of her face seemed to suggest a life–long familiarity with the "infinite soul"; but Margaret Fuller was sound at heart, and when she talked on those subjects which interested her, no one could be more self–forgetful or thoroughly in earnest. At times, she seemed like an inspired prophetess, and if she had lived two thousand years earlier, she might have been remembered as a sibyl. [Footnote: See Appendix B.]

"The Blithedale Romance" is written with a freer pen and less carefully than "The House of the Seven Gables," and is so much the better; for the author's state of mind in which he is writing will always affect the reader more or less, and if the former feels under a slight constraint the latter will also. A writer cannot be too exact in ascertaining the truth,—Macaulay to the contrary,—but he can trouble himself too much as to the expression of it. At the same time, "The Blithedale Romance" is the least poetic of Hawthorne's more serious works (which is the same as saying that it is more like a novel), for the reason that Hawthorne in this instance was closer to his subject. It is also more of a personal reminiscence, and less an effort of the imagination. He has included in it a number of descriptive passages taken from his Brook Farm diary; most notably the account of that sylvan masquerade, in which Coverdale finds his former associates engaged on his return to Blithedale in the autumn. Perhaps this is the reason why the book has so pleasant a flavor—a mellow after–thought of old associations.

An air of mystery adds an enchantment to a work of art, whether in poetry, painting, or sculpture,—perhaps also in music; but there is a difference in kind between mystery and uncertainty. We do not like to be left half in the dark, in regard to things which we think we ought to know. There is a break in Hawthorne's chain of evidence against Hollingsworth and Zenobia, which might possibly have been filled to advantage. He would certainly have been non–suited, if his case had been carried into court. We are permitted to suppose that Zenobia, in order to clear her path of a successful rival, assists the mountebank, Westervelt, to entrap Priscilla, over whom he possesses a kind hypnotic power, and to carry her off for the benefit of his mountebank exhibitions; but it remains a supposition and nothing more. We cannot but feel rejoiced, when Hollingsworth steps onto the platform and releases Priscilla from the psychological net–work in which she is involved, and from which she has not sufficient will–power to free herself. He certainly deserves her hand and fortune; but, as to his condemnatory charges against Zenobia, which led directly to her suicide,—what could they have been? Was there nothing more than the trick she had attempted upon Priscilla? And if he accused her of that only, why should he suffer perpetual remorse on account of her death? Surely there was need of further explanation here, for the catastrophe and its consequences are out of all proportion to the apparent cause.

His account of the recovery of Zenobia's body is a close transcript of the search for that unfortunate school–mistress, who drowned herself in Concord River; and it is possible that, if Hawthorne had not been present on that occasion, the plot might have terminated in some other manner.

The story closes without a ray of hope for Hollingsworth; but the reader can perceive one in the generous devotion of his single–minded wife, even if Hawthorne did not.

CHAPTER XII. THE LIVERPOOL CONSULATE: 1852–1854

Why Hawthorne returned to Concord in 1852 is more of a mystery than the suicide of Zenobia. Horace Mann also left Newton, to be President of Antioch College (and to die there in the cause of feminine education), in the autumn of that year; but this could hardly have been expected six months earlier. Hawthorne was not very favorably situated at Newton, being rather too near the railroad; but there was plenty of land on the top of the hill, where he might have built himself a house, and in the course of twelve years his property would have quadrupled in value. A poet will not be less of a poet, but more so, for understanding the practical affairs of life. Or he might have removed to Cambridge, where Longfellow, always foremost in kind offices, would have been like a guardian angel to him, and where he could have made friends like Felton and Agassiz, who would have been much more in harmony with his political views. Ellery Channing was the only friend he appears to have retained in Concord, and it was not altogether a favorable place to bring up his children; but the natural topography of Concord is unusually attractive, and it may be suspected that he was drawn thither more from the love of its pine solitudes and shimmering waters, than from any other motive.

The house he purchased was nearly a mile from the centre of the town, and has ever since been known by the name of the Wayside. After Hawthorne's return from Europe in 1860, he remodelled it somewhat, so that it has a more dignified aspect than when he first took possession of it. Alcott, who occupied it for some years previously, had adorned it with that species of rustic architecture in which he was so skilful. The house was half surrounded by a group of locust trees, much in fashion seventy years ago, and had been set so close against the hill–side, that a thicket of stunted pines and other wild growth rose above the roof like a crest. Bronson Alcott was his next–door neighbor,— almost too strong a contrast to him,—and Emerson's house was half a mile away; so that these three families formed a group by themselves in that portion of Concord.

Hawthorne wrote a letter to his sister Elizabeth, describing his new acquisition, and expressing satisfaction in it. It was the first house that he had ever owned; and it is no small comfort to a man to live under his own roof, even though it be a humble one. At this time, however, he did not remain at the Wayside but a single year. After that, the house stood empty until the untimely death of Horace Mann, August 2, 1859, when Mrs. Mann came to Concord with her three boys, and occupied it until Hawthorne's return from Europe.

[Illustration: THE WAYSIDE]

It may as well be noticed here, that, during the eight years which Hawthorne spent altogether in Concord, he accomplished little literary work, and none of any real importance. It is impossible to account for this, except upon those psychological conditions which sometimes affect delicately balanced minds. Whether the trouble was in the social atmosphere of the place, or in its climatic conditions, perhaps Hawthorne himself could not have decided; but there must have been a reason for it of some description. Julian Hawthorne states that his father had a plan at this time of writing another romance, of a more cheerful tone than "The Blithedale Romance," but the full current of his poetic activity was suddenly brought to a standstill by an event that nobody would have dreamed of.

Hawthorne had hardly established himself in his new abode, when Franklin Pierce was nominated for the presidency by the Democratic party. The whole country was astonished, for no such nomination had ever been made before, and it is probable that Pierce himself shared largely in this. The New Hampshire delegation had presented his name to the convention, in order to procure him distinction in his own State, but without expectation that he would become a serious candidate. Like the nomination of Hayes in 1876, it resulted from the jealousy of the great party leaders,—always an unfortunate position for a public man to be placed in. Theodore Parker said, "Any one is now in danger of becoming President."

Hawthorne evidently felt this, for he wrote to Bridge, "I do not consider Pierce the brightest man in the country, for there are twenty more so." It would have been a mild statement if he had said two hundred. Pierce wanted him, of course, to write a campaign biography, and communicated with him to that effect; but Hawthorne disliked meddling in such matters, and at first declined to do it, although it was expected to be highly remunerative. Pierce, however, insisted, for Hawthorne's reputation was now much beyond his own, and he felt that a biography by so distinguished a writer would confer upon him great dignity in the eyes of the world; and as Hawthorne felt already much indebted to Pierce, he finally consented,—although a cheap spread–eagle affair would have served the purpose of his party quite as well. The book had to be written in haste, and just at the time when Hawthorne wished to take a little leisure. There were so few salient points in Pierce's life, that it was almost like making a biography out of nothing, and as for describing him as a hero, that was quite impossible. It was fortunate that he knew so much of Pierce's early life, and also that Pierce had kept a diary during the Mexican War, which formed a considerable portion of the biography.

The book is worth reading, although written in this prosaic manner. Hawthorne states in the preface, frankly and manfully, that he objected to writing it, and this ought to be an excuse sufficient for his doing so—if excuse be needed. He does not attempt to represent his friend as a great statesman, but rather as a patriotic country gentleman, who is interested in public affairs, and who rises from one honorable position to another through a well–deserved popularity. This would seem to have been the truth; and yet there was a decided inconsistency in Franklin Pierce's life, which Hawthorne represents plainly enough, although he makes no comment thereon.

The Life and Genius of Nathaniel Hawthorne

Franklin Pierce's father was captain of a militia company in 1798, when war was declared against the French Directory, for seizing and confiscating American merchant ships, contrary to the law of nations. There could not have been a more just occasion for war, but Captain Pierce resigned his commission, because he considered it wrong to fight against a republic; and Hawthorne approves of him for this. Franklin Pierce, however, resigned his seat in the Senate in 1842, on account of the interests of his family, alleging that "he would never enter public life again, unless the needs of his country imperatively demanded it," yet four years later he organized a regiment for the invasion of Mexico,—not only for making war upon a republic, but an unjust and indefensible war. General Grant's opinion ought to be conclusive on this latter point, for he belonged to the same political party as Pierce and Hawthorne. Certainly, Pierce's services were not required for the defence of his native land.

To do Hawthorne justice, there can be no doubt that in his heart he disapproved of this; for in one of his sketches written at the Old Manse, he speaks censoriously of "those adventurous spirits who leave their homes to emigrate to Texas." He evidently foresaw that trouble would arise in that direction, and perhaps Ellery Channing assisted him in penetrating the true inwardness of the movement.

It will be remembered that in Franklin Pierce's youth, he was exceptionally interested in military manouvres, and this may have been one of the inducements which led him into the Mexican War; but young men who are fond of holiday epaulets do not, for obvious reasons, make the best fighters. Pierce's military career was not a distinguished one; for, whether he was thrown from his horse in his first engagement, or, as the Whigs alleged, fell from it as soon as he came under fire, it is certain that he did not cover himself with glory, as the phrase was at that time. But we can believe Hawthorne, when he tells us that Pierce took good charge of the troops under his command, and that he was kind and considerate to sick and wounded soldiers. That was in accordance with his natural character.

It was impossible at that time to avoid the slavery question in dealing with political subjects, and what Hawthorne said on this point, in the life of General Pierce, attracted more attention than the book itself. Like Webster he considered slavery an evil, but he believed it to be one of those evils which the human race outgrows, by progress in civilization,—like the human sacrifices of the Gauls perhaps,—and he greatly deprecated the anti–slavery agitation, which only served to inflame men's minds and make them unreasonable.

There were many sensible persons in the Northern States at that time, like Hawthorne and Hillard, who sincerely believed in this doctrine, but they do not seem to have been aware that there was a pro–slavery agitation at the South which antedated Garrison's *Liberator* and which was much more aggressive and vehement than the anti–slavery movement, because there were large pecuniary interests connected with it. The desperate grasping of the slave–holders for new territory, first in the Northwest and then in the Southwest, was not because they were in any need of land, but because new slave States increased their political power. Horatio Bridge says, relatively to this subject:

"No Northern man had better means for knowing the dangers impending, previous to the outbreak of the war, than had General Pierce. Intimately associated—as he was—with the strong men of the South, in his Cabinet and in Congress, he saw that the Southerners were determined, at all hazards, to defend their peculiar institution of slavery, which was imperilled by the abolitionists."

If Franklin Pierce was desirous of preserving the Union, why did he give Jefferson Davis a place in his Cabinet, and take him for his chief adviser? Davis was already a pronounced secessionist, and had been defeated in his own State on that issue. In subserviency to Southern interests, no other Northern man ever went so far as Franklin Pierce, nor did Garrison himself accomplish so much toward the dissolution of the Union. He was an instance in real life of Goldsmith's "good–natured man," and the same qualities which assisted him to the position of President prevented his administration from being a success. Presidents ought to be made of firmer and sterner material.

Hawthorne had barely finished with the proofs of this volume, when he received the saddest, most harrowing news that ever came to him. After her mother's death, in 1849, Louisa Hawthorne had gone to live with her aunt, Mrs. John Dike; and in July, 1852, Mr. Dike went with her on an excursion to Saratoga and New York City. On the morning of July 27, they left Albany on the steamboat "Henry Clay," which, as is well known, never reached its destination. When nearing Yonkers, a fire broke out near the engines, where the wood–work was saturated with oil, and instantly the centre of the vessel was in a bright blaze. Mr. Dike happened to be on the forward deck at the moment, but Louisa Hawthorne was in the ladies' cabin, and it was impossible to reach her. The captain of the Henry Clay immediately ran the vessel on shore, so that Mr. Dike and those who were with him escaped to land, but Louisa and more than seventy others, who threw themselves into the water, were drowned. It would seem to have been impossible to save her.

The death of Hawthorne's mother may be said to have come in the course of Nature, and his mind was prepared for it; but Louisa had been the playmate of his childhood, and her death seemed as unnecessary as it was sharp and sudden. It happened almost on the third anniversary of his mother's death, and these were the only two occasions in Hawthorne's life, when the Dark Angel hovered about his door.

Rebecca Manning says: "Louisa Hawthorne was a most delightful, lovable, interesting woman—not at all 'commonplace,' as has been stated. Her death was a great sorrow to all her friends. Her name was Maria Louisa, and she was often called Maria by her mother and sister and aunts."

Depressed and unnerved, in the most trying season of the year, Hawthorne went in the latter part of August to visit Franklin Pierce at Concord, New Hampshire; but there a severe torrid wave came on, so that Pierce advised him to go at once to the Isles of Shoals, promising to follow in a few days, if his numerous engagements would permit him.

The Isles of Shoals have the finest summer climate on the Atlantic Ocean; an atmosphere at once quieting and strengthening, and always at its best when it is hottest on the main–land. Hawthorne found a pair of friends ready–made there, and prepared to receive him,—Levi Thaxter, afterwards widely known as the apostle of Browning in America, and his wife, Celia, a poetess in the bud, only sixteen, but very bright, original, and pleasant. They admired Hawthorne above all living men, and his sudden advent on their barren island seemed, as Thaxter afterward expressed it, like a supernatural presence. They became good companions in the next two weeks; climbing the rocks, rowing from one island to another,—bald pieces of rock, like the summits of mountains rising above the surface of the sea,—visiting the light–house, the monument to Captain John Smith, Betty Moody's Cave, the graves of the Spanish sailors, the trap dikes of ancient lava, and much else. Every day Hawthorne wrote a minute account in his diary of his various proceedings there, including the observation of a live shark, which came into the cove by the hotel, a rare spectacle on that coast. General Pierce did not make his appearance, however, and on September 15, Hawthorne returned to his own home.

The Life and Genius of Nathaniel Hawthorne

The election of Pierce to the presidency was as remarkable as his nomination. In 1848, General Taylor, the victor of a single battle, but a man of little education, was nominated for the presidency over the heads of the finest orators and ablest statesmen in America, and was enthusiastically elected. General Scott, Franklin Pierce's opponent, defeated the Mexicans in four decisive battles, captured the capital of the country, and conducted one of the most skilful military expeditions of the past century. He was a man of rare administrative ability, and there is no substantial argument against his character. We have Grant's testimony that it was pleasant to serve under him. Yet he was overwhelmingly defeated at the polls by a militia general without distinction, military or civil.

Hawthorne was naturally delighted at the result of the election; unfortunate as it afterwards proved for his country. He derived a threefold satisfaction from it, in the success of his friend, in the defeat of the Whigs, and in the happy prospects which it opened for himself. He could now return to the Salem Custom House in triumph,—as the wisest man might be tempted to do,—but he looked forward to something that would be more advantageous to his family. He had already written on October 18 to Horatio Bridge:

"Before undertaking it [the biography] I made an inward resolution, that I should accept no office from him; but, to say the truth, I doubt whether it would not be rather folly than heroism to adhere to this purpose, in case he should offer me anything particularly good. We shall see. A foreign mission I could not afford to take. The consulship at Liverpool, I might." [Footnote: Bridge 130]

We may conclude from this, that Pierce had already intimated the Liverpool consulate, which at that time was supposed to be worth twenty–five thousand dollars a year in fees. It was an excellent plan for the President of the United States to have such a gift at his disposal, to reward some individual like Hawthorne, to whom the whole nation was indebted to an extent that could never be repaid; but it is a question whether it would not have been as well, in this particular case, for Hawthorne to have remained in his own country. If he could have written five or six romances more, this would have secured him a good competency, and would have assured a sufficient income for his family after his death. As it happened, the Liverpool consulate did not prove so profitable as was anticipated.

The Life and Genius of Nathaniel Hawthorne

With such "great expectations" before him, Hawthorne could do no serious work that winter, so he occupied himself leisurely enough, with writing a sequel to his "Wonder Book," which he called "Tanglewood Tales," apparently after the thicket which surmounted the hill above his residence. This was finished early in March, and given to Ticknor & Company to publish when they saw fit. As it is a book intended for children, the consideration of it need not detain us.

Early in April, 1853, Hawthorne was appointed and confirmed to the Liverpool consulate, and on the 14th he went to Washington, as he tells us, for the first time, to thank the President in person. Otherwise he has divulged nothing concerning this journey, except that he was introduced to a larger number of persons than he could remember the names or faces of, and received ten times as many invitations as he could accept. If Charles V. honored himself with posterity by picking up the paint–brush which Titian had dropped on the floor, President Pierce might have done himself equal credit by making Hawthorne his guest at the White House; but if he did not go so far as this, it cannot be doubted that he treated Hawthorne handsomely. There were giants at Washington in those days. Webster and Clay were gone, but Seward was the Charles Fox and Sumner the Edmund Burke of America; Chase and Marcy were not much less in intellectual stature. Hawthorne must have met them, but we hear nothing of them from him.

Hawthorne delayed his departure for England, until the most favorable season arrived, for his fragile wife and infant children to cross the "rolling forties." At length, on July 6, two days after his forty–ninth birthday, he sailed from Boston in the "Niagara," and with *placida onda prospero il vento*, in about twelve days they all arrived safely at their destination.

The great stone docks of Liverpool, extending along its whole water–front, give one a strong impression of the power and solidity of England. Otherwise the city is almost devoid of interest, and travellers customarily pass through it, to take the next train for Oxford or London, without further observation, unless it be to give a look at the conventional statue of Prince Albert on an Arab horse. Liverpool is not so foggy a place as London, but it has a damper and less pleasant climate, without those varied attractions and substantial enjoyments which make London one of the most pleasant residences and most interesting of cities.

London fog is composed of soft–coal smoke, which, ascending from innumerable chimneys, is filtered in the upper skies, and then, mixed with vapor, is cast back upon the city by every change of wind. It is not unpleasant to the taste, and seems to be rather healthful than otherwise; but all the vapors which sail down the Gulf Stream, and which are not condensed on the Irish coast in the form of rain, collect about the mouth of the Mersey, so that the adjacent country is the best watered portion of all England, Cornwall possibly excepted. There is plenty of wealth in Liverpool, and all kinds of private entertainments, but in no other city of its size are there so few public entertainments, and the only interesting occupation that a stranger might find there, would be to watch the strange and curious characters in the lower classes, faces and figures that cannot be caricatured, emerging from cellar–ways or disappearing through side–doors. Go into an alehouse in the evening and, beside the pretty barmaid, who deserves consideration as much for her good behavior as for her looks, you will see plainly enough where Dickens obtained his *dramatis personae* for "Barnaby Rudge" and "The Old Curiosity Shop." Either in Liverpool or in London you can see more grotesque comedy characters in a day, than you could meet with in a year in America. These poor creatures are pressed down, and squeezed out into what they are, under the superincumbent weight of an enormous leisure class.

Such was the environment in which Hawthorne was obliged to spend the ensuing four years. He soon, however, discovered a means to escape from the monotonous and labyrinthine streets of the city, by renting an imitation castle at Rock Ferry,—a very pretty place, much like Dobbs Ferry, on the Hudson, although the river is not so fine,—where his wife and children enjoyed fresh air, green grass, and all the sunshine attainable, and whence he could reach the consulate every morning by the Mersey boat. We find them located there before September 1.

Of the consulate itself, Hawthorne has given a minute pictorial description in "Our Old Home," from which the following extract is especially pertinent to our present inquiry:

"The Consulate of the United States in my day, was located in Washington Buildings (a shabby and smoke–stained edifice of four stories high, thus illustriously named in honor of our national establishment), at the lower corner of Brunswick Street, contiguous to the Goree Arcade, and in the neighborhood of some of the oldest docks. This was by no means a polite or elegant portion of England's great commercial city, nor were the apartments of the American official so splendid as to indicate the assumption of much consular pomp on his part. A narrow and ill–lighted staircase gave access to an equally narrow and ill–lighted passage–way on the first floor, at the extremity of which, surmounting a door frame, appeared an exceedingly stiff pictorial representation of the Goose and Gridiron, according to the English idea of those ever–to–be–honored symbols. The staircase and passage–way were often thronged of a morning, with a set of beggarly and piratical–looking scoundrels (I do no wrong to our countrymen in styling them so, for not one in twenty was a genuine American), purporting to belong to our mercantile marine, and chiefly composed of Liverpool Blackballers, and the scum of every maritime nation on earth; such being the seamen by whose assistance we then disputed the navigation of the world with England. These specimens of a most unfortunate class of people were shipwrecked crews in quest of bed, board, and clothing, invalids asking permits for the hospital, bruised and bloody wretches complaining of ill–treatment by their officers, drunkards, desperadoes, vagabonds, and cheats, perplexingly intermingled with an uncertain proportion of reasonably honest men. All of them (save here and there a poor devil of a kidnapped landsman in his shore–going rags) wore red flannel shirts, in which they had sweltered or shivered throughout the voyage, and all required consular assistance in one form or another."

The position of an American consul in a large foreign seaport, especially at Liverpool, is anything but a sinecure, and in fact requires a continual exercise of judgment much beyond the average duties of a foreign minister. The difficulty also of being continually obliged to distinguish between true and false applications for charity, especially when the false are greatly in excess of the true, and among a class of persons notably given to mendacious tricks, is one of the most unpleasant conditions in which a tender–hearted man can find himself. As curious studies in low life, the rascality of these nautical mendicants may often have been interesting, and even amusing, to Hawthorne, but as a steady pull they must have worn hard on his nerves, even though his experienced clerk served as a breakwater to a considerable portion. It has already been noticed that Hawthorne was a conscientious office–holder, and he never trusted to others any duties which he was able to attend to in person. Moreover, although he was a man of reserved manners, there was an exceptionally tender, sympathetic heart behind this impenetrable exterior, and it may be suspected that he relieved many instances of actual distress, which could not be brought within the government regulations. He may have suffered like the ghost in Dickens's "Haunted Man," on account of those whom he could not assist. It is certain that he aged more, in appearance at least, during these four years, than at any similar period of his life.

The Life and Genius of Nathaniel Hawthorne

It is no wonder, therefore, that, after a visit to the English lakes, the following summer, Hawthorne wrote to his friend, Henry Bright, from Liverpool:

"I have come back only for a day or two to this black and miserable hole. I do not mean to apply these two adjectives to my consulate, but to the whole of Liverpool."

Yet it should be recollected that there were nearly a million of persons in Liverpool, who were obliged to spend their lives there, for good and evil fortune; and, as Emerson says, we can never think too lightly of our own difficulties.

Neither did Hawthorne find the news from America particularly interesting. On March 30, 1854, he wrote to Bridge:

"I like my office well enough, but my official duties and obligations are irksome to me beyond expression. Nevertheless, the emoluments will be a sufficient inducement to keep me here, though they are not above a quarter part what some people suppose them.

"It sickens me to look back to America. I am sick to death of the continual fuss and tumult and excitement and bad blood which we keep up about political topics. If it were not for my children, I should probably never return, but—after quitting office—should go to Italy, and live and die there. If Mrs. Bridge and you would go too, we might form a little colony amongst ourselves, and see our children grow up together. But it will never do to deprive them of their native land, which I hope will be a more comfortable and happy residence in their day than it has been in ours."

[Footnote: J. Hawthorne, ii. 65.]

The last sentence in this ought to be printed in italics, for it is the essence of patriotism. The "fuss and tumult" in America were due, for the time being, to the apple of discord which Douglas had cast into the Senate, by his Kansas–Nebraska bill. Hawthorne was too far away to distinguish the full force and insidious character of that measure, but if he had been in Concord, we believe he would have recognized (as so many did who never had before) the imminent danger to the Union, from the repeated concessions to the slave power. After he had become disenthralled from his allegiance to party, we find him in his letters to Bridge, taking broad views on political subjects.

An event was soon to happen, well calculated to disenthrall him. The Congress of 1854, after passing the Kansas–Nebraska bill, resolved, in order to prove its democratic spirit, to economize in the representation of our government to foreign powers. On April 14, the good–hearted, theoretical O'Sullivan arrived in Liverpool, on his way to be minister to Portugal, and warned Hawthorne that there was a bill before Congress to reduce the consulate there to a salaried position. This was a terrible damper on Hawthorne's great expectations, and on April 17 he wrote again to Bridge, protesting against the change: [Footnote: Bridge, 135, 136.]

"I trust, in Heaven's mercy, that no change will be made as regards the emoluments of the Liverpool consulate—unless indeed a salary is to be given in addition to the fees, in which case I should receive it very thankfully. This, however, is not to be expected; and if Liverpool is touched at all, it will be to limit its emoluments by a fixed salary— which will render the office not worth any man's holding. It is impossible (especially for a man with a family and keeping any kind of an establishment) not to spend a vast deal of money here. The office, unfortunately, is regarded as one of great dignity, and puts the holder on a level with the highest society, and compels him to associate on equal terms with men who spend more than my whole income on the mere entertainments and other trimmings and embroidery of their lives. Then I feel bound to exercise some hospitality towards my own countrymen. I keep out of society as much as I decently can, and really practice as stern an economy as I ever did in my life; but, nevertheless, I have spent many thousands of dollars in the few months of my residence here, and cannot reasonably hope to spend less than six thousand per annum, even after all the expenditure of setting up an establishment is defrayed."

In addition to this, he states that his predecessor in office, John J. Crittenden, never received above fifteen thousand dollars in fees, of which he saved less than half.

We can trust this to be the plain truth in regard to the Liverpool consulate, and if twenty–five thousand a year was ever obtained from it, there must have been some kind of deviltry in the business. Congress proved inexorable,—as it might not have been, had Hawthorne possessed the influence of a prominent politician like Crittenden. It was a direct affront to the President from his own party, and Pierce did not dare to veto the bill.

What O'Sullivan said to Hawthorne on other subjects may be readily inferred from Hawthorne's next letter to Bridge, in which he begs him to remain in Washington for

Pierce's sake, and says:

"I feel a sorrowful sympathy for the poor fellow (for God's sake don't show him this), and hate to have him left without one true friend, or one man, who will speak a single honest word to him."

It is not very clear how Horatio Bridge could counteract the influence of Jefferson Davis and Caleb Cushing, but this shows that Franklin Pierce's weakness as an administrator was already painfully apparent to his friends, and that even Hawthorne could no longer disguise it to himself.

CHAPTER XIII. HAWTHORNE IN ENGLAND: 1854–1858

Hawthorne's life in England was too generally monotonous to afford many salient points to his biographer. It was monotonous in his official duties, in his pleasure–trips, and in his social experiences. He found one good friend in Liverpool, Mr. Henry Bright, to whom he had already been introduced in America, and he soon made another in Mr. Francis Bennoch, who lived near the same city. They were both excellent men, and belonged to that fine class of Englishmen who possess a comfortable income, but live moderately, and prefer cultivating their minds and the society of their friends, to clubs, yachting, horse–racing, and other forms of external show. They were not distinguished, and were too sensible to desire distinction. Henry Bright may have been the more highly favored in Hawthorne's esteem, but they both possessed that tact and delicacy of feeling which is rare among Englishmen, and by accepting Hawthorne simply as a man like themselves, instead of as a celebrity, they won that place in his confidence from which so many had been excluded.

Otherwise, Hawthorne contracted no friendships among distinguished Englishmen of letters, like that between Emerson and Carlyle; and from first to last he saw little of them. He had no sooner landed than he was greeted with a number of epistles from sentimental ladies, or authors of a single publication, who claimed a spiritual kinship with him, because of their admiration for his writings. One of them even addressed him as "My dear brother." These he filed away with a mental reservation to give the writers as wide a circuit as he possibly could. He attended a respectable number of dinner parties in both Liverpool and London, at which he remained for the most part a silent and unobtrusive guest. He was not favored with an invitation to Holland House, although he met Lady Holland on one occasion, and has left a description of her, not more flattering than others that have been preserved for us. He also met Macaulay and the Brownings at Lord Houghton's; but for once Macaulay would not talk. Mrs. Browning evidently pleased Hawthorne very much. [Footnote: J. Hawthorne, ii. 129.]

The great lights of English literature besides these,—Tennyson, Carlyle, Ruskin, Thackeray, Dickens,—he was never introduced to, although he saw Tennyson in a picture–gallery at Manchester, and has left a description of him, such as might endure to the end of time. Neither did he make the acquaintance of those three luminaries, Froude, Marian Evans, and Max Muller, who rose above the horizon, previous to his return to America. That he was not presented at Court was a matter of course. There was nothing which he could have cared for less.

After his return he published a volume of English sketches, which he entitled "Our Old Home," but he seems to have felt actually less at home in England than in any other country that he visited. In that book, and also in his diary, the even tenor of his discourse is interrupted here and there by fits of irritability which disclose themselves in the use of epithets such as one would hardly expect from the pen of Hawthorne. If we apply to him the well–known proverb with respect to the Russians, we can imagine that under similar conditions an inherited sailor–like tendency in him came to the surface. We only remember one such instance in his American Note–book, that in which he speaks of Thoreau's having a face "as homely as sin."

[Footnote: The general effect of Thoreau's face was by no means unpleasant.]

Hawthorne did not carry with him to Europe that narrow provincialism, which asserts itself in either condemning or ridiculing everything that differs essentially from American ways and methods. On the contrary, when he compares the old country with the new,—for instance, the English scenery with that of New England,—Hawthorne is usually as fair, discriminating, and dispassionate as any one could wish, and perhaps more so than some would desire. His judgment cannot be questioned in preferring the American elm, with its wine–glass shape, to the rotund European species; but he admires the English lake country above anything that he has seen like it in his own land. "Centuries of cultivation have given the English oak a domestic character," while American trees are still to be classed with the wild flowers which bloom beneath their outstretched arms.

Matthew Arnold spoke of his commentaries on England as the writing of a man chagrined; but what could have chagrined Hawthorne there? The socially ambitious man may become chagrined, if he finds that doors are closed to him, and so may an unappreciated would–be genius. But Hawthorne's position as an author was already more firmly established than Matthew Arnold's ever could be; and as for social ambition, no writer since Shakespeare has been so free from it. It seems more probable that the difficulty with Hawthorne in this respect was due to his old position on the slavery question, which now began to bear bitter fruit for him. All Englishmen at that time, with the exception of Carlyle, Froude, and the nobility, were very strongly anti–slavery, —the more so, as it cost them nothing to have other men's slaves liberated,—and the English are particularly blunt, not to say *gauche*, in introducing topics of conversation which are liable to become a matter of controversy. At the first dinner–party I attended in London some thirty–odd years ago, I had scarcely tasted the soup, before a gentleman opposite asked me: "What progress are you making in the United States toward free trade? Can you tell me, sir?" He might as well have asked me what progress we were making in the direction of monarchy. Fortunately for Hawthorne, his good taste prevented him from introducing the slavery question in his publications, excepting in the life of Pierce, but for this same reason his English acquaintances in various places were obliged to discover his opinions at first hand, nor is it very likely that they were slow to do this. Phillips and Garrison had been to England and through England, and their dignified speeches had made an excellent impression. Longfellow, Emerson, Lowell and Whittier had spoken with no uncertain sound, protesting against what they considered a great national evil. How did it happen that Hawthorne was an exception?

Through his kind friend Mr. Bennoch, he fell in with a worthy whom it would have been just as well to have avoided—the proverbial–philosophy poet, Martin Farquhar Tupper; not a genuine poet, nor considered as such by trustworthy critics, but such a good imitation, that he persuaded himself and a large portion of the British public, including Queen Victoria, that he was one. Hawthorne has given an account of his visit to this man, [Footnote: J. Hawthorne, ii. 114.] second only in value to his description of Tennyson; for it is quite as important for us to recognize the deficiencies of the one, as it is to know the true appearance of the other. It is an unsparing study of human nature, but if a man places himself on a pedestal for all people to gaze at, it is just this and nothing more that he has to expect. Hawthorne represents him as a kindly, domestic, affectionate, bustling little man, who kept on bustling with his hands and tongue, even while he was seated—a man of no dignity of character or perception of his deficiency of it. This all does well enough, but when Hawthorne says, "I liked him, and laughed in my sleeve at him, and was utterly weary of him; for certainly he is the ass of asses," we feel that he has gone too far, and suspect that there was some unpleasantness connected with the occasion, of which we are not informed. The word "ass," as applied to a human being, is not current in good literature, unless low comedy be entitled to that position, and coming from Hawthorne, of all writers, it seems like an oath from the mouth of a woman. Tupper, who was quite proud of his philanthropy, was also much of an abolitionist, and he may have trodden on Hawthorne's metaphysical toes half a dozen times, without being aware of what he was doing. Altogether, it seems like rather an ill return for Tupper's hospitality; but Hawthorne himself did not intend it for publication, and on the whole one does not regret that it has been given to the public. We have been, however, anticipating the order of events.

During the summer of 1854, the Hawthorne family made a number of unimportant expeditions, visiting mediaeval abbeys and ruinous castles,—especially one to Chester and Eton Hall, which was not quite worth the fees they paid to the janitors. An ancient walled city is much of a novelty to an American for the first time, but, having seen one, you have seen them all, and Chester Cathedral does not stand high in English architecture. On September 14, O'Sullivan appeared again, and they all went into the Welsh mountains, where they examined the old fortresses of Rhyl and Conway, which were built by Edward Longshanks to hold the Welshmen in check. Those relics of the feudal system are very impressive, not only on account of their solidity and the great human forces which they represent, but from a peculiar beauty of their own, which modern fortifications do not possess at all. They seem to belong to the ground they stand on, and the people who live about them look upon them as cherished landmarks. They are the monuments of an heroic age, and Hawthorne's interest in them was characteristic of his nature.

O'Sullivan returned to Lisbon early in October, and on the 5th of that month, Hawthorne found himself obliged to make a speech at an entertainment on board a merchant vessel called the "James Barnes," which had been built in Boston for a Liverpool firm of ship-owners. He considered this the most serious portion of his official duty,—the necessity of making after-dinner speeches at the Mayor's or other public tables. He writes several pages on the subject in a humorously complainant tone, congratulating himself that on the present occasion he has succeeded admirably, for he has really said nothing, and that is precisely what he intended to do. After–dinner speeches are like soap–bubbles: they are made of nothing, signify nothing, float for a moment in the air, attract a momentary attention, and then disappear. But the difficulty is, to make an apparent something out of nothing, to say nothing that will offend anybody, and to say something that will be different from what others say. It is truly a hard situation in which to place even a very talented man, and, as Longfellow once remarked, those were most fortunate who made their speeches first, and could then enjoy their dinner, while their successors were writhing in agony. However, there are those who like it, and having practised it to perfection, can do it better than anything else. Hawthorne analyzes his sensations, after finishing his speech, with rare self–perception. "After sitting down, I was conscious of an enjoyment in speaking to a public assembly, and felt as if I should like to rise again. It is something like being under fire,—a sort of excitement, not exactly pleasure, but more piquant than most pleasures." Was it President Jackson, or Senator Benton, who said that fighting a duel was very much like making one's maiden speech?

Mrs. Hawthorne thus describes the residence of the President of the Chamber of Commerce at Liverpool: [Footnote: Mrs. Lathrop, 238.] "We were ushered into the drawing–room, which looked more like a brilliant apartment in Versailles than what I had expected to see. The panels were richly gilt, with mirrors in the centre, and hangings of gilded paper; and the broad windows were hung with golden–colored damask; the furniture was all of the same hue; with a carpet of superb flowers; and vases of living flowers standing everywhere; and a chandelier of diamonds (as to indefatigable and vivid shining), and candlesticks of the same,—not the long prisms like those on Mary's astral, but a network of crystals diamond–cut."

This was the coarse commercial taste of the time, previous to the reforms of Ruskin and Eastlake. The same might be said of Versailles. There is no true elegance in gilding and glass–work, including mirrors, unless they be sparingly used.

The Hawthornes were equally overpowered by a dinner–party given by a millionaire and country squire of Liscard Vale; "two enormous silver dish–covers, with the gleam of Damascus blades, putting out all the rest of the light;" and after the fish, these were replaced by two other enormous dishes of equal brilliancy. The table was shortly covered with an array of silver dishes, reflecting the lights above in dazzling splendor. At one end of the table was a roast goose and at the other a boiled turkey; while "cutlets, fricassees, ragouts, tongue, chicken—pies," and much else, filled the intermediate spaces, and the sideboard groaned under a round of beef "like the dome of St. Peter's." It was fortunate that the American consul came to this Herculean repast with an excellent appetite.

Henry Bright was their chief refuge from this flummery, as Hawthorne called it; "an extremely interesting, sincere, earnest, independent, warm and generous hearted man; not at all dogmatic; full of questions, and with ready answers. He is highly cultivated, and writes for the *Westminster*,"—a man who respected formalities and could preserve decorum in his own household, but liked a simple, unostentatious mode of living—in brief, he was a true English gentleman. Mrs. Hawthorne has drawn his portrait with only less skill than her husband:

"His eyes are large, bright, and prominent, rather indicating great facility of language, which he has. He is an Oxford scholar, and has decided literary tastes. He is delicately strung, and is as transparent—minded and pure—hearted as a child, with great enthusiasm and earnestness of character; and, though a Liberal, very loyal to his Queen and very admiring of the aristocracy."

He appears to have been engaged in the Australian carrying trade, and owned the largest sailing vessel afloat.

Hawthorne went to an exhibition of English landscape paintings, and he remarked that Turner's seemed too ethereal to have been painted by mortal hands,—the finest compliment that Turner could have received, for in delicate effects of light and shade,—in painting the atmosphere itself,—he has no rival.

In January, James Buchanan, who was then minister to England, came to visit Hawthorne, and talked with him about the presidency,—for which he considered himself altogether too old; but at the same time he did not suggest the renomination of Franklin Pierce. This, of course, disclosed his own ambition, and as Hawthorne's impartial pen—and—ink sketch of him may not be recognized by many readers, on account of the form in which it appears in the note-books, we append it here, with the regret that Hawthorne could not have treated his friend Pierce in an equally candid manner.

"I like Mr.—. He cannot exactly be called gentlemanly in his manners, there being a sort of rusticity about him; moreover, he has a habit of squinting one eye, and an awkward carriage of his head; but, withal, a dignity in his large person, and a consciousness of high position and importance, which give him ease and freedom. Very simple and frank in his address, he may be as crafty as other diplomatists are said to be; but I see only good sense and plainness of speech,—appreciative, too, and genial enough to make himself conversable. He talked very freely of himself and of other public people, and of American and English affairs. He returns to America, he says, next October, and then retires forever from public life."

A certain amount of rusticity would seem to have been essential to a presidential candidate during the middle of the past century.

During this dismal winter Hawthorne was beset more than ever, by nautical mendicants of all countries,—Hungarians, Poles, Cubans, Spanish Americans, and French Republicans, who, unhappily for him, had discovered that the American consul was a tender-hearted man. He had, beside, to deal with a number of difficult cases of maltreated American sailors,—the more difficult, because both parties to the suits were greatly given to lying, even on occasions when it would have been more expedient for them to tell the truth. He has recorded one such in his diary, that deserves more than a superficial consideration.

An American bark was on the point of sailing, when the captain cast ashore a bruised and battered-looking man, who made his way painfully to the consulate, and begged Hawthorne for a permit to be placed in the hospital. He called himself the son of a South Carolina farmer, and stated that he had gone on board this vessel with a load of farm products, but had been impressed by the captain for the voyage, and had been so maltreated, that he thought he would die,—and so he did, not long afterward, at the hospital. Letters were found upon him, substantiating the statement concerning his father, but it was discovered, from the same source, that he was a jail-bird, and the tattooed figures upon his arms showed that he had been a sailor of many years' standing, although he had denied this to the consul. Hawthorne speaks of him as an innocent man, the victim of criminal brutality little less than murder; it is certainly difficult to account for such severe ill-treatment, but the man was clearly a bad character, and it is also true that sea-captains do not interfere with their deck-hands without some kind of provocation. The man clung desperately to life up to the last moment, and the letters he carried with him indicated that he was more intelligent than the average of the nautical fraternity.

In June, Hawthorne went with his family to Leamington, of which he afterward published an account in the *Atlantic Monthly*, criticised at the time for the manner in which he referred to English ladies, as "covering a large area of Nature's foot–stool"; but this element in Hawthorne's English writing has already been considered. From Leamington he went, early in July, to the English lakes, especially Windermere, and fortunately found time to thoroughly enjoy them. He enjoyed them not only for their scenery, which he preferred to that of New England, but also as illustrations to many descriptive passages in Wordsworth's poetry, which serves the same purpose in the guidebook of that region, as "Childe Harold" serves in the guidebooks for Italy and Greece. Hawthorne also was interested in such places for the sake of their associations. He describes Wordsworth's house, the grounds about it, and the cemetery where he lies, with the accuracy of a scientific report. He finds the grass growing too high about the head–stone of Wordsworth's grave, and plucks it away with his own hands, reflecting that it may have drawn its nourishment from his mortal remains. We may suppose that he preserved this grass, and it is only from such incidental circumstances that we discover who were Hawthorne's favorites among poets and other distinguished writers. He twice visited Wordsworth's grave.

Their first two winters in Liverpool had not proved favorable to Mrs. Hawthorne's health She had contracted a disorder in her throat from the prevailing dampness, which threatened to become chronic, and her husband felt that it would not be prudent for her to remain there another winter. He thought of resigning and returning to America. Then he thought of exchanging his consulship for one in southern Europe, although the salaries of the more southern consulates were hardly sufficient to support a married man. Then he thought of exchanging places with O'Sullivan, but he hardly knew languages well enough for an ambassador. The doctors, however, had advised Mrs. Hawthorne to spend a winter at Madeira, and she courageously solved the problem by proposing to go there alone with her daughters, for which Lisbon and O'Sullivan would serve as a stepping–stone by the way. There are wives who would prefer such an expedition to spending a winter in England with their husbands, but Mrs. Hawthorne was not of that mould, and in her case it was a brave thing to do.

Accordingly, on the second Monday in October, Mrs. Hawthorne and her two daughters sailed for Lisbon. She was presented at court there; concerning which occasion she wrote a lengthy and very interesting account to her husband, published in her son's biography. The King of Portugal held a long conversation with her and Minister O'Sullivan, and she describes him as dressed in a flamboyant manner,—a scarlet uniform, lavishly ornamented with diamonds. With how much better taste did the Empress of Austria receive the President of the French Republic,—in a simple robe of black velvet, fastened at her throat with a diamond brooch. One can envy Mrs. Hawthorne a winter at Madeira, for there is no place in Europe pleasanter for that purpose, unless it be Rome. Meanwhile, her husband spent the winter with his son (who was now old enough to be trusted safely about the streets), at a sea–captains' boarding–house in Liverpool. There, as in Salem, he felt himself most companionable in such company, as he had been accustomed to it from boyhood; and it appears that at this time he was in the habit of composing fables for the entertainment of Julian, not unlike the yarns which sailors often spin to beguile landsmen. [Footnote: J. Hawthorne, ii. 75.]

Hawthorne found his third winter in Liverpool dismal enough without his wife and the two little girls, and this feeling was considerably increased by his dislike for the sea–captains' boarding–house keeper, [Footnote: English Note–book, November 28, 1855.]with whom he was living, and concerning whom he remarks, that a woman in England "is either decidedly a lady or decidedly not." She would not have annoyed him so much, had it not been for "her bustle, affectation, intensity, and pretension of literary taste." The race of landladies contains curious specimens, although we have met with some who were real ladies nevertheless. Thackeray's description of a French boarding–house keeper in "The Adventures of Philip" goes to every heart. Hawthorne writes much in his diary, at this juncture, of his friend Francis Bennoch, who clearly did the best he could, as a man and a brother, to make life cheerful for his American friend; a true, sturdy, warm–hearted Englishman.

Christmas was celebrated at Mrs. Blodgett's, after the fashion of a second–rate English house of entertainment. The servants hung mistletoe about in various places, and woe to the unlucky wight that was caught under it. Hawthorne presents an amusing picture of his boy Julian, nine years old, struggling against the endearments of a chamber–maid, and believes that he himself was the only male person in the house that escaped. [Footnote: English Note–book, December, 1855.]If any man would be sure to escape that benediction, he would have been the one; for no one could be more averse to public demonstrations of affection.

Hawthorne was witness to a curious strategic manouvre between President Pierce and Minister Buchanan, which, however, he was not sufficiently familiar with practical politics to perceive the full meaning of. On the way to Southampton with his wife in October, they called on Buchanan in London, and were not only civilly but kindly received. Mrs. Hawthorne wished to view the Houses of Parliament while they were in session, and the ambassador made a knot in his handkerchief, so as to be sure to remember his promise to her. He informed Hawthorne at that time of his desire to return to America, but stated that the President had just written to him, requesting him to remain until April, although he was determined not to do so. He excused himself on the plea of old age, and Hawthorne seems to have had a suspicion of the insincerity of this, but concluded on reflection not to harbor it. Pierce knew already that Buchanan was his most dangerous rival for renomination, and desired that he should remain as far off as possible; while Buchanan was aware that, if he intended to be on the ground, he must not return so late as to attract public attention. There were so many presidential aspirants that Pierce may have found it difficult to supply Buchanan's place, for the time being.

Buchanan delayed a respectful length of time, and then handed in his resignation. His successor, George M. Dallas, arrived at Liverpool during the second week of March, and Hawthorne who does not mention him by name, called upon him at once, and gives us this valuable portrait of him.

"The ambassador is a venerable old gentleman, with a full head of perfectly white hair, looking not unlike an old–fashioned wig; and this, together with his collarless white neckcloth and his brown coat, gave him precisely such an aspect as one would expect in a respectable person of pre–revolutionary days. There was a formal simplicity, too, in his manners, that might have belonged to the same era. He must have been a very handsome man in his youthful days, and is now comely, very erect, moderately tall, not overburdened with flesh; of benign and agreeable address, with a pleasant smile; but his eyes, which are not very large, impressed me as sharp and cold. He did not at all stamp himself upon me as a man of much intellectual or characteristic vigor. I found no such matter in his conversation, nor did I feel it in the indefinable way by which strength always makes itself acknowledged. Buchanan, though somehow plain and uncouth, yet vindicates himself as a large man of the world, able, experienced, fit to handle difficult circumstances of life, dignified, too, and able to hold his own in any society." [Footnote: English Note–book, March, 1856.]

Morton McMichael, whose statue now stands in Fairmount Park, once related this incident concerning Dallas, at a meeting of the Philadelphia Hock Club. Somewhere about 1850 Dallas was invited to deliver a 4th of July oration at Harrisburg, where McMichael was also requested to read the Declaration of Independence. McMichael performed his part of the ceremony, and sat down; then Dallas arose and thanked the assembly for honoring him with such an invitation, but confessed to some difficulty in considering what he should say, for an occasion which had been celebrated by so many famous orators; but that a few nights since, while he was lying awake, it occurred to him what he should say to them. After this he proceeded to read his address from a newspaper printed in 1841, which the audience could not see, but which McMichael, from his position on the platform, could see perfectly well.

Hawthorne's description suggests a man somewhat like this; but the opinion of the Hock Club was that Dallas was not greatly to blame; for how could any man make two distinct and original 4th of July orations?

The 1st of April 1856, Hawthorne and Bennoch set off on a bachelor expedition of their own, first to visit Tupper at Albany, as has been already related, and then going to view a muster of British troops at Aldershot; thence to Battle Abbey, which Hawthorne greatly admired, and the field of Hastings, where England's greatness began in defeat. He does not mention the battle, however, in his diary, and it may be remarked that, generally, Hawthorne felt little interest in historical subjects. After this, they went to London, where Bennoch introduced Hawthorne at the Milton Club and the Reform Club. At the former, he again encountered Martin F. Tupper, and became acquainted with Tom Taylor, the editor of *Punch*, as well as other writers and editors, of whom he had not previously heard. The Club was by no means Miltonic, and one would suppose not exactly the place where Hawthorne would find himself much at home. Neither were the proceedings altogether in good taste. Bennoch opened the ball with a highly eulogistic speech about Hawthorne, and was followed by some fifty others in a similar strain, so that the unfortunate incumbent must have wished that the earth would open and let him down to the shades of night below. On such an occasion, even a feather weight becomes a burden. Oh, for a boy, with a tin horn!

Neither did Hawthorne apparently find his peers at the Reform Club. Douglas Jerrold, who reminded him somewhat of Ellery Channing, was the most notable writer he met there. There was, however, very little speech–making, and plenty of good conversation. Unfortunately, he offended Jerrold, by using the word "acrid" as applied to his writing, instead of some other word, which he could not think of at the moment. The difficulty, however, was made up over a fresh bottle of Burgundy, and with the help of Hawthorne's unlimited good—will, so that they parted excellent friends, and much the better for having known each other. Either Jerrold or some other present told Hawthorne that the English aristocracy, for the most part hated, despised, and feared men of literary genius. Is it not much the same in America?

After these two celebrations, and attending the Lord Mayor's banquet, where he admired the beautiful Jewess whom he has described as Miriam in "The Marble Faun," Hawthorne returned to Liverpool; and early in May took another recess, with a Mr. Bowman, to York, Edinburgh, the Trossachs, Abbotsford, and all the haunts of Scott and Burns; with his account of which a large portion of the second volume of English Note—books is filled; so that, if Scotland should sink into the sea, as a portion is already supposed to have done in antediluvian times, all those places could be reconstructed through Hawthorne's description of them.

This expedition lasted nearly three weeks, and on June 12 Hawthorne received word that his wife, with Una and Rose, had already landed at Southampton. He hastened at once to meet them, greatly rejoiced to find Mrs. Hawthorne entirely restored to health. They had been separated for more than seven months.

They first proceeded to Salisbury, to see the cathedral and Stonehenge,—the former, very impressive externally, but not so satisfactory within; and the latter, a work of man emerging out of Nature. Then they went to London, to enjoy the June season, and see the regular course of sights in that huge metropolis. They visited St. Paul's, the Tower, Guildhall, the National Gallery, the British Museum, Westminster Abbey, and the Houses of Parliament, apparently finding as much satisfaction in this conventional occupation as they did in the social entertainments of London. At the house of Mr. S. C. Hall, a noted entertainer of those days, Hawthorne became acquainted with the most celebrated singer of her time, or perhaps of all time; namely, Jenny Lind. No modern orator has held such a sway over the hearts of men and women, as that Swedish nightingale,—for the purity of her voice seemed no more than the emanation of her lofty nature. Hawthorne describes her as a frank, sincere person, rather tall,—certainly no beauty, but with sense and self—reliance in her aspect and manners. She immediately gave Hawthorne an illustration of her frankness by complaining of the unhealthy manner in which Americans, and especially American women, lived. This seems like a prosaic subject for such a person, but it was natural enough; for a concert singer has to live like a race—horse, and this would be what would constantly strike her attention in a foreign country. Hawthorne rallied to the support of his countrywomen, and believed that they were, on the whole, as healthy and long–lived as Europeans. This may be so now, but there has been great improvement in the American mode of living, during the past fifty years, and we can imagine that Jenny Lind often found it difficult to obtain such food as she required.

That she should have requested an introduction to Hawthorne is significant of her interest in American literature, and suggests a taste as refined and elevated as her music.

It was on Hawthorne's wedding–day this happened, and a few days later he was invited to a select company at Monckton Milnes's, which included Macaulay, the Brownings, and Professor Ticknor. He found both the Brownings exceedingly pleasant and accessible, but was somewhat startled to find that Mrs. Browning was a believer in spiritism—not such a sound and healthy intelligence as the author of "Middle–march," and he might have been still more so, if he had known that she and her husband were ardent admirers of Louis Napoleon. That was something which an American in those days could not quite understand. However, he found her an exceedingly pleasant companion. After dinner they looked over several volumes of autographs, in which Oliver Cromwell's was the only one that would to–day be more valuable than Hawthorne's own.

A breakfast at Monckton Milnes's usually included the reading of a copy of verses of his own composition, but perhaps he had not yet reached that stage on the present occasion.

Hawthorne heard such varied and conflicting accounts of Charles Dickens that he hardly knew whether he would like to meet him or not. He wanted to see Tennyson when he was at the Isle of Wight, but feared that his visit might be looked on as an intrusion, by a person who lived so retired a life,—judging perhaps from his own experience. While at Windermere he paused for a moment in front of Harriet Martineau's cottage, but on second thought he concluded to leave the good deaf lady in peace.

Conway speaks of Hawthorne's social life in England as a failure; but failure suggests an effort in some direction or other, and Hawthorne made no social efforts. Being lionized was not his business. He had seen enough of it during the London season of 1856, and after that he retired into his domestic shell, cultivating the acquaintance of his wife and children more assiduously than ever, so that even his two faithful allies, Bright and Bennoch, found it difficult to withdraw him from it. Watching the development of a fine child is much more satisfactory than any course of fashionable entertainments—even than Lowell's twenty–nine dinner–parties in the month of June. Nothing becomes more tedious than long–continued pleasure–seeking, with post–prandial speeches and a constant effort to be agreeable.

Hawthorne remained in England fully seventeen months after this, and made a number of excursions; especially one to Oxford, where he and his family were dined by a former mayor of the city, and where he greatly admired the broad verdant grounds and Gothic architecture of the colleges; and also a second journey to Edinburgh and the Trossachs, undertaken for the benefit of Mrs. Hawthorne and Una. But we hear no more of him in London society, and it only remains for us to chronicle his exceptional kindness to an unfortunate American woman.

It seems strange that the first doubt in regard to the authorship of Shakespeare should have originated on this side of the Atlantic. If Dante was a self–educated poet, there seems no good reason why Shakespeare should not have been; and if the greatest of French writers earned his living as an actor, why should not the greatest of English writers have done the same? That would seem to be much more in harmony with the central idea of American life—the principle of self–helpfulness; but this is a skeptical epoch, and the tendency of our political institutions is toward skepticism of character and distrust of tradition. Hence we have Delia Bacon, Holmes, and Donnelly.

Hawthorne has given future generations an account of Delia Bacon, which will endure as the portrait of a gifted and interesting woman, diverted from the normal channels of feminine activity by the force of a single idea; but he makes no mention of his efforts in her behalf. He found her in the lodgings of a London tradesman, and although she received him in a pleasant and lady–like manner, he quickly perceived that her mind was in an abnormal condition, and that it was positively dangerous to discuss her favorite topic in a rational manner. He had a feeling that the least opposition on his part to the Baconian theory would result in his expulsion from the room, yet he found her conversation interesting, and recognized that if her conclusions were erroneous she had nevertheless unearthed valuable historic material, which ought to be given to the world. He loaned her money, which he did not expect to be repaid, and exerted himself to find a publisher for her, recollecting perhaps the vows he had made to the gods in the days of his own obscurity. He mentions in his diary calling on the Rutledges for this purpose—where he saw Charles Reade, a tall, strong–looking man, just leaving the office. He also wrote to Ticknor &Fields, and finally did get Miss Bacon's volume brought out in London. The critics treated it in a contemptuous manner, as a desecration of Shakespeare's memory; and Hawthorne was prepared for this, but it opened a new era in English bibliography. Shortly after the publication of her book Miss Bacon became insane.

To many this appeared like a Quixotic adventure, but now we can see that it was not, and that it was necessary in its way to prove the generosity of Hawthorne. We can readily infer from it what he might have done with ampler means, and what he must often have wished to do. To be sure, the truest kindness to Delia Bacon would have been to have purchased a ticket on a Cunard steamer for her, after her own funds had given out, and to have persuaded her to return to her own country; but those who have dealt with persons whose whole vitality is absorbed in a single idea, can testify how difficult, if not impossible, this would have been. It redounds the more to Hawthorne's credit that although Elizabeth Peabody was converted to Delia Bacon's theory, Hawthorne himself never entertained misgivings as to the reality of Shakespeare as a poet and a dramatist.

He had doubts, however, and I felt the same in regard to the authenticity of the verses on Shakespeare's marble slab. It is fortunate that Miss Bacon's purpose of opening the tomb at Stratford was not carried out, but that is no reason why it should not be opened in a properly conducted manner, for scientific purposes—in order to discover all that is possible concerning so remarkable and mysterious a personality. Raphael's tomb has been opened, and why should not Shakespeare's be also?

At the Democratic convention in 1856 the Southern delegates wished to renominate Franklin Pierce, but the Northern delegates refused their agreement to this, because they knew that in such a case they would be liable to defeat in their own districts. James Buchanan was accordingly nominated, and Pierce's fears in regard to him were fully realized. He was elected in November, and the following June appointed Beverly Tucker to succeed Hawthorne as consul at Liverpool. Hawthorne resigned his office on July 1, 1857, and went with his family on a long tour in Scotland. Two weeks earlier he had written a memorial to the Secretary of State concerning the maltreatment of a special class of seamen, which deserved more consideration than it received from the government at Washington.

The Life and Genius of Nathaniel Hawthorne

The gold discoveries in California had induced a large immigration to America from the British Isles, and many who went thither in hopes of bettering their fortunes became destitute from lack of employment, and attempted to work their passage back to Liverpool in American sailing vessels. It is likely that they often represented themselves as more experienced mariners than they actually were, and there were also a good many stowaways who might expect little mercy; but there was no court in England that could take cognizance of their wrongs,—in order to obtain justice they would have to return to America,—and it cannot be doubted that the more brutal sort of officers took advantage of this fact. The evil became so notorious that the British minister at Washington requested Pierce's administration to have legislation enacted that would cover this class of cases, but the President declined to interfere. This may have been prudent policy, but Hawthorne felt for the sufferers, and the memorial that he submitted to our government on their account has a dignity, a clearness and cogency of statement, worthy of Blackstone or Marshall. It is in marked contrast to the evasive reply of Secretary Cass, both for its fine English and for the directness of its logic. It is published at length in Julian Hawthorne's biography of his father, and is unique for the insight which it affords as to Hawthorne's mental ability in this direction. We may infer from it that if he had made a study of jurisprudence, he might have risen to the highest position as a writer on law.

Hawthorne's English Note–books are the least interesting of that series, on account of the literal descriptions of castles, abbeys, scenery and palaces, with which they abound. The perfectly cultivated condition of England and Scotland, so far as he went in the latter country, is not stimulating to the imagination; for, as he says somewhere, even the trees seemed to be thoroughly domesticated. They are excellent reading for Americans who have never been to England, or for those who wish to renew their memories in regard to certain places there—perhaps better for the latter than for the former; and there are fine passages in them, especially his descriptions of the old abbeys and Gothic cathedrals, which seem to have delighted him more than the gardens at Blenheim and Eton, and to have brought to the surface a rare quality in his nature, or otherwise hidden in its depths,—his enthusiasm. Never before did words fail him until he attempted to describe the effect of a Gothic cathedral,—the time–honored mystery of its arches, the sober radiance of its stained windows, and the solemn aspiration of its lofty vault. As Schiller says, they are the monuments of a mighty civilization of which we know only too little.

The Life and Genius of Nathaniel Hawthorne

Hawthorne's object in writing these detailed accounts of his various expeditions becomes apparent from a passage in his Note-book, of the date of August 21, 1856, in which he says: "In my English romance, an American might bring a certain tradition from over the sea, and so discover the cross which had been long since forgotten." It may have been his intention from the first to write a romance based on English soil, but that soil was no longer productive of such intellectual fruit, except in the form in which Dickens dug it up, like peat, out of the lower classes. We find Francis Bennoch writing to Hawthorne after his return to America, [Footnote: Mrs. Lathrop, 310.] hoping to encourage him in this direction, but without apparent effect. Instead of a romance, he made a collection of essays from those portions of his diary which were most closely connected together, enlarging them and rounding them out, which he published after his return to America, in the volume we have often referred to as "Our Old Home." But as truthful studies of English life and manners Mrs. Hawthorne's letters, though not always sensible, are much more interesting than her husband's diary.

When Doctor Johnson was inquired of by a lady why he defined "pastern" in his Dictionary as the knee of a horse, he replied, "Ignorance, madam, pure ignorance;" and if Hawthorne had been asked a year afterwards why he went to Scotland in the summer of 1857, instead of to the Rhine and Switzerland, he might have given a similar excuse. In this way he missed the grandest and some of the most beautiful scenery in Europe. He could not, however, have been ignorant of the attractions of Paris, and yet he lingered in England until the following January, and then went over to that metropolis of fashion at a most unseasonable time. He had, indeed, planned to leave England in October, [Footnote: English Note-book, December, 1857.] and does not explain why he remained longer. He made a last visit to London in November, where he became reconciled to his fellow-townsmen of Salem, in the person of Edward Silsbee, of whom he writes as "a man of great intelligence and true feeling, absolutely brimming over with ideas." Mr. Silsbee was an amateur art critic and connoisseur, who often made himself serviceable to American travellers in the way of a gentleman-cicerone. He went with the Hawthorne family to the Crystal Palace, where there were casts of all famous statues, models of architecture, and the like, and gave Hawthorne his first lesson in art criticism. Hawthorne indicated a preference for Michel Angelo's statue of Giuliano de Medici, called "Il Pensero;" also for the "Perseus" of Cellini, and the Gates of the Florentine Baptistery by Lorenzo Ghiberti. If we except the other statues of Michel Angelo, these are the most distinguished works in sculpture of the modern world.

CHAPTER XIV. ITALY

Hawthorne went to Italy as naturally as the salmon ascends the rivers in spring. His artistic instinct drew him thither as the original home of modern art and literature, and perhaps also his interest in the Latin language, the single study which he cared for in boyhood. Does not romance come originally from Roma,—as well as Romulus? He wished to stand where Casar stood, to behold the snowy Soracte of Horace, and to read Virgil's description of an Italian night on Italian ground. It is noticeable that he cared little or nothing for the splendors of Paris, the glittering peaks of Switzerland, medical–musical Vienna, or the grand scholarship and homely sweetness of old Germany.

Of all the Anglo–Saxon writers who have celebrated Italy, Byron, Shelley, Rogers, Ruskin and the two Brownings, none were more admirably equipped for it than Hawthorne. We cannot read "The Romance of Monte Beni" without recognizing a decidedly Italian element in his composition,—not the light–hearted, subtle, elastic, fiery Italian, such as we are accustomed to think them, but the tenderly feeling, terribly earnest Tuscan, like Dante and Savonarola. The myrtle and the cypress are both emblematic of Italian character, and there was more of the latter than the former, though something of either, in Hawthorne's own make–up.

The Hawthornes left London on January 6, and, reaching Paris the following day, they made themselves comfortable at the Hotel du Louvre. However, they only remained there one week, during which it was so cold that they saw little and enjoyed little. They went to Notre Dame, the Louvre, the Madeleine, and the Champs Elysees, but without being greatly impressed by what they beheld. Hawthorne does not mention a single painting or statue among the art treasures of the Louvre, which if rivalled elsewhere are certainly unsurpassed; but Hawthorne began his studies in this line by an examination of the drawings of the old masters, and confesses that he was afterward too much fatigued to appreciate their finished paintings.

On January 19 they reached Marseilles, and two days later they embarked on that dreary winter voyage, so pleasant at an earlier season, for Civita Vecchia; and on the 20th they rolled into the Eternal City, with such sensations as one may imagine. On the 24th they located themselves for the season in the Palazzo Larazani, Via Porta Pinciana. [Footnote.

The Life and Genius of Nathaniel Hawthorne

Italian Note–book.]

Nemo similis Homeri.—There is nothing like the charm of a first visit to Rome. The first sight of the Forum, with its single pathetic column, brings us back to our school–days, to the study of Casar and the reading of Plutarch; and the intervening period drops out of our lives, taking all our care and anxiety with it. In England, France, Germany, we feel the weight of the present, but in Rome the present is like a glass window through which we view the grand procession of past events. What *is*, becomes of less importance than what was, and for the first time we feel the true sense of our indebtedness to the ages that have gone before. We bathe deep in the spirit of classical antiquity, and we come out refreshed, enlarged and purified. We return to the actualities of to–day with a clearer understanding, and better prepared to act our part in them.

Hawthorne did not feel this at first. He arrived in inclement weather, and it was some weeks before he became accustomed to the climatic conditions—so different from any northern atmosphere. He hated the filth of the much–neglected city, the squalor of its lower classes, the narrowness of its streets, and the peculiar pavement, which, as he says makes walking in Rome a penitential pilgrimage. He goes to the carnival, and his penetrating glance proves it to be a sham entertainment.

But in due course he emerges from this mood; he rejoices in the atmospheric immensity of St. Peter's; he looks out from the Pincian hill, and sees *Nivea Soracte* as Horace beheld it; and he is overawed (if Hawthorne could be) by the Forum of Trajan and the Column of Antoninus. He makes a great discovery, or rediscovery, that Phidias's colossal statues of Castor and Pollux on the Monte Cavallo are the finest figures in Rome. They are late Roman copies, but probably from Phidias,—not by Lysippus or Praxiteles; and he felt the presence of Michel Angelo in the Baths of Diocletian. It is not long before he goes to the Pincian in the afternoon to play at jack–stones with his youngest daughter.

William W. Story, the American sculptor, would seem to have been a former acquaintance. His father, the famous law lecturer, lived in Salem during Hawthorne's youth, but afterward removed to Cambridge, where the younger Story was educated, and there married an intimate friend of Mrs. James Russell Lowell. This brought him into close relations with Lowell, Longfellow, and their most intimate friends. He was something of a poet, and more of a sculptor, but, inheriting an independent fortune and living in the Barberini Palace, he soon became more of an Englishman than an American, a tendency which was visibly increased by a patent of nobility bestowed on him by the King of Naples.

Hawthorne soon renewed William Story's acquaintance, and found him modelling the statue of Cleopatra, of which Hawthorne has given a somewhat idealized description in "The Marble Faun." This may have interested him the more from the fact that he witnessed its development under the sculptor's hands, and saw that distinguished historical person emerge as it were out of the clay, like a second Eve; but he makes a mental reservation that it would be better if English and American sculptors would make a freer use of their chisels—of which more hereafter. Story was a light–hearted, discursive person, with a large amount of bric–a–brac information, who could appreciate Hawthorne either as a genius or as a celebrity. He soon became Hawthorne's chief companion and social mainstay in Rome, literally a *vade mecum*, and we may believe that he exercised more or less influence over Hawthorne's judgment in matters of art.

Hawthorne listened to Story, and read Mrs. Jameson, although Edward Silsbee had warned him against her as an uncertain authority; but Hawthorne depended chiefly on his own investigations. He and his wife declined an invitation to Mrs. Story's masquerade, and lived very quietly during this first winter in Rome, making few acquaintances, but seeing a good deal of the city. They went together to all the principal churches and the princely galleries; and beside this Hawthorne traversed Rome from one end to the other, and across in every direction, sometimes alone, or in company with Julian, investigating everything from the Mamartine prison, in which Jugurtha was starved, to the catacombs of St. Calixtus and the buffaloes on the Campagna. The impression which Conway gives, that he went about sight–seeing and drinking sour wine with Story and Lothrop Motley, is not quite correct, for Motley did not come to Rome until the following December, and then only met Hawthorne a few times, according to his own confession. [Footnote: Mrs. Lathrop, 406.] We must not forget, however, that excellent lady and skilful astronomer, Miss Maria Mitchell, who joined the Hawthorne party in Paris, and became an indispensable accompaniment to them the rest of the winter.

Hawthorne also became acquainted with Buchanan Read, who afterward painted that stirring picture of General Sheridan galloping to the battle of Cedar Run; and on March 12 Mr. Read gave a party, at his Roman dwelling, of painters and sculptors, which Hawthorne attended, and has entered in full, with the moonlight excursion afterward, in "The Marble Faun." There Hawthorne met Gibson, to whom he refers as the most distinguished sculptor of the time. So he was, in England, but there were much better sculptors in France and in Germany. Gibson's personality interested Hawthorne, as it well might, but he saw clearly that Gibson was merely a skilful imitator of the antique, or, as he calls him, a pagan idealist. He also made acquaintance with two American sculptors, a Yankee and a girlish young woman, whose names are prudently withheld; for he afterward visited their studios, and readily discovered that they had no real talent for their profession.

If we feel inclined to quarrel with Hawthorne anywhere, it is in his disparagement of Crawford. There might be two opinions in regard to the slavery question, but there never has been but one as to the greatest of American artists. It was a pity that his friend Hillard could not have been with Hawthorne at this time to counteract the jealous influences to which he was exposed. He writes no word of regret at the untimely death of Crawford, but goes into his studio after that sad event and condemns his work. Only the *genre* figure of a boy playing marbles, gives him any satisfaction there; although a plea of extenuation might be entered in Hawthorne's favor, for statues of heroic size could not be seen to greater disadvantage than when packed together in a studio. The immense buttons on the waistcoats of our revolutionary heroes seem to have startled him on his first entrance, and this may be accepted as an indication of the rest. Yet the tone of his criticism, both in the "Note-book" and in "The Marble Faun," is far from friendly to Crawford. He does not refer to the statue of Beethoven, which was Crawford's masterpiece, nor to the statue of Liberty, which now poses on the lantern of the Capitol at Washington,— much too beautiful, as Hartmann says, for its elevated position, and superior in every respect to the French statue of Liberty in New York harbor.

Hawthorne had already come to the conclusion that there was a certain degree of poison in the Roman atmosphere, and in April he found the climate decidedly languid, but he had fallen in love with this pagan capital and he hated to leave it. Mrs. Anna Jameson arrived late in April; a sturdy, warm-hearted Englishwoman greatly devoted to art, for which her books served as elementary treatises and pioneers to the English and Americans of those days. She was so anxious to meet Hawthorne that she persuaded William Story to bring him and his wife to her lodgings when she was too ill to go forth. They had read each other's writings and could compliment each other in all sincerity, for Mrs. Jameson had also an excellent narrative style; but Hawthorne found her rather didactic, and although she professed to be able "to read a picture like a book," her conversation was by no means brilliant. She had contracted an unhappy marriage early in life, and found an escape from her sorrows and regrets in this elevated interest.

It was just before leaving Rome that Hawthorne conceived the idea of a romance in which the "Faun" of Praxiteles should come to life, and play a characteristic part in the modern world; the catastrophe naturally resulting from his coming into conflict with a social organization for which he was unfitted. This portion of Hawthorne's diary is intensely interesting to those who have walked on classic ground.

On May 24 Hawthorne commenced his journey to Florence with a *vetturino* by easy stages, and one can cordially envy him this portion of his Italian sojourn; with his devoted wife and three happy children; travelling through some of the most beautiful scenery in the world,—nearly if not quite equal to the Rhineland—without even the smallest cloud of care and anxiety upon his sky, his mind stored with mighty memories, and looking forward with equal expectations to the prospect before him,—*bella Firenze*, the treasure–house of Italian cities; through sunny valleys, with their streams and hill–sides winding seaward; up the precipitous spurs of the Apennines, with their old baronial castles perched like vultures' nests on inaccessible crags; passing through gloomy, tortuous defiles, guarded by Roman strongholds; and then drawn up by white bullocks over Monte Somma, and to the mountain cities of Assisi and Perugia, older than Rome itself; by Lake Trasimenus, still ominous of the name of Hannibal; over hill–sides silver–gray with olive orchards; always a fresh view and a new panorama, bounded by the purple peaks on the horizon; and over all, the tender blue of the Italian sky. Hawthorne may have felt that his whole previous life, all he had struggled, lived and suffered for, was but a preparation for this one week of perfectly harmonious existence. Such vacations from earthly troubles come but rarely in the most fortunate lives, and are never of long duration.

When they reached Florence, they found it, as Rose Hawthorne says, very hot—much too hot to enjoy the city as it should be enjoyed. Her reminiscences of their life at Florence, and especially of the Villa Manteuto, have a charming freshness and virginal simplicity, although written in a somewhat high–flown manner. She succeeds, in spite of her peculiar style, in giving a distinct impression of the old chateau, its surroundings, the life her family led there, and of the wonderful view from Bellosguardo. One feels that beneath the disguise of a fashionable dress there is an innocent, sympathetic, and pure–spirited nature.

The Life and Genius of Nathaniel Hawthorne

The Hawthornes arrived in Florence on the afternoon of June 3, and spent the first night at the Albergo della Fontano, and the next day obtained apartments in the Casa del Bello, opposite Hiram Powers' studio, and just outside of the Porta Romana. Hawthorne made Mr. Powers' acquaintance even before he entered the city, and Powers soon became to him what Story had been in Rome. The Brownings were already at Casa Guidi,—still noted in the annals of English poesy,—and called upon the Hawthornes at the first notice of their arrival. Alacrity or readiness would seem to have been one of Robert Browning's prominent characteristics. Elizabeth Browning's mind was as much occupied with spiritism as when Hawthorne met her two years previously at Monckton Milnes's breakfast; an unfortunate proclivity for a person of frail physique and delicate nerves. Neither did she live very long after this. Her husband and Hawthorne both cordially disapproved of these mesmeric practices; but Mrs. Browning could not be prevented from talking on the subject, and this evidently produced an ecstatic and febrile condition of mind in her, very wearing to a poetic temperament. Hawthorne heartily liked Browning himself, and always speaks well of him; but there must also have been an undercurrent of disagreement between him and so ardent an admirer of Louis Napoleon, and he recalls little or nothing of what Browning said to him. This continued till the last of June, when Robert and Elizabeth left Florence for cooler regions.

Meanwhile Hawthorne occupied himself seriously with seeing Florence and studying art, like a man who intends to get at the root of the matter. Florence afforded better advantages than Rome for the study of art, not only from the superiority of its collections, but because there the development of mediaeval art can be traced to its fountain—source. He had no textbooks to guide him,—at least he does not refer to any,—and his investigations were consequently of rather an irregular kind, but it was evidently the subject which interested him most deeply at this time. His Note—book is full of it, and also of discussions on sculpture with Hiram Powers, in which Hawthorne has frequently the best of the argument.

In fact Powers looked upon his art from much too literal a stand—point. He agreed with Hawthorne as to the fine expression of the face of Michel Angelo's "Giuliano de Medici," [Footnote: As Hawthorne did not prepare his diary for publication, it would not be fair to hold him responsible for the many instances of bad Italian in the Note—book, which ought to have been edited by some one who knew the language.] but affirmed that it was owing to a trick of overshadowing the face by the projecting visor of Giuliano's helmet. Hawthorne did not see why such a device did not come within the range of legitimate art, the truth of the matter being that Michel Angelo left the face unfinished; but the expression of the statue is not in its face, but in the inclination of the head, the position of the arms, the heavy droop of the armor, and in fact in the whole figure. Powers' "Greek Slave," on the contrary, though finely modelled and sufficiently modern in type, has no definite expression whatever.

Hawthorne found an exceptional interest in the "Venus de Medici," now supposed to have been the work of one of the sons of Praxiteles, and its wonderful symmetry gives it a radiance like that of the sun behind a summer cloud; but Powers cooled down his enthusiasm by objecting to the position of the ears, the vacancy of the face, the misrepresentation of the inner surface of the lips, and by condemning particularly the structure of the eyes, which he declared were such as no human being could see with. [Footnote: Italian Note-book, June 13, 1858.] Hawthorne was somewhat puzzled by these subtleties of criticism, which he did not know very well how to answer, but he still held fast to the opinion that he was fundamentally right, and retaliated by criticising Powers' own statues in his diary.

The Greeks, in the best period of their favorite art, never attempted a literal reproduction of the human figure. Certain features, like the nostrils, were merely indicated; others, like the eyelashes, often so expressive in woman, were omitted altogether; hair and drapery were treated in a schematic manner. In order to give an expression to the eyes, various devices were resorted to. The eyelids of the bust of Pericles on the Acropolis had bevelled edges, and the eyeballs of the "Apollo Belvedere" are exceptionally convex, to produce the effect of looking to a distance, although the human eye when gazing afar off becomes slightly contracted. The head of the "Venus de Medici" is finely shaped, but small, and her features are pretty, rather than beautiful; but her eyes are exceptional among all feminine statues for their tenderness of expression—swimming, as it were, with love; and it is the manner in which this effect is produced that Powers mistook for bad sculpture. Hiram Powers' most exceptional proposition was to the effect that the busts of the Roman emperors were not characteristic portraits. Hawthorne strongly dissented from this; and he was in the right, for if the character of a man can be read from marble, it is from those old blocks. Hawthorne has some admirable remarks on this point.

Such was Hawthorne's internal life during his first month at Florence. He was full of admiration for the cathedral, the equestrian statue of Cosmo de Medici, the "David" of Michel Angelo, the Loggia de Lanzi, Raphael's portrait of Julius II., the "Fates" of

Michel Angelo, and many others; yet he confesses that the Dutch, French, and English paintings gave him a more simple, natural pleasure,—probably because their subjects came closer to his own experience.

A strange figure of an old man, with "a Palmer–like beard," continually crossed Hawthorne's path, both in Rome and in Florence, where he dines with him at the Brownings'. His name is withheld, but Hawthorne informs us that he is an American editor, a poet; that he voted for Buchanan, and was rejoicing in the defeat of the Free–soilers,—"a man to whom the world lacks substance because he has not sufficiently cultivated his emotional nature;" and "his personal intercourse, though kindly, does not stir one's blood in the least." Yet Hawthorne finds him to be good–hearted, intelligent, and sensible. This can be no other than William Cullen Bryant. [Footnote: Italian Note–book, ii. 15.]

In the evening of June 27 the Hawthornes went to call on a Miss Blagden, who occupied a villa on Bellosguardo, and where they met the Brownings, and a Mr. Trollope, a brother of the novelist. It could not have been the Villa Manteuto, which Miss Blagden rented, for we hear of her at Bellosguardo again in August, when Hawthorne was living there himself; and after this we do not hear of the Brownings again.

Hawthorne's remark on Browning's poetry is one of the rare instances in which he criticises a contemporary author:

"I am rather surprised that Browning's conversation should be so clear, and so much to the purpose at the moment, since his poetry can seldom proceed far, without running into the high grass of latent meanings and obscure allusions."

It is precisely this which has prevented Browning from achieving the reputation that his genius deserves. We wish that Hawthorne could have favored us with as much literary criticism as he has given us of art criticism, and we almost lose patience with him for his repeated canonization of General Jackson—St. Hickory—united with a disparagement of Washington and Sumner; but although Hawthorne's insight into human nature was wonderful in its way, it would seem to have been confined within narrow boundaries. At least he seems to have possessed little insight into grand characters and magnanimous natures. He wishes now that Raphael could have painted Jackson's portrait. So, conversely, Shakespeare belittles Casar in order to suit the purpose of his play. Which of

The Life and Genius of Nathaniel Hawthorne

Shakespeare's male characters can be measured beside George Washington? There is not one of them, unless Kent in "King Lear." Strong, resolute natures, like Washington, Hamilton, Sumner, are not adapted to dramatic fiction, either in prose or in verse.

A Florentine summer is about equal to one in South Carolina, and now, when Switzerland can be reached by rail in twenty–four hours, no American or Englishman thinks of spending July and August there; but in Hawthorne's time it was a long and expensive journey over the Pennine Alps; Hawthorne's physique was as well attempered to heat as to cold; and he continued to frequent the picture–galleries and museums after all others had ceased to do so; although he complains in his diary that he had never known it so hot before, and that the flagstones in the street reflect the sun's rays upon him like the open doors of a furnace.

At length, in an entry of July 27, he says:

"I seldom go out nowadays, having already seen Florence tolerably well, and the streets being very hot, and myself having been engaged in sketching out a romance, [Footnote: "The Marble Faun."] which whether it will ever come to anything is a point yet to be decided. At any rate, it leaves me little heart for journalizing, and describing new things; and six months of uninterrupted monotony would be more valuable to me just now, than the most brilliant succession of novelties."

This is the second instance in which we hear of a romance based on the "Faun" of Praxiteles, and now at last he appears to be in earnest.

It may be suspected that his entertaining friend, Hiram Powers, was the chief obstacle to the progress of his new plot, and it is rather amusing to believe that it was through the agency of Mr. Powers, who cared for nothing so much as Hawthorne's welfare, that this impediment was removed. Five days later, Hawthorne and his household gods, which were chiefly his wife and children, left the Casa del Bello for the Villa Manteuto where they remained in peaceful retirement until the first of October.

On the tower of the Villa he could enjoy whatever enlivening breezes came across to Florence from the mountains to the north and east. When the *tramontana* blew, he was comfortable enough. Thunder–storms also came frequently, with the roar of heaven's artillery reverberating from peak to peak, and enveloping Bellosguardo in a dense vapor, like the smoke from Napoleon's cannon; after which they would career down the valley of the Arno to Pisa, flashing and cannonading like a victorious army in pursuit of the enemy.

The beauty of the summer nights at Florence amply compensates for the sultriness of the days,—especially if they be moonlight nights,—and the bright starlight of the Mediterranean is little less beautiful. Travellers who only see Italy in winter, know not what they miss. Hawthorne noticed that the Italian sky had a softer blue than that of England and America, and that there was a peculiar luminous quality in the atmosphere, as well as a more decided difference between sunshine and shadow, than in countries north of the Alps. The atmosphere of Italy, Spain, and Greece is not like any American air that I am acquainted with. During the summer season, all Italians whose occupation will permit them, sleep at noon,—the laborers in the shadows of the walls,—and sit up late at night, enjoying the fine air and the pleasant conversation which it inspires. Hawthorne found the atmosphere of Tuscany favorable for literary work, even in August.

On the 4th of that month he looked out from his castle wall late at night and noticed the brilliancy of the stars,—also that the Great Dipper exactly overhung the valley of the Arno. At that same hour the astronomer Donati was sweeping the heavens with his telescope at the Florentine observatory, and it may have been ten days later that he discovered in the handle of the Dipper the great comet which will always bear his name,—the most magnificent comet of modern times, only excepting that of 1680, which could be seen at noonday. It first became visible to the naked eye during the last week of August, as a small star with a smaller tail, near the second star from the end of the handle of the Dipper; after which it grew apace until it extended nearly from the horizon to the zenith, with a tail millions of miles in length. This, however, did not take place until near the time of Hawthorne's departure from Florence. In his case it proved sorrowfully enough a harbinger of calamity.

Hawthorne blocked out his sketch of "The Romance of Monte Beni" in a single month, and then returned to the churches and picture-galleries. He could not expect to revisit Italy in this life, and prudently concluded to make the most of it while the opportunity lasted. He notices the peculiar fatigue which sight-seeing causes in deep natures, and becomes unspeakably weary of it, yet returns to it again next day with an interest as fresh as before.

Neither did he lack for society. William Story came over to see him from Siena, where he was spending the summer, exactly as Hawthorne describes the visit of Kenyon to Donatello in his romance. Mr. and Mrs. Powers came frequently up the hill in the cool of the evening, and Miss Blagden also proved an excellent neighbor. Early in September the "spirits" appeared again in great force. Mrs. Hawthorne discovered a medium in her English governess; table–rappings and table–tippings were the order of the evening; and some rather surprising results were obtained through Miss Shepard's fingers. [Footnote: J. Hawthorne, i. 31.] Powers related a still more surprising performance [Footnote: Italian Note–book.] that he had witnessed, which was conducted by D. D. Home, an American mountebank, who hoaxed more crowned heads, princes, princesses, and especially English duchesses than Cagliostro himself. Hawthorne felt the repugnance of the true artist to this uncanny business, and his thorough detestation of the subject commends itself to every sensible reader. He came to the conclusion that the supposed revelations of spirits were nothing more than the mental vagaries of persons in the same room, conveyed in some occult manner to the brain of the medium. The governess, Miss Shepard, agreed with him in this, but she could give no explanation as to the manner in which the response came to her. Twenty years of scientific investigations have added little or nothing to this diagnosis of Hawthorne's, nor are we any nearer to an explanation of the simple fact; which is wonderful enough in its way. Hawthorne compares the revelations of mediums to dreams, but they are not exactly like them, for they are at the same time more rational and less original or spontaneous than dreams. In my dreams my old friends often come back to me and speak in their characteristic manner,—more characteristic perhaps than I could represent them when awake,—but the responses of mediums are either evasive or too highly generalized to be of any particular value. The story of Mary Runnel, or Rondel, which Julian Hawthorne narrates, is an excellent case in point. Hawthorne had probably heard of that flirtation of his grandfather some time in his youth, and the fact was unconsciously latent in his mind; but nothing that Mary divulged at Bellosguardo was of real interest to him or to the others concerned. The practice of spiritism, hypnotism, or Christian Science opens a wide door for superstition and imposture to walk in and seat themselves by our firesides.

About a year before this, Congress had given Hiram Powers a commission to model a colossal statue of *America* for the Capitol at Washington. This he had done, and the committee in charge accepted his design,—Hawthorne also writes admiringly of it,—but it was also necessary to receive the approval of the President, and this Buchanan with his peculiar obstinacy refused to give. Powers was left without compensation for a whole year of arduous labor, and Hawthorne for once was thoroughly indignant. He wrote in his diary:

"I wish our great Republic had the spirit to do as much, according to its vast means, as Florence did for sculpture and architecture when it was a republic.... And yet the less we attempt to do for art the better, if our future attempts are to have no better result than such brazen troopers as the equestrian statue of General Jackson, or even such naked respectabilities as Greeneough's Washington."

Perhaps Powers' "America" was a fortunate escape, and yet it does not seem right that any enlightened government should set such a pitfall for honest men to stumble into. There certainly ought to be some compensation in such cases. The experience of history hitherto has been that, whereas painting and literature have nourished under all forms of government, sculpture has only attained its highest excellence in republics like Athens, Rhodes, Florence, and Nuremberg; so that upon this line of argument there is good hope for America in the future.

CHAPTER XV. HAWTHORNE AS ART CRITIC: 1858

Nearly one–third of the Italian Note–book is devoted to the criticisms or descriptions of paintings, statues, and architecture, for which we can be only too thankful as coming from such a bright, penetrating, and ingenious intelligence. It is much in their favor that Hawthorne had not previously undertaken a course of instruction in art; that he wrote for his own benefit, and not for publication; and that he was not biased by preconceived opinions. It cannot be doubted that he was sometimes influenced by the opinions of Story, Powers, and other artists with whom he came in contact; but this could have happened only in particular cases, and more especially in respect to modern works of art. When Hawthorne visited the galleries he usually went alone, or only accompanied by his wife.

The only opportunities for the study of aesthetics or art criticism, fifty years ago, were to be found in German universities. Kugler's handbook of painting was the chief authority in use, rather academic, but correct enough in a general way. Ruskin, a more eloquent and discriminating writer, had devoted himself chiefly to celebrating the merits of Turner and Tintoretto, but was never quite just to Florentine art. Mrs. Jameson followed closely after

Kugler, and was the only one of these that Hawthorne appears to have consulted. Winckelmann's history of Greek sculpture, which was not a history in the proper sense of the word, had been translated by Lodge, but Hawthorne does not mention it, and it would not have been much assistance to him if he had read it. Like Winckelmann and Lessing, however, he admired the "Laocoon,"—an admiration now somewhat out of fashion.

There can be no final authority in art, for the most experienced critics still continue to differ in their estimates of the same painting or statue. More than this, it is safe to affirm that any one writer who makes a statement concerning a certain work of art at a given time, would have made a somewhat different statement at another time. In fact, this not unfrequently happens in actual practice; for all that any of us can do is, to reproduce the impression made on us at the moment, and this depends as much on our own state of mind, and on our peculiarities, as on the peculiarities of the picture or statue that we criticise. It is the same in art itself. If Raphael had not painted the "Sistine Madonna" at the time he did, he would have produced a different work. It was the concentration of that particular occasion, and if any accident had happened to prevent it, that pious and beautiful vision would have been lost to the world.

It requires years of study and observation of the best masters to become a trustworthy art critic, and then everything depends of course upon the genius of the individual. It has happened more than once that a wealthy American, with a certain kind of enthusiasm for art, has prepared himself at a German university, has studied the science of connoisseurship, and has become associate member of a number of foreign societies, only to discover at length that he had no talent for the profession. Hawthorne enjoyed no such advantages, nor did he even think of becoming a connoisseur. His whole experience in the art of design might be included within twelve months, and his original basis was nothing better than his wife's water–color painting and the mediocre pictures in the Boston Athenaeum; but he brought to his subject an eye that was trained to the closest observation of Nature and a mind experienced beyond all others [Footnote: At least at that time.] in the mysteries of human life. He begins tentatively, and as might be expected makes a number of errors, but quite as often he hits the nail, where others have missed it. He learns by his mistakes, and steadily improves in critical faculty. Hawthorne's Italian Note–book is a unique record, in which the development of a highly organized mind has advanced from small beginnings to exceptional skill in a fresh department of activity.

The Life and Genius of Nathaniel Hawthorne

Hawthorne brought with him to Italy the Yankee preference for newness and nicety, which our forefathers themselves derived from their residence in Holland, and there is no city in Europe where this sentiment could have troubled him so much as in Rome. He disliked the dingy picture–frames, the uncleanly canvases, the earth–stains and broken noses of the antique statues, the smoked–up walls of the Sistine Chapel, and the cracks in Raphael's frescos. He condemns everything as rubbish which has not an external perfection; forgetting that, as in human nature, the most precious treasures are sometimes allied with an ungainly exterior. Yet in this he only echoes the impressions of thousands of others who have gone to the Vatican and returned disconsolate, because amid a perplexing multitude of objects they knew not where to look for consummate art. One can imagine if an experienced friend had accompanied Hawthorne to the Raphael stanza, and had pointed out the figures of the Pope, the cardinal, and the angelic boys in the "Mass at Bolsena," he would have admired them without limitation. He quickly discovered Raphael's "Transfiguration," and considered it the greatest painting that the world contains.

The paintings in the princely collections in Rome are, with the exception of those in the Borghese gallery, far removed from princely. A large proportion of their best paintings had long since been sold to the royal collections of northern Europe, and had been replaced either by copies or by works of inferior masters. In the Barberini palace there are not more than three or four paintings such as might reasonably detain a traveller, and it is about the same in the Ludovisi gallery. There was not a grain of affectation in Hawthorne; he never pretended to admire what he did not like, nor did he strain himself into liking anything that his inner nature rebelled against.

Hawthorne's taste in art was much in advance of his time. His quick appreciation of the colossal statues of Castor and Pollux on the Quirinal is the best proof of this. Ten years later it was the fashion in Rome to deride those statues, as a late work of the empire and greatly lacking in artistic style. Brunn, in his history of ancient sculpture, attributes them to the school of Lysippus, a contemporary of Alexander, which Brunn certainly would not have done if he had possessed a good eye for form. Vasari, on the contrary, a surer critic, considered them worthy to be placed beside Michel Angelo's "David"; but it remained for Furtwangler to restore them to their true position as a work of the Periclean age, although copied by Italian sculptors. They must have been the product of a single mind, [Footnote: On the base of one is *Opus Phidiae*, and on that of the other, *Opus Praxitelis.*] either Phidias, Alcameres, or the elder Praxiteles—if there ever was such a person; and they have the finest figures of any statues in Rome (much finer than the dandified "Apollo Belvedere") and also the most spirited action.

Hawthorne went to the Villa Ludovisi to see the much-vaunted bas-relief of Antinous, which fifty years ago was considered one of the art treasures of the city; but a more refined taste has since discovered that in spite of the rare technical skill, its hard glassy finish gives it a cold and conventional effect. Hawthorne returned from it disappointed, and wrote in his diary:

"This Antinous is said to be the finest relic of antiquity next to the Apollo and the Laocoon; but I could not feel it to be so, partly, I suppose, because the features of Antinous do not seem to me beautiful in themselves; and that heavy, downward look is repeated till I am more weary of it than of anything else in sculpture."

The Greek artist of Adrian's time attempted to give the face a pensive expression, but only succeeded in this heavy downward look.

Hawthorne felt the same disappointment after his first visit to the sculpture-gallery of the Vatican. "I must confess," he wrote, "taking such transient glimpses as I did, I was more impressed with the extent of the Vatican, and the beautiful order in which it is kept and its great sunny, open courts, with fountains, grass, and shrubs ... than with the statuary." The Vatican collection has great archaeological value, but, with the exception of the "Laocoon," the "Meleager," the "Apollo," and a few others, little or no artistic value. The vast majority of the statues there are either late Roman works or cheap Roman copies of second-rate Hellenic statues. Some of them are positively bad and others are archaic, and Hawthorne was fully justified in his disatisfaction with them. He noticed, however, a decided difference between the original "Apollo" and the casts of it with which he was familiar. On a subsequent visit he fails to observe the numerous faults in Canova's "Perseus," and afterwards writes this original statement concerning the "Laocoon":

"I felt the Laocoon very powerfully, though very quietly; an immortal agony with a strange calmness diffused through it, so that it resembles the vast age of the sea, calm on account of its immensity; as the tumult of Niagara, which does not seem to be tumult, because it keeps pouring on forever and ever."

The Life and Genius of Nathaniel Hawthorne

Professor E. A. Gardner and the more fastidious school of critics have recently decided that the action of the "Laocoon" is too violent to be contained within the proper boundaries of sculpture; but Hawthorne controverts this view in a single sentence. The action is violent, it is true, but the *impression* which the statue makes on him is not a violent one; for the greatness of the art sublimates the motive. It is a tragedy in marble, and Pliny, who had seen the works of Phidias and Praxiteles, placed Agesander's "Laocoon" above them all. This, however, is a Roman view. What Hawthorne wrote in his diary should not always be taken literally. When he declares that he would like to have every artist that perpetrates an allegory put to death, he merely expresses the puzzling effects which such compositions frequently exercise on the weary–minded traveller; and when he wishes that all the frescos on Italian walls could be obliterated, he only repeats a sentiment of similar strain. Perhaps we should class in the same category Hawthorne's remark concerning the Elgin marbles in the British Museum, that "it would be well if they were converted into paving– stones." There are no grander monuments of ancient art than those battered and headless statues from the pediment of the Parthenon (the figures of the so–called "Three Fates" surpass the "Venus of Melos"), and archaeologists are still in dispute as to what they may have represented; but the significance of the subject before him was always the point in which Hawthorne was interested. Julian Hawthorne says of his father, in regard to a similar instance:

"Of technicalities,—difficulties overcome, harmony of lines, and so forth,—he had no explicit knowledge; they produced their effect upon him of course, but without his recognizing the manner of it. All that concerned him was the sentiment which the artist had meant to express; the means and method were comparatively unimportant." [Footnote: J. Hawthorne, ii. 193.]

The technicalities of art differ with every clime and every generation. They belong chiefly to the connoisseur, and have their value, but the less a critic thinks of them in making a general estimate of a painting or statue, the more likely he is to render an impartial judgment. Hawthorne's analysis of Praxiteles's "Faun," in his "Romance of Monte Beni," being a subject in which he was particularly interested, is almost without a rival in the literature of its kind; and this is the more remarkable since the copy of the "Faun" in the museum of the Capitol is not one of the best, at least it is inferior to the one in the Glyptothek at Munich. It seems as if Hawthorne had penetrated to the first conception of it in the mind of Praxiteles.

The Life and Genius of Nathaniel Hawthorne

The Sistine Chapel, like the Italian scenery, only unfolds its beauties on a bright day, and Hawthorne happened to go there when the sky was full of drifting clouds, a time when it is difficult to see any object as it really is. It may have been on this account that he entirely mistook the action of the Saviour in Michel Angelo's "Last Judgment." Christ has raised his arm above his head in order to display the mark where he was nailed to the cross, and Hawthorne presumed this, as many others have done, to be an angry threatening gesture of condemnation, which would not accord with his merciful spirit. He appreciated the symmetrical figure of Adam, and the majestic forms of the prophets and sibyls encircling the ceiling, and if he had seen the face of the Saviour in a fair light, he might have recognized that such divine calmness of expression could not coexist with a vindictive motive. This, however, can be seen to better advantage in a Braun photograph than in the painting itself.

Hawthorne goes to the Church of San Pietro in Vincolo to see Michel Angelo's "Moses," but he does not moralize before it, like a certain Concord artist, on "the weakness of exaggeration;" nor does he consider, like Ruskin, that its conventional horns are a serious detriment. On the contrary he finds it "grand and sublime, with a beard flowing down like a cataract; a truly majestic figure, but not so benign as it were desirable that such strength should hold." An Englishman present remarked that the "Moses" had very fine features,— "a compliment," says Hawthorne, "for which the colossal Hebrew ought to have made the Englishman a bow."

[Footnote: Italian Note–book, p. 164.]

Perhaps the Englishman really meant that the face had a noble expression. The somewhat satyr–like features of the "Moses" would seem to have been unconsciously adopted, together with the horns, from a statue of the god Pan, which thus serves as an intermediate link between the "Moses" and the "Faun" of Praxiteles; but he who cannot appreciate Michel Angelo's "Moses" in spite of this, knows nothing of the Alpine heights of human nature.

Of all the paintings that Hawthorne saw in Rome none impressed him so deeply as Guido's portrait of Beatrice Cenci, and none more justly. If the "Laocoon" is the type of an old Greek tragedy, a strong man strangled in the coils of Fate, the portrait of Beatrice represents the tragedy of mediaeval Italy, a beautiful woman crushed by the downfall of a splendid civilization. The fate of Joan of Arc or of Madame Roland was merciful compared to that of poor Beatrice. Religion is no consolation to her, for it is the Pope himself who signs her death–warrant. She is massacred to gratify the avarice of the Holy See. Yet in this last evening of her tragical life, she does find strength and consolation in her dignity as a woman. Never was art consecrated to a higher purpose; Guido rose above himself; and, as Hawthorne says, it seems as if mortal man could not have wrought such an effect. It has always been the most popular painting in Rome, but Hawthorne was the first to celebrate its unique superiority in writing, and his discourse upon it in various places leaves little for those that follow.

It may have been long since discovered that Hawthorne's single weakness was a weakness for his friends; certainly an amiable weakness, but nevertheless that is the proper name for it. When Phocion was Archon of Athens, he said that a chief magistrate should know no friends; and the same should be true of an authoritative writer. Hawthorne has not gone so far in this direction as many others have who had less reason to speak with authority than he; but he has indicated his partiality for Franklin Pierce plainly enough, and his over–praise of Hiram Powers and William Story, as well as his under–praise of Crawford, will go down to future generations as something of an injustice to those three artists.

[Illustration: GUIDO RENI'S PORTRAIT OF BEATRICE CENCI, PAINTED WHILE SHE WAS IN PRISON, WHICH SUGGESTED TO HAWTHORNE THE PLOT OF "THE MARBLE FAUN"]

It is not necessary to repeat here what Hawthorne wrote concerning Powers' Webster. The statue stands in front of the State House at Boston, and serves as a good likeness of the famous orator, but more than that one cannot say for it. The face has no definable expression, and those who have looked for a central motive in the figure will be pleased to learn what it is by reading Hawthorne's description of it, as he saw it in Powers' studio at Florence. A sculptor of the present day can find no better study for his art than the attitudes and changes of countenance in an eloquent speaker; but which of them can be said to have taken advantage of this? Story made an attempt in his statue of Everett, but even his most indulgent friends did not consider it a success. His "George Peabody," opposite the Bank of England, could not perhaps have been altogether different from what it is.

The Life and Genius of Nathaniel Hawthorne

What chiefly interested Story in his profession seems to have been the modelling of unhappy women in various attitudes of reflection. He made a number of these, of which his "Cleopatra" is the only one known to fame, and in the expression of her face he has certainly achieved a high degree of excellence. Neither has Hawthorne valued it too highly, —the expression of worldly splendor incarnated in a beautiful woman on the tragical verge of an abyss. If she only were beautiful! Here the limitations of the statue commence. Hawthorne says, "The sculptor had not shunned to give the full, Nubian lips and other characteristics of the Egyptian physiognomy."

Here he follows the sculptor himself, and it is remarkable that a college graduate like William Story should have made so transparent a mistake. Cleopatra was not an Egyptian at all. The Ptolemies were Greeks, and it is simply impossible to believe that they would have allied themselves with a subject and alien race. This kind of small pedantry has often led artists astray, and was peculiarly virulent during the middle of the past century. The whole figure of Story's "Cleopatra" suffers from it. Hawthorne says again, "She was draped from head to foot in a costume minutely and scrupulously studied from that of ancient Egypt." In fact, the body and limbs of the statue are so closely shrouded as to deprive the work of that sense of freedom of action and royal abandon which greets us in Shakespeare's and Plutarch's "Cleopatra." Story might have taken a lesson from Titian's matchless "Cleopatra" in the Cassel gallery, or from Marc Antonio's small woodcut of Raphael's "Cleopatra."

Perhaps it is not too much to say of Crawford that he was the finest plastic genius of the Anglo–Saxon race. His technique may not have been equal to Flaxman's or St. Gaudens', but his designs have more of grandeur than the former, and he is more original than the latter. There are faults of modelling in his "Orpheus," and its attitude resembles that of the eldest son of Niobe in the Florentine gallery,— although the Niobe youth looks upward and Orpheus is peering into darkness,—its features are rather too pretty; but the statue has exactly what Powers' "Greek Slave" lacks, a definite motive,—that of an earnest seeker,—which pervades it from head to foot; and it is no imaginary pathos that we feel in its presence. There is, at least, no imitation of the antique in Crawford's "Beethoven," for its conception, the listening to internal harmonies, would never have occurred to a Greek or a Roman. Even Hawthorne admits Crawford's skill in the treatment of drapery; and this is very important, for it is in his drapery quite as much as in the nude that we recognize the superiority of Michel Angelo to Raphael; and the folds of Beethoven's mantle are as rhythmical as his own harmonies. The features lack something of firmness, but it is altogether a statue in the grand manner.

Hawthorne is rather too exacting in his requirements of modern sculptors. Warrington Wood, who commenced life as a marble–worker, always employed Italian workmen to carve his statues, although he was perfectly able to do it himself, and always put on the finishing touches,—as I presume they all do. Bronze statues are finished with a file, and of course do not require any knowledge of the chisel.

In regard to the imitation of antique attitudes, there has certainly been too much of it, as Hawthorne supposes; but the Greeks themselves were given to this form of plagiarism, and even Praxiteles sometimes adopted the motives of his predecessors; but Hawthorne praises Powers, Story, and Harriet Hosmer above their merits.

The whole brotherhood of artists and their critical friends might rise up against me, if I were to support Hawthorne's condemnation of modern Venuses, and "the guilty glimpses stolen at hired models." They are not necessarily guilty glimpses. To an experienced artist the customary study from a naked figure, male or female, is little more than what a low–necked dress at a party would be to many others. Yet the instinct of the age shrinks from this exposure. We can make pretty good Venuses, but we cannot look at them through the same mental and moral atmosphere as the contemporaries of Scopas, or even with the same eyes that Michel Angelo saw them. We feel the difference between a modern Venus and an ancient one. There is a statue in the Vatican of a Roman emperor, of which every one says that it ought to wear clothes; and the reason is because the face has such a modern look. A raving Bacchante may be a good acquisition to an art museum, but it is out of place in a public library. A female statue requires more or less drapery to set off the outlines of the figure and to give it dignity. We feel this even in the finest Greek work—like the "Venus of Cnidos."

In this matter Hawthorne certainly exposes his Puritanic education, and he also places too high a value on the carving of button–holes and shoestrings by Italian workmen. Such things are the fag–ends of statuary.

His judgment, however, is clear and convincing in regard to the tinted Eves and Venuses of Gibson. Whatever may have been the ancient practice in this respect, Gibson's experiment proved a failure. Nobody likes those statues; and no other sculptor has since followed Gibson's example. The tinting of statues by the Greeks did not commence until the time of Aristotle, and does not seem to have been very general. Their object evidently was, not so much to imitate flesh as to tone down the crystalline glare of the new marble. Pausanias speaks of a statue in Arcadia, the drapery of which was painted with vermilion, "so as to look very gay." This was of course the consequence of a late and degraded taste. That traces of paint should have been discovered on Greek temples is no evidence that the marble was painted when they were first built.

It may be suspected that Hawthorne was one of the very few who have seen the "Venus de Medici" and recognized the true significance of the statue. The vast majority of visitors to the Uffizi only see in it the type of a perfectly symmetrical woman bashfully posing for her likeness in marble, but Hawthorne's perception in it went much beyond that, and the fact that he attempts no explanation of its motive is in accordance with the present theory. He also noticed that statues had sometimes exercised a potent spell over him, and at others a very slight influence.

Froude says that a man's modesty is the best part of him. Notice that, ye strugglers for preferment, and how beautifully modest Hawthorne is, when he writes in his Florentine diary:

"In a year's time, with the advantage of access to this magnificent gallery, I think I might come to have some little knowledge of pictures. At present I still know nothing; but am glad to find myself capable, at least, of loving one picture better than another. I am sensible, however, that a process is going on, and has been ever since I came to Italy, that puts me in a state to see pictures with less toil, and more pleasure, and makes me more fastidious, yet more sensible of beauty where I saw none before."

Hawthorne belongs to the same class of amateur critics as Shelley and Goethe, who, even if their opinions cannot always be accepted as final, illuminate the subject with the radiance of genius and have an equal value with the most experienced connoisseurs.

* * * * *

The return of the Hawthornes to Rome through Tuscany was even more interesting than their journey to Florence in the spring, and they enjoyed the inestimable advantage of a *vetturino* who would seem to have been the Sir Philip Sidney of his profession, a compendium of human excellences. There are such men, though rarely met with, and we may trust Hawthorne's word that Constantino Bacci was one of them; not only a skilful driver, but a generous provider, honest, courteous, kindly, and agreeable. They went first to Siena, where they were entertained for a week or more by the versatile Mr. Story, and where Hawthorne wrote an eloquent description of the cathedral; then over the mountain pass where Radicofani nestles among the iron–browed crags above the clouds; past the malarious Lake of Bolsena, scene of the miracle which Raphael has commemorated in the Vatican; through Viterbo and *Sette Vene*; and finally, on October 16, into Rome, through the Porta' del Popolo, designed by Michel Angelo in his massive style, —Donati's comet flaming before them every night. Thompson, the portrait painter, had already secured a furnished house, No. 68 Piazza Poli, for the Hawthornes, to which they went immediately.

Since the death of Julius Casar, comets have always been looked upon as the forerunners of pestilence and war, but wars are sometimes blessings, and Donati's discovery proved a harbinger of good to Italy, —but to the Hawthornes, a prediction of evil. Continually in Hawthorne's Italian journal we meet with references to the Roman malaria, as if it were a subject that occupied his thoughts, and nowhere is this more common than during the return–journey from Florence. Did it occur to him that the lightning might strike in his own house? No sensible American now would take his children to Rome unless for a very brief visit; and yet William Story brought up his family there with excellent success, so far as health was concerned.

We can believe that Hawthorne took every possible precaution, so far as he knew, but in spite of that on November 1 his eldest daughter was seized with Roman fever, and for six weeks thereafter lay trembling between life and death, so that it seemed as if a feather might turn the balance.

She does not appear to have been imprudent. Her father believed that the "old hag" breathed upon her while she was with her mother, who was sketching in the Palace of the Casars; but the Palatine Hill is on high ground, with a foundation of solid masonry, and was guarded by French soldiers, and it would have been difficult to find a more cleanly spot in the city. A German count, who lived in a villa on the Calian Hill, close by, considered his residence one of the most healthful in Rome. Miss Una had a passionate attachment for the capital of the ancient world; and it seems as if the evil spirit of the place had seized upon her, as the Ice Maiden is supposed to entrap chamois hunters in the Alps.

188

One of the evils attendant on sickness in a foreign country is, the uncertainty in regard to a doctor, and this naturally leads to a distrust and suspicion of the one that is employed. Even so shrewd a man as Bismarck fell into the hands of a charlatan at St. Petersburg and suffered severely in consequence. Hawthorne either had a similar experience, or, what came to the same thing, believed that he did. He considered himself obliged to change doctors for his daughter, and this added to his care and anxiety. During the next four months he wrote not a word in his journal (or elsewhere, so far as we know), and he visibly aged before his wife's eyes. He went to walk on occasion with Story or Thompson, but it was merely for the preservation of his own health. His thoughts were always in his daughter's chamber, and this was so strongly marked upon his face that any one could read it. Toward the Ides of March, Miss Una was sufficiently improved to take a short look at the carnival, but it was two months later before she was in a condition to travel, and neither she nor her father ever wholly recovered from the effects of this sad experience.

CHAPTER XVI. "THE MARBLE FAUN": 1859–1860

What the Roman carnival was a hundred and fifty years ago, when the Italian princes poured out their wealth upon it, and when it served as a medium for the communication of lovers as well as for social and political intrigue, which sometimes resulted in conflicts like those of the Montagues and Capulets, can only be imagined. Goethe witnessed it from a balcony in the Corso, and his carnival in the second part of "Faust" was worked up from notes taken on that occasion; but it is so highly poetized that little can be determined from it, except as a portion of the drama. By Hawthorne's time the aristocratic Italians had long since given up their favorite holiday to English and American travellers,—crowded out, as it were, by the superiority of money; and since the advent of Victor Emmanuel, the carnival has become so democratic that you are more likely to encounter your landlady's daughter there than any more distinguished person. Hawthorne's description of it in "The Marble Faun" is not overdrawn, and is one of the happiest passages in the book.

The carnival of 1859 was an exceptionally brilliant one. The Prince of Wales attended it with a suite of young English nobles, who, always decorous and polite on public occasions, nevertheless infused great spirit into the proceedings. Sumner and Motley were there, and Motley rented a balcony in a palace, to which the Hawthornes received general and repeated invitations. On March 7, Miss Una was driven through the Corso in a barouche, and the Prince of Wales threw her a bouquet, probably recognizing her father, who was with her; and to prove his good intentions he threw her another, when her carriage returned from the Piazza, del Popolo. The present English sovereign has always been noted for a sort of journalistic interest in prominent men of letters, science, and public affairs, and it is likely that he was better informed in regard to the Hawthornes than they imagined. Hawthorne himself was too much subdued by his recent trial to enter into the spirit of the carnival, even with a heart much relieved from anxiety, but he sometimes appeared in the Motleys' balcony, and sometimes went along the narrow sidewalk of the Corso, "for an hour or so among the people, just on the edges of the fun." Sumner invited Mrs. Hawthorne to take a stroll and see pictures with him, from which she returned delighted with his criticisms and erudition.

A few days later Franklin Pierce suddenly appeared at No. 68 Piazza Poli, with that shadow on his face which was never wholly to leave it. The man who fears God and keeps his commandments will never feel quite alone in the world; but for the man who lives on popularity, what will there be left when that forsakes him? Hawthorne was almost shocked at the change in his friend's appearance; not only at his gray hair and wrinkled brow, but at the change in his voice, and at a certain lack of substance in him, as if the personal magnetism had gone out of him. Hawthorne went to walk with him, and tried to encourage him by suggesting another term of the presidency, but this did not help much, for even Pierce's own State had deserted him,—a fact of which Hawthorne may not have been aware. The companionship of his old friend, however, and the manifold novelty of Rome itself, somewhat revived the ex–President, as may be imagined; and a month later he left for Venice, in better spirits than he came.

They celebrated the Ides of March by going to see Harriet Hosmer's statue of Zenobia, which was afterward exhibited in America. Hawthorne immediately detected its resemblance to the antique,—the figure was in fact a pure plagiarism from the smaller statue of Ceres in the Vatican,—but Miss Hosmer succeeded in giving the face an expression of injured and sorrowing majesty, which Hawthorne was equally ready to appreciate.

On this second visit to Rome he became acquainted with a sculptor, whose name is not given, but who criticised Hiram Powers with a rather suspicious severity. He would not allow Powers "to be an artist at all, or to know anything of the laws of art," although acknowledging him to be a great bust–maker, and to have put together the "Greek Slave" and the "Fisher–Boy" very ingeniously. "The latter, however (he says), is copied from the Spinario in the *Tribune* of the Uffizi; and the former made up of beauties that had no reference to one another; and he affirms that Powers is ready to sell, and has actually sold, the 'Greek Slave,' limb by limb, dismembering it by reversing the process of putting it together. Powers knows nothing scientifically of the human frame, and only succeeds in representing it, as a natural bone–doctor succeeds in setting a dislocated limb, by a happy accident or special providence." [Footnote: Italian Note–book, 483.]

We may judge, from "the style, the matter, and the drift" of this discourse, that it emanated from the same sculptor who is mentioned, in "Nathaniel Hawthorne and His Wife," as having traduced Margaret Fuller and her husband Count Ossoli. As Tennyson says, "A lie that is half a truth is ever the blackest of lies," and this fellow would seem to have been an adept in unveracious exaggeration. It is remarkable that Hawthorne should have given serious attention to such a man; but an English critic said in regard to this same incident that if Hawthorne had been a more communicative person, if he had talked freely to a larger number of people, he would not have been so easily prejudiced by those few with whom he was chiefly intimate. To which it could be added, that he might also have taken broader views in regard to public affairs.

Hawthorne was fortunate to have been present at the discovery of the St. Petersburg "Venus," the twin sister of the "Venus de Medici," which was dug up in a vineyard outside the Porta Portese. The proprietor of the vineyard, who made his fortune at a stroke by the discovery, happened to select the site for a new building over the buried ruins of an ancient villa, and the "Venus" was discovered in what appeared to Hawthorne as an old Roman bath–room. The statue was in more perfect preservation than the "Venus de Medici," both of whose arms have been restored, and Hawthorne noticed that the head was larger and the face more characteristic, with wide–open eyes and a more confident expression. He was one of the very few who saw it before it was transported to St. Petersburg, and a thorough artistic analysis of it is still one of the *desiderata*. The difference in expression, however, would seem to be in favor of the "Venus de Medici," as more in accordance with the ruling motive of the figure.

Miss Una Hawthorne had not sufficiently recovered to travel until the last of May, when they all set forth northward by way of Genoa and Marseilles, in which latter place we find them on the 28th, enjoying the comfort and elegance of a good French hotel. Thence they proceeded to Avignon, but did not find much to admire there except the Rhone; so they continued to Geneva, the most pleasant, homelike resting place in Europe, but quite deficient in other attractions.

It seems as if Hawthorne's Roman friends were somewhat remiss in not giving him better advice in regard to European travelling. At Geneva he was within a stone's throw of Chamounix, and hardly more than that of Strasburg Cathedral, and yet he visited neither. Why did he go out of his way to see so little and to miss so much? He went across the lake to visit Lausanne and the Castle of Chillon, and he was more than astonished at the view of the Pennine Alps from the deck of the steamer. He had never imagined anything like it; and he might have said the same if he had visited Cologne Cathedral. Instead of that, however, he hurried through France again, with the intention of sailing for America the middle of July; but after reaching London he concluded to remain another year in England, to write his "Romance of Monte Beni," and obtain an English copyright for it.

He left Geneva on June 15, and as he turned his face northward, he felt that Henry Bright and Francis Bennoch were his only real friends in Great Britain. There could hardly have been a stronger contrast than these two. Bright was tall, slender, rather pale for an Englishman, grave and philosophical. Bennoch was short, plump, lively and jovial, with a ready fund of humor much in the style of Dickens, with whom he was personally acquainted. Yet Hawthorne recognized that Bright and Bennoch liked him for what he was, in and of himself, and not for his celebrity alone.

Bright was in London when Hawthorne reached there, and proposed that they should go together to call on Sumner, [Footnote: J. Hawthorne, ii. 223.] who had been cured from the effects of Brooks's assault by an equally heroic treatment; but Hawthorne objected that as neither of them was Lord Chancellor, Sumner would not be likely to pay them much attention; to which Bright replied, that Sumner had been very kind to him in America, and they accordingly went. Sumner was kind to thousands,—the kindest as well as the most upright man of his time,— and no one in America, except Longfellow, appreciated Hawthorne so well; but he was the champion of the anti-slavery movement and the inveterate opponent of President Pierce. I suppose a man's mind cannot help being colored somewhat by such conditions and influences.

Hawthorne wished for a quiet, healthful place, where he could write his romance without the disturbances that are incident to celebrity, and his friends recommended Redcar, on the eastern coast of Yorkshire, a town that otherwise Americans would not have heard of. He went there about the middle of July, remaining until the 5th of October, but of his life there we know nothing except that he must have worked assiduously, for in that space of time he nearly finished a book containing almost twice as many pages as "The Scarlet Letter." Meanwhile Mrs. Hawthorne entertained the children and kept them from interfering with their father (in his small cottage), by making a collection of sea–mosses, which Una and Julian gathered at low tides, and which their mother afterward dried and preserved on paper. On October 4th Una Hawthorne wrote to her aunt, Elizabeth Peabody:

"Our last day in Redcar, and a most lovely one it is. The sea seems to reproach us for leaving it. But I am glad we are going, for I feel so homesick that I want constant change to divert my thoughts. How troublesome feelings and affections are."

[Footnote: Mrs. Lathrop, 35 a.]

One can see that it was a pleasant place even after the days had begun to shorten, which they do very rapidly in northern England. From Redcar, Hawthorne went to Leamington, where he finished his romance about the first of December, and remained until some time in March, living quietly and making occasional pedestrian tours to neighboring towns. He was particularly fond of the walk to Warwick Castle, and of standing on the bridge which crosses the Avon, and gazing at the walls of the Castle, as they rise above the trees—"as fine a piece of English scenery as exists anywhere; the gray towers and long line of windows of the lordly castle, with a picturesquely varied outline; ancient strength, a little softened by decay." It is a view that has often been sketched, painted and engraved.

The romance was written, but had to be revised, the least pleasant portion of an author's duties,—unless he chooses to make the index himself. This required five or six weeks longer, after which Hawthorne went to London and arranged for its publication with Smith &Elder, who agreed to bring it out in three volumes—although two would have been quite sufficient; but according to English ideas, the length of a work of fiction adds to its importance. Unfortunately, Smith &Elder also desired to cater to the more prosaic class of readers by changing the name of the romance from "The Marble Faun" to "Transformation," and they appear to have done this without consulting Hawthorne's wishes in the matter. It was simply squeezing the title dry of all poetic suggestions; and it would have been quite as appropriate to change the name of "The Scarlet Letter" to "The

Clergyman's Penance," or to call "The Blithedale Romance" "The Suicide of a Jilt." If Smith &Elder considered "The Marble Faun" too recondite a title for the English public, what better name could they have hit upon than "The Romance of Monte Beni"? Would not the Count of Monte Beni be a cousin Italian, as it were, to the Count of Monte Cristo? We are thankful to observe that when Hawthorne published the book in America, he had his own way in regard to this point.

It was now that a new star was rising in the literary firmament, not of the "shooting" or transitory species, and the genius of Marian Evans (George Eliot) was casting its genial penetrating radiance over Great Britain and the United States. She was as difficult a person to meet with as Hawthorne himself, and they never saw one another; but a friend of Mr. Bennoch, who lived at Coventry, invited the Hawthornes there in the first week of February to meet Bennoch and others, and Marian Evans would seem to have been the chief subject of conversation at the table that evening. What Hawthorne gathered concerning her on that occasion he has preserved in this compact and discriminating statement:

"Miss Evans (who wrote 'Adam Bede') was the daughter of a steward, and gained her exact knowledge of English rural life by the connection with which this origin brought her with the farmers. She was entirely self– educated, and has made herself an admirable scholar in classical as well as in modern languages. Those who knew her had always recognized her wonderful endowments, and only watched to see in what way they would develop themselves. She is a person of the simplest manners and character, amiable and unpretending, and Mrs. B——spoke of her with great affection and respect."

There is actually more of the real George Eliot in this summary than in the three volumes of her biography by Mr. Cross.

Thorwaldsen's well–known simile in regard to the three stages of sculpture, the life, the death and the resurrection, also has its application to literature. The manuscript is the birth of an author's work, and its revision always seems like taking the life out of it; but when the proof comes, it is like a new birth, and he sees his design for the first time in its true proportions. Then he goes over it as the sculptor does his newly–cast bronze, smoothing the rough places and giving it those final touches which serve to make its expression clearer. Hawthorne was never more to be envied than while correcting the proof of "The Marble Faun" at Leamington. The book was given to the public at

Easter–time; and there seems to have been only one person in England that appreciated it, even as a work of art—John Lothrop Motley. The most distinguished reviewers wholly failed to catch the significance of it; and even Henry Bright, while warmly admiring the story, expressed a dissatisfaction at the conclusion of it,—although he could have found a notable precedent for that in Goethe's "Wilhelm Meister." The *Saturday Review*, a publication similar in tone to the New York *Nation*, said of "Transformation:"

[Footnote: J. Hawthorne, ii. 250.]

"A mystery is set before us to unriddle; at the end the author turns round and asks us what is the good of solving it. That the impression of emptiness and un–meaningness thus produced is in itself a blemish to the work no one can deny. Mr. Hawthorne really trades upon the honesty of other writers. We feel a sort of interest in the story, slightly and sketchily as it is told, because our experience of other novels leads us to assume that, when an author pretends to have a plot, he has one."

The *Art Journal* said of it: [Footnote: J. Hawthorne, ii. 249.]

"We are not to accept this book as a story; in that respect it is grievously deficient. The characters are utterly untrue to nature and to fact; they speak, all and always, the sentiments of the author; their words also are his; there is no one of them for which the world has furnished a model."

And the London *Athenaeum* said: [Footnote: Ibid., ii. 244.]

"To Mr. Hawthorne truth always seems to arrive through the medium of the imagination.... His hero, the Count of Monte Beni, would never have lived had not the Faun of Praxiteles stirred the author's admiration.... The other characters, Mr. Hawthorne must bear to be told, are not new to a tale of his. Miriam, the mysterious, with her hideous tormentor, was indicated in the Zenobia of 'The Blithedale Romance.' Hilda, the pure and innocent, is own cousin to Phoebe in 'The House of the Seven Gables'."

If the reviewer is to be reviewed, it is not too much to designate these criticisms as miserable failures. They are not even well written. Henry Bright seemed to be thankful that they were no worse, for he wrote to Hawthorne: "I am glad that sulky *Athenaeum* was so civil; for they are equally powerful and unprincipled." The writer in the

Athenaeum evidently belonged to that class of domineering critics who have no literary standing, but who, like bankers' clerks, arrogate to themselves all the importance of the establishment with which they are connected. Fortunately, there are few such in America. No keen–witted reader would ever confound the active, rosy, domestic Phoebe Pyncheon with the dreamy, sensitive, and strongly subjective Hilda of "The Marble Faun;" and Hawthorne might have sent a communication to the *Athenaeum* to refresh the reviewer's memory, for it was not Zenobia in "The Blithedale Romance" who was dogged by a mysterious persecutor, but her half–sister—Priscilla. Shakespeare's Beatrice and his Rosalind are more alike (for Brandes supposes them to have been taken from the same model) than Zenobia and Miriam; and the difference between the persecutors of Priscilla and Miriam, as well as their respective methods, is world–wide; but there are none so blind as those who are enveloped in the turbid medium of their self–conceit.

The pure–hearted, chivalrous Motley read these reviews, and wrote to Hawthorne a vindication of his work, which must have seemed to him like a broad belt of New England sunshine in the midst of the London fog. In reference to its disparagement by so–called authorities, Motley said: [Footnote: Mrs. Lathrop, 408.]

"I have said a dozen times that nobody can write English but you. With regard to the story which has been slightingly criticised, I can only say that to me it is quite satisfactory. I like those shadowy, weird, fantastic, Hawthornesque shapes flitting through the golden gloom which is the atmosphere of the book. I like the misty way in which the story is indicated rather than revealed. The outlines are quite definite enough, from the beginning to the end, to those who have imagination enough to follow you in your airy flights; and to those who complain——

"I beg your pardon for such profanation, but it really moves my spleen that people should wish to bring down the volatile figures of your romance to the level of an everyday novel. It is exactly the romantic atmosphere of the book in which I revel."

The calm face of Motley, with his classic features, rises before us as we read this, illumined as it were by "the mild radiance of a hidden sun." He also had known what it was to be disparaged by English periodicals; and if it had not been for Froude's spirited assertion in his behalf, his history of the Dutch Republic might not have met with the celebrity it deserved. He was aware of the difference between a Hawthorne and a Reade or a Trollope, and knew how unfair it would be to judge Hawthorne even by the same standard as Thackeray. He does not touch in this letter on the philosophical character of the work, although that must have been evident to him, for he had said enough without it; but one could wish that he had printed the above statement over his own name, in some English journal.

American reviewers were equally puzzled by "The Marble Faun," and, although it was generally praised here, the literary critics treated it in rather a cautious manner, as if it contained material of a dangerous nature. The *North American*, which should have devoted five or six pages to it, gave it less than one; praising it in a conventional and rather unsympathetic tone. Longfellow read it, and wrote in his diary, "A wonderful book; but with the old, dull pain in it that runs through all Hawthorne's writings." There was always something of this dull pain in the expression of Hawthorne's face.

ANALYSIS OF "THE MARBLE FAUN"

It is like a picture, or a succession of pictures, painted in what the Italians call the *sfumato*, or "smoky" manner. The book is pervaded with the spirit of a dreamy pathos, such as constitutes the mental atmosphere of modern Rome; not unlike the haze of an Indian summer day, which we only half enjoy from a foreboding of the approach of winter. All outlines are softened and partially blurred in it, as time and decay have softened the outlines of the old Roman ruins. We recognize the same style with which we are familiar in "The Scarlet Letter," but influenced by a change in Hawthorne's external impressions.

It is a rare opportunity when the work of a great writer can be traced back to its first nebulous conception, as we trace the design of a pictorial artist to the first drawing that he made for his subject. Although we cannot witness the development of the plot of this romance in Hawthorne's mind, it is much to see in what manner the different elements of which it is composed, first presented themselves to him, and how he adapted them to his purpose.

The first of these in order of time was the beautiful Jewess, whom he met at the Lord Mayor's banquet in London; who attracted him by her *tout ensemble*, but at the same time repelled him by an indefinable impression, a mysterious something, that he could not analyze. There would seem, however, to have been another Jewess connected with the character of Miriam; for I once heard Mrs. Hawthorne narrating a story in which she stated that she and her husband were driving through London in a cab, and passing close to the sidewalk in a crowded street they saw a beautiful woman, with black hair and a ruddy complexion, walking with the most ill– favored and disagreeable looking Jew that could be imagined; and on the woman's face there was an expression of such deep–seated unhappiness that Hawthorne and his wife turned to each other, and he said, "I think that woman's face will always haunt me." I did not hear the beginning of Mrs. Hawthorne's tale, but I always supposed that it related to "The Marble Faun," and it would seem as if the character of Miriam was a composite of these two daughters of Israel, uniting the enigmatical quality of one with the unfortunate companionship of the other, and the beauty of both.

As previously noticed, the portrait of Beatrice Cenci excited a deeply penetrating interest in Hawthorne, and his reflections on it day after day would naturally lead him to a similar design in regard to the romance which he was contemplating. The attribution of a catastrophe like Beatrice's to either of the two Jewesses, would of course be adventitious, and should be considered in the light of an artistic privilege.

The "Faun" of Praxiteles in the museum of the Capitol next attracted his attention. This is but a poor copy of the original; but he penetrated the motive of the sculptor with those deep–seeing eyes of his, and there is no analysis of an ancient statue by Brunn or Furtwangler that equals Hawthorne's description of this one. It seems as if he must have looked backward across the centuries into the very mind of Praxiteles, and he was, in fact, the first critic to appreciate its high value. The perfect ease and simple beauty of the figure belong to a higher grade of art than the Apollo Belvedere, and Hawthorne discovered what Winckelmann had overlooked. He immediately conceived the idea of bringing the faun to life, and seeing how he would behave and comport himself in the modern world—in brief, to use the design of Praxiteles as the mainspring of a romance. In the evening of April 22, 1858, he wrote in his journal:

[Illustration: STATUE OF PRAXITELES' RESTING FAUN, WHICH HAWTHORNE HAS DESCRIBED AND BROUGHT TO LIFE IN THE CHARACTER OF DONATELLO]

"I looked at the Faun of Praxiteles, and was sensible of a peculiar charm in it; a sylvan beauty and homeliness, friendly and wild at once. It seems to me that a story, with all sorts of fun and pathos in it, might be contrived on the idea of their species having become intermingled with the human race; a family with the faun blood in them, having prolonged itself from the classic era till our own days. The tail might have disappeared, by dint of constant intermarriages with ordinary mortals; but the pretty hairy ears should occasionally reappear in members of the family; and the moral instincts and intellectual characteristics of the faun might be most picturesquely brought out, without detriment to the human interest of the story."

This statue served to concentrate the various speculative objects which had been hovering before Hawthorne's imagination during the past winter, and when he reached Florence six weeks later, the chief details of the plot were already developed in his mind.

Hilda and Kenyon are, of course, subordinate characters, like the first walking lady and the first walking gentleman on the stage. They are the sympathetic friends who watch the progress of the drama, continually hoping to be of service, but still finding themselves powerless to prevent the catastrophe. It was perhaps their unselfish interest in their mutual friends that at length taught them to know each other's worth, so that they finally became more than friends to one another. True love, to be firmly based, requires such a mutual interest or common ground on which the parties can meet,—something in addition to the usual attraction of the sexes. Mrs. Hawthorne has been supposed by some to have been the original of Hilda; and by others her daughter Una.

Conway holds an exceptional opinion, that Hilda was the feminine counterpart of Hawthorne himself; but Hilda is only too transparent a character, while Hawthorne always was, and still remains, impenetrable; and there was enough of her father in Miss Una, to render the same objection applicable in her case. Hilda seems to me very much like Mrs. Hawthorne, as one may imagine her in her younger days; like her in her mental purity, her conscientiousness, her devotion to her art,—which we trust afterwards was transformed into a devotion to her husband,— her tendency to self-seclusion, her sensitiveness and her lack of decisive resolution. She is essentially what they call on the stage an *ingenue* character; that is, one that remains inexperienced in the midst of experience; and it is in this character that she contributes to the catastrophe of the drama.

If Hawthorne appears anywhere in his own fiction, it is not in "The Blithedale Romance," but in the role of Kenyon. Although Kenyon's profession is that of a sculptor, he is not to be confounded with the gay and versatile Story. Neither is he statuesque, as the English reviewer criticised him. He is rather a shadowy character, as Hawthorne himself was shadowy, and as an author always must be shadowy to his readers; but Kenyon is to Hawthorne what Prospero is to Shakespeare, and if he does not make use of magic arts, it is because they no longer serve their purpose in human affairs. He is a wise, all–seeing, sympathetic mind, and his active influence in the play is less conspicuous because it is always so quiet, and so correct.

It will be noticed that the first chapter and the last chapter of this romance have the same title: "Miriam, Hilda, Kenyon, Donatello." This is according to their respective ages and sexes; but it is also the terms of a proportion,—as Miriam is to Hilda, so is Kenyon to Donatello. As the experienced woman is to the inexperienced woman, so is the experienced man to the inexperienced man. This seems simple enough, but it has momentous consequences in the story. Donatello, who is a type of natural but untried virtue, falls in love with Miriam, not only for her beauty, but because she has acquired that worldly experience which he lacks. Hilda, suddenly aroused to a sense of her danger in the isolated life she is leading, accepts Kenyon as a protector. The means in this proportion come together and unite, because they are the mean terms, and pursue a medium course. The extremes fly apart and are separated, simply because they are extremes. But there is a spiritual bond between them, invisible, but stronger than steel, which will bring them together again—at the Day of Judgment, if not sooner.

All tragedy is an investigation or exemplification of that form of human error which we call sin; a catastrophe of nature or a simple error of judgment may be tragical, but will not constitute a tragedy without the moral or poetic element.

In "The Scarlet Letter," we have the sin of concealment and its consequences. The first step toward reformation is confession, and without that, repentance is little more than a good intention.

In "The House of the Seven Gables," Hawthorne has treated the sin of hypocrisy—a smiling politician who courts popularity and pretends to be everybody's friend, and agrees with everybody,—only with a slight reservation. There may be occasions on which hypocrisy is a virtue; but the habit of hypocrisy for personal ends is like a dry rot in the heart of man.

In "The Blithedale Romance," we find the sin of moral affectation. Neither Hollingsworth nor Zenobia is really what they pretend themselves to be. Their morality is a hollow shell, and gives way to the first effective temptation. Zenobia betrays Priscilla; and is betrayed in turn by Hollingsworth,—as well as the interests of the association which had been committed to his charge.

The kernel of "The Marble Faun" is *original sin*. It is a story of the fall of man, told again in the light of modern science. It is a wonderful coincidence that almost in the same months that Hawthorne was writing this romance, Charles Darwin was also finishing his work on the "Origin of Species;" for one is the moral counterpart of the other. Hawthorne did not read scientific and philosophical books, but he may have heard something of Darwin's undertaking in England, as well as Napoleon's prophetic statement at St. Helena, that all the animals form an ascending series, leading up to man. [Footnote: Dr. O'Meara's "A Voice from St. Helena."] The skeleton of a prehistoric man discovered in the Neanderthal cave, which was supposed to have proved the Darwinian theory, does not suggest a figure similar to the "Faun" of Praxiteles, but the followers of Darwin have frequently adverted to the Hellenic traditions of fauns and satyrs in support of their theory. Hawthorne, however, has made a long stride beyond Darwin, for he has endeavored to reconcile this view of creation with the Mosaic cosmogony; and it must be admitted that he has been fairly successful. The lesson that Hawthorne teaches is, that evil does not reside in error, but in neglecting to be instructed by our errors. It is this which makes the difference between a St. Paul and a Nero. The fall of man was only apparent; it was really a rise in life. The Garden of Eden prefigures the childhood of the human race. Do we not all go through this idyllic moral condition in childhood, learning through our errors that the only true happiness consists in self–control? Do not all judicious parents protect their children from a knowledge of the world's wickedness, so long as it is possible to prevent it,—and yet not too long, for then they would become unfitted for their struggle with the world, and in order to avoid the pitfalls of mature life they must know where the pitfalls are. It is no longer essential for the individual to pass through the Cain and Abel experience—that has been accomplished by the race as a whole; but it is quite possible to imagine an incipient condition of society in which the distinction of justifiable homicide in self–defence (which is really the justification of war between nations) has not yet obtained.

Hawthorne's Donatello is supposed to belong, in theory at least, to that primitive era; but it is not necessary to go back further than the feudal period to look for a man who never has known a will above his own. Donatello seizes Miriam's tormentor and casts him down the Tarpeian Rock,—from the same instinct, or clairvoyant perception, that a hound springs at the throat of his master's enemy. When the deed is done he recognizes that the punishment is out of all proportion to the offence,—which is in itself the primary recognition of a penal code,— and more especially that the judgment of man is against him. He realizes for the first time the fearful possibilities of his nature, and begins to reflect. He is a changed person; and if not changed for the better yet with a possibility of great improvement in the future. His act was at least an unselfish one, and it might serve as the argument for a debate, whether Donatello did not do society a service in ridding the earth of such a human monstrosity. Hawthorne has adjusted the moral balance of his case so nicely, that a single scruple would turn the scales.

The tradition among the Greeks and Romans, of a Golden Age, corresponds in a manner to the Garden of Eden of Semitic belief. There may be some truth in it. Captain Speke, while exploring the sources of the Nile, discovered in central Africa a negro tribe uncontaminated by European traders, and as innocent of guile as the antelopes upon their own plains; and this suggests to us that all families and races of men may have passed through the Donatello stage of existence.

Hawthorne's master–stroke in the romance is his description or analysis of the effect produced by this homicide on the different members of the group to which he has introduced us. The experienced and worldly–wise Kenyon is not informed of the deed until his engagement to Hilda, but he has sufficient reason to suspect something of the kind from the simultaneous disappearance of Donatello and the model, as well as from the sudden change in Miriam's behavior. Yet he does not treat Donatello with any lack of confidence. He visits him at his castle of Monte Beni, which is simply the Villa Manteuto somewhat idealized and removed into the recesses of the Apennines; he consoles him in his melancholy humor; tries to divert him from gloomy thoughts; and meanwhile watches with a keen eye and friendly solicitude for the *denouement* of this mysterious drama. If he had seen what Hilda saw, he would probably have left Rome as quickly as possible, never to return; and Donatello's fate might have been different.

The effect on the sensitive and inexperienced Hilda was like a horrible nightmare. She cannot believe her senses, and yet she has to believe them. It seems to her as if the fiery pit has yawned between her and the rest of the human race. Her position is much like that of Hamlet, and the effect on her is somewhat similar. She thrusts Miriam from her with bitterness; yet forms no definite resolutions, and does she knows not what; until, overburdened by the consciousness of her fatal secret, she discloses the affair to an unknown priest in the church of St. Peter. Neither does she seem to be aware at any time of the serious consequences of this action.

Miriam, more experienced even than Kenyon, is not affected by the death of her tormentor so much directly as she is by its influence on Donatello. Hitherto she had been indifferently pleased by his admiration for her; now the tables are turned and she conceives the very strongest attachment for him. She follows him to his castle in disguise, dogs his footsteps on the excursion which he and Kenyon make together, shadows his presence again in Rome, and is with him at the moment of his arrest. This is all that we know of her from the time of her last unhappy interview with Hilda. Her crime consisted merely in a look,—the expression of her eyes,—and the whole world is free to her; but her heart is imprisoned in the same cell with Donatello. There is not a more powerful ethical effect in Dante or Sophocles.

A certain French writer [Footnote: Name forgotten, but the fact is indelible.] blames Hilda severely for her betrayal of Miriam (who was at least her best friend in Rome), and furthermore designates her as an immoral character. This, we may suppose, is intended for a hit at New England Puritanism; and from the French stand–point, it is not unfair. Hilda represents Puritanism in its weakness and in its strength. It is true, what Hamlet says, that "conscience makes cowards of us all," but only true under conditions like those of Hamlet,—desperate emergencies, which require exceptional expedients. On the contrary, in carrying out a great reform like the abolition of slavery, the education of the blind, or the foundation of national unity, a man's conscience becomes a tower of strength to him. As already intimated, what Hilda ought to have done was, to leave Rome at once, and forever; but she is no more capable of forming such a resolution, than Hamlet was of organizing a conspiracy against his usurping uncle. When, however, the priest steps out from the confessional–box and attempts to make a convert of Hilda,—for which indeed she has given him a fair opening,—she asserts herself and her New England training, with true feminine dignity, and in fact has decidedly the best of the argument. It is a trying situation, in which she develops unexpected resources. Hawthorne's genius never shone forth more brilliantly than in this scene at St. Peter's. It is Shakespearian.

Much dissatisfaction was expressed when "The Marble Faun" was first published, at the general vagueness of its conclusion. Hawthorne's admirers wished especially for some clearer explanation of Miriam's earlier life, and of her relation to the strange apparition of the catacombs. He answered these interrogatories in a supplementary chapter which practically left the subject where it was before—an additional piece of mystification. In a letter to Henry Bright he admitted that he had no very definite scheme in his mind in regard to Miriam's previous history, and this is probably the reason why his readers feel this vague sense of dissatisfaction with the plot. I have myself often tried to think out a prelude to the story, but without any definite result. Miriam's persecuting model was evidently a husband who had been forced upon her by her parents, and would not that be sufficient to account for her moods of gloom and despondency? Yet Hawthorne repeatedly intimates that there was something more than this. Let us not think of it. If the tale was not framed in mystery, Donatello would not seem so real to us. Do not the characters in "Don Quixote" and "Wilhelm Meister" spring up as it were out of the ground? They come we know not whence, and they go we know not whither. It is with these that "The Marble Faun" should be classed and compared, and not with "Middle–march," "Henry Esmond," or "The Heart of Midlothian."

[Illustration: TORRE MEDIAVALLE DELLA SCIMMIA (HILDA'S TOWER), OF THE VIA PORTOGHESE AT ROME, WHERE HAWTHORNE REPRESENTS HILDA TO HAVE LIVED AND TENDED THE LAMP AT THE VIRGIN'S SHRINE ON THE TOP OF THE TOWER]

Goethe said, while looking at the group of the "Laocoon," "I think that young fellow on the right will escape the serpents." This was not according to the story Virgil tells, but it is true to natural history. Similarly, it is pleasant to think that the Pope's mercy may ultimately have been extended to Donatello. We can imagine an aged couple living a serious, retired life in the castle of Monte Beni, childless, and to a certain extent joyless, but taking comfort in their mutual affection, and in acts of kindness to their fellow–mortals.

In order to see Hilda's tower in Rome, go straight down from the Spanish Steps to the Corso, turn to the right, and you will soon come to the Via Portoghese (on the opposite side), where you will easily recognize the tower on the right hand. The tower is five stories in height, set in the front of the palace, and would seem to be older than the building about it; the relic, perhaps, of some distinguished mediaeval structure. The odd little shrine to the Virgin, a toy–like affair, still surmounts it; but its lamp is no longer burning. It was fine imagination to place Hilda in this lofty abode.

CHAPTER XVII. HOMEWARD BOUND: 1860–1862

There is no portion of Hawthorne's life concerning which we know less than the four years after his return from England to his native land. He was so celebrated that every eye was upon him; boys stopped their games to see him pass by, and farmers stood still in the road to stare at him. He was Hawthorne the famous, and every movement he made was remembered, every word spoken by him was recorded or related, and yet altogether it amounts to little enough. Letters have been preserved in number,—many of his own and others from his English friends, and those from his wife to her relatives; but they do not add much to the picture we have already formed in our minds of the man. As he said somewhere, fame had come too late to be a satisfaction to him, but on the contrary more of an annoyance. Hawthorne left Leamington the last of March, and transferred his family to Bath, which he soon discovered to be the pleasantest English city he had lived in yet,—symmetrically laid out, like a Continental city, and built for the most part of a yellowish sandstone; not unlike in appearance the travertine of which St. Peter's at Rome is built. The older portion of the city lies in a hollow among the hills, like an amphitheatre, and the more recent additions rise upon the hill–sides above it to a considerable height. This is the last note of enthusiasm in his writings; and in the next entry in his diary, which was written at Lothrop Motley's house, Hertford Street, London, May 16, he makes this ominous confession: "I would gladly journalize some of my proceedings, and describe things and people, but I find the same coldness and stiffness in my pen as always since our return to England." It is only too evident that from this time literary composition, which had been the chief recreation of his youth, and in which he had always found satisfaction until now, was no longer a pleasure to him. It is the last entry in his journal, at least for more than two years, and whatever writing he accomplished in the mean time was done for the sake of his wife and children. Dickens had a similar experience the last year of his life. Clearly, Hawthorne's nervous force was waning.

On May 15, Hawthorne and Motley were invited to dine by Earl Dufferin, that admirable diplomat and one of the pleasantest of men. In fact, if there was a person living who could make Hawthorne feel perfectly at his ease, it was Dufferin. Motley provided some entertainment or other for his guest every day, and Hawthorne confessed that the stir and activity of London life were doing him "a wonderful deal of good." What he seems to have needed at this time was a vigorous, objective employment that would give his circulation a start in the right direction; but how was he to obtain that?

He enjoyed one last stroll with Henry Bright through Hyde Park and along the Strand, and found time to say a long farewell to Francis Bennoch: the last time he was to meet either of them on this side of eternity.

He returned to Bath the 1st of June, and ten days later they all embarked for Boston,—as it happened, by a pleasant coincidence, with the same captain with whom they had left America seven years before. Mrs. Hawthorne's sister, Mrs. Horace Mann, prepared their house at Concord for their reception, and there they arrived at the summer solstice.

The good people of Concord had been mightily stirred up that spring, by an attempt to arrest Frank B. Sanborn and carry him forcibly to Washington,—contrary to law, as the Supreme Court of the State decided the following day. The marshal who arrested him certainly proceeded more after the manner of a burglar than of a civil officer, hiding himself with his *posse comitatus* in a barn close to Sanborn's school-house, watching his proceedings through the cracks in the boards, and finally arresting him at night, just as he was going to bed; but the alarm was quickly sounded, and the whole male population of the place, including Emerson, turned out like a swarm of angry hornets, and the marshal and his posse were soon thankful to escape with their bones in a normal condition. A few nights later, the barn, which was owned by a prominent official in the Boston Custom House, was burned to the ground (the fire-company assisting), as a sacrifice on the altar of personal liberty.

The excitement of this event had not yet subsided when the arrival of the Hawthorne family produced a milder and more amiable, but no less profound, sensation in the old settlement; and this was considerably increased by the fact that for the first month nothing was seen of them, except a sturdy-looking boy fishing from a rock in Concord River, opposite the spot where his father and Channing had discovered the unfortunate school-mistress. Old friends made their calls and were cordially received, but Hawthorne himself did not appear in public places; and it was soon noticed that he did not take the long walks which formerly carried him to the outer limits of the town. He was sometimes met on the way to Walden Pond, either alone or in company with his son; but Bronson Alcott more frequently noticed him gliding along in a ghost-like manner by the rustic fence which separated their two estates, or on the way to Sleepy Hollow. When the weather became cooler he formed a habit of walking back and forth on the hill-side above his house, where the bank descends sharply like a railroad–cut, with dwarf pines and shrub oaks on the further side of it. He wore a path there, which is described in "Septimius Felton," and it is quite possible that the first inception of that story entered his mind while looking down upon the Lexington road beneath him, and imagining how it appeared while filled with marching British soldiers.

About July 10, 1860, the scholars of Mr. Sanborn's school, male and female, gave an entertainment in the Town Hall, not unlike Harvard Class Day. Mrs. Hawthorne and her eldest daughter appeared among the guests, and attracted much attention from the quiet grace and dignity of their manners; but there was an expression of weariness on Miss Una's face, which contrasted strangely with the happy, blithesome looks of the school–girls. Some idea of the occasion may be derived from a passing remark of Mrs. Hawthorne to a Harvard student present: "My daughter will be happy to dance with you, sir, if I can only find her."

In September Hawthorne wrote to James T. Fields: [Footnote: Mrs. J. T. Fields, 118.]

"We are in great trouble on account of our poor Una, in whom the bitter dregs of that Roman fever are still rankling, and have now developed themselves in a way which the physicians foreboded. I do not like to write about it, but will tell you when we meet. Say nothing."

Miss Una was evidently far from well, and her father's anxiety for her sensibly affected his mental tone.

He was invited at once to join the Saturday Club, popularly known at that time as the Atlantic Club, because its most conspicuous members were contributors to that periodical. Hawthorne did not return in season to take part in the Club's expedition to the Adirondack Mountains, concerning which Doctor Holmes remarked that, considering the number of rifles they carried, it was fortunate that they all returned alive. The meetings of the Club came but once a month, and as the last train to Concord was not a very late one, Judge Hoar had his carryall taken down to Waltham on such occasions, and thence he, with Hawthorne and Emerson, drove back to Concord through the woods in the darkness or moonlight; and Hawthorne may have enjoyed this as much as any portion of the entertainment.

The Life and Genius of Nathaniel Hawthorne

A club whose membership is based upon celebrity reminds one rather of a congregation of stags, all with antlers of seven tines. There was every shade of opinion, political, philosophical and religious, represented in the Saturday Club, and if they never fought over such subjects it was certainly much to their credit. Very little has been divulged of what took place at their meetings; but it is generally known that in the winter of 1861 Longfellow was obliged to warn his associates that if they persisted in abusing Sumner he should be obliged to leave their company; Sumner being looked upon by the Democrats and more timid Republicans as the chief obstacle to pacification; as if any one man could prop a house up when it was about to fall. After the War began, this naturally came to an end, and Sumner was afterwards invited to join the Club, with what satisfaction to Hoar, Lowell, and Holmes it might be considering rather curiously to inquire. We can at least feel confident that Hawthorne had no share in this. He did not believe in fighting shadows, and he at least respected Sumner for his frankness and disinterestedness.

Such differences of opinion, however, are not conducive to freedom of discussion. Henry James, Sr., lifts the veil for a moment in a letter to Emerson, written about this time, [Footnote: Memoir of Bronson Alcott; also the "Hawthorne Centenary."] and affords us a picture of Hawthorne at the Saturday Club, which might bear the designation of a highly–flavored caricature. According to Mr. James, John M. Forbes, the Canton millionaire, preserved the balance at one end of the table, while Hawthorne, an oasis in a desert, served as the nearest approach to a human being, at the other. "How he buried his eyes in his plate and ate with such a voracity! that no one should dare to ask him a question."

We do not realize the caricaturist in Henry James, Jr., so readily, on account of his elastic power of expression; but the relationship is plain and apparent. Both father and son ought to have been baptized in the Castalian Fount. There are those who have been at table with both Hawthorne and the elder James, and without the slightest reflection on Mr. James, have confessed their preference for the quiet composure and simple dignity of Hawthorne. In truth Hawthorne's manners were above those of the polished courtier or the accomplished man of fashion: they were poetic manners, and in this respect Longfellow most nearly resembled him of all members of the Club; although Emerson also had admirable manners and they were largely the cause of his success. It would have done no harm if Emerson had burned this letter after its first perusal, but since it is out of the bag we must even consider it as it deserves.

The Life and Genius of Nathaniel Hawthorne

Hawthorne must have enjoyed the meetings of the Club or he would not have attended them so regularly. He wrote an account of the first occasion on which he was present, giving an accurate description of the dinner itself and enclosing a diagram of the manner in which the guests were seated, but without any commentary on the proceedings of the day. It was, after all, one of the nerve–centres of the great world, and an agreeable change from the domestic monotony of the Wayside. Thackeray would have descried rich material for his pen in it, but Hawthorne's studies lay in another direction. Great men were not his line in literature.

Meanwhile Mrs. Hawthorne and her daughter were transforming their Concord home into a small repository of the fine arts. Without much that would pass by the title of elegance, they succeeded in giving it an unpretentious air of refinement, and one could not enter it without realizing that the materials of a world–wide culture had been brought together there. Hawthorne soon found the dimensions of the house too narrow for the enlarged views which he had brought with him from abroad, and he designed a tower to be constructed at one corner of it, similar to, if not so lofty as that of the Villa Manteuto. This occupied him and the dilatory Concord carpenter for nearly half a year; and meanwhile chaos and confusion reigned supreme. There was no one whose ears could be more severely offended by the music of the carpenter's box and the mason's trowel than Hawthorne, and he knew not whether to fly his home or remain in it. Not until all this was over could he think seriously of a new romance.

He made his study in the upper room of the tower; a room exactly twenty feet square, with a square vaulted ceiling and five windows,—too many, one would suppose, to produce a pleasant effect of light,—and walls papered light yellow. There he could be as quiet and retired as in the attic of his Uncle Robert Manning's house in Salem. Conway states that he wrote at a high desk, like Longfellow, and walked back and forth in the room while thinking out what he was going to say. The view from his windows extended across the meadows to Walden woods and the Fitchburg railroad track, and it also commanded the Alcott house and the road to Concord village. It was in this work–shop that he prepared "Our Old Home" for the press and wrote the greater part of "Septimius Felton" and "The Dolliver Romance."

The War was a new source of distraction. It broke out before the tower was finished, stimulating Hawthorne's nerves, but disturbing that delicate mental equilibrium upon which satisfactory procedure of his writing depended. On May 26, 1861, he wrote to

The Life and Genius of Nathaniel Hawthorne

Horatio Bridge:

"The war, strange to say, has had a beneficial effect upon my spirits, which were flagging wofully before it broke out. But it was delightful to share in the heroic sentiment of the time, and to feel that I had a country,—a consciousness which seemed to make me young again. One thing as regards this matter I regret, and one thing I am glad of. The regrettable thing is that I am too old to shoulder a musket myself, and the joyful thing is that Julian is too young." [Footnote: J. Hawthorne, ii. 276.]

Hawthorne's patriotism was genuine and deep-seated. He was not the only American whom the bombardment of Fort Sumter had awakened to the fact that he had a country. What we have always enjoyed, we do not think of until there is danger of losing it. In the same letter, he confesses that he does not quite understand "what we are fighting for, or what definite result can be expected. If we pummel the South ever so hard, they will love us none the better for it; and even if we subjugate them, our next step should be to cut them adrift."

There were many in those times who thought and felt as Hawthorne did. Douglas said in the Senate, "Even if you coerce the Southern States and bring them back by force, it will not be the same Union." A *people* does not necessarily mean a *nation*; for the idea of nationality is of slow growth, and is in a manner opposed to the idea of democracy; for if the right of government depends on the consent of the governed, the primary right of the governed must be to abrogate that government whenever they choose to do so. Hawthorne was simply a consistent democrat; but time has proved the fallacy of Douglas's statement, and that a forcible restoration of the Union was entirely compatible with friendliness and mutal good-will between the different sections of the country,—after slavery, which was the real obstacle to this, had been eliminated. If the States east of the Alleghanies should attempt to separate from the rest of the nation, it would inevitably produce a war similar to that of 1861.

Hawthorne even went to the length at this time of proposing to arm the negroes, and preparing them "for future citizenship by allowing them to fight for their own liberties, and educating them through heroic influences." [Footnote: The "Hawthorne Centenary," 197.] When George L. Stearns was organizing the colored regiments in Tennessee in 1863 he wrote concerning his work, in almost exactly these terms; and the inference is plain that Hawthorne might have been more of a humanitarian if his early associations had been different.

Such an original character as Bronson Alcott for a next–door neighbor could not long escape Hawthorne's penetrating glance. Alcott was an interesting personality, perfectly genuine, frank, kindly and imperturbably good–humored. He had a benevolent aspect, and in general appearance so much resembled the portraits of Benjamin Franklin that his ingenious daughters made use of him in charades and theatricals for that purpose. Hawthorne had known him many years earlier, and had spoken very pleasantly of him in his first publication of "The Hall of Fantasy." He even said, "So calm and gentle was he, so quiet in the utterance of what his soul brooded upon, that one might readily conceive his Orphic Sayings to well up from a fountain in his breast, which communicated with the infinite abyss of thought,"—rather an optimistic view for Hawthorne. Alcott's philosophy had the decided merit, which Herbert Spencer's has not, of a strong affirmation of a Great First Cause, and our direct responsibility thereto: but it was chiefly the philosophy of Plotinus; and his constant reiteration of a "lapse" in human nature from divine perfection (which was simply the Donatello phase expressed in logic), with the various corollaries deduced from it, finally became as wearisome as the harp with a single string. Whether he troubled Hawthorne in that way, is rather doubtful, for even as a hobby–rider, Alcott was a man of Yankee shrewdness and considerable tact. Rose Hawthorne says that "he once brought a particularly long poem to read, aloud to my mother and father; a seemingly harmless thing from which they never recovered." What poem this could have been I have no idea, but in his later years Alcott wrote some excellent poetry, and those who ought to know do not think that he bored Hawthorne very severely. They frequently went to walk together, taking Julian for a make–weight, and Hawthorne could easily have avoided this if he had chosen. There are times for all of us when our next–door neighbors prove a burden; and it cannot be doubted that in most instances this is reciprocal. [Footnote: Rose Hawthorne, however, writes charmingly of the Alcotts. Take this swift sketch, among others: "I imagine his slightly stooping, yet tall and well–grown figure, clothed in black, and with a picturesque straw hat, twining itself in and out of forest aisles, or craftily returning home with gargoyle–like stems over his shoulders."]

Alcott was a romance character of exceptional value, and Hawthorne recognized this, but did not succeed in inventing a plot that would suit the subject. The only one of Hawthorne's preparatory sketches given to the public—in which we see his genius in the "midmost heat of composition"—supposes a household in which an old man keeps a crab–spider for a pet, a deadly poisonous creature; and in the same family there is a boy whose fortunes will be mysteriously affected in some manner by this dangerous insect. He did not proceed sufficiently to indicate for us how this would turn out, but he closes the sketch with the significant remark, "In person and figure Mr. Alcott"; from which it may be inferred that the crab–spider was intended to symbolize Alcott's philosophy, and the catastrophe of the romance would naturally result from the unhealthy mental atmosphere in which the boy grew up,— a catastrophe which in Alcott's family was averted by the practical sagacity of his daughters. The idea, however, became modified in its application.

It is with regret that we do not allot a larger space to this important sketch, for it is clearly an original study (like an artist's drawing) of the unfinished romance which was published in 1883 under the title of "Doctor Grimshawe's Secret." Long lost sight of in the mass of Hawthorne's manuscripts, this last of his posthumous works was reviewed by the critics with some incredulity, and Lathrop had the hardihood to publicly assert that no such romance by Hawthorne's pen existed, thereby casting a gratuitous slander on his own brother–in–law. We may have our doubts in regard to the authorship of Shakespeare's plays, for we have no absolute standard by which to judge of Shakespeare's style, but the "style, the matter, and the drift" of "Doctor Grimshawe's Secret" are so essentially Hawthornish that a person experienced in judging of such matters should not hesitate long in deciding that it belongs in the same category with "Fanshawe" and "The Dolliver Romance." It is even possible to determine, from certain peculiarities in its style, the exact period at which it was written; which must have been shortly after Hawthorne's return from Europe. In addition to this, if further evidence were required, its close relationship to the aforementioned sketch is a fact which no sophistry can reason away. [Footnote: This sketch was published in the *Century*, January, 1883.]

The bloody footstep suggested to Hawthorne by the antediluvian print in the stone step at Smithell's Hall, in Lancashire, serves as the key–note of this romance; but the eccentric recluse, the big crab–spider, the orphaned grandchild, and even Bronson Alcott also appear in it. Alcott, however,—and his identity cannot be mistaken,—does not play the leading part in the piece, but comes in at the fifth chapter, only to disappear mysteriously in the eighth; the orphan boy is companioned by a girl of equal age, and these two bright spirits, mutually sustaining each other, cast a radiance over the old Doctor in his dusty, frowsy, cobwebby study, which brings out the external appearance and internal peculiarities of the man, in the most vivid manner. The dispositions and appearances of the two children are also contrasted, as Raphael might have drawn and contrasted them, if he had painted a picture on a similar subject.

The crab–spider is one of the most horrible of Nature's creations. Hawthorne saw one in the British Museum and it seems to have haunted his imagination ever afterward. Why the creature should have been introduced into this romance is not very clear, for it plays no part in the development of the plot. The spider hangs suspended over the old Doctor's head like the sword of Damocles, and one would expect it to descend at the proper moment in the narrative, and make an end of him with its nippers; but Doctor Grimshawe dies a comparatively natural death, and the desiccated body of the spider is found still clinging to the web above him. The man and the insect were too closely akin in the modes and purposes of their lives for either to outlast the other. There is nothing abnormal in the fact of Doctor Grimshawe's possessing this dangerous pet; for all kinds of poisonous creatures have a well–known fascination for the medical profession. Doctor Holmes amused himself with a rattlesnake.

In spite of its unpleasant associations with spiders and blood–stains, "Doctor Grimshawe's Secret" is one of the most interesting of Hawthorne's works, containing much of his finest thought and most characteristic description. The portrait of the grouty old Doctor himself has a solidity of impast like Shakespeare's Falstaff, and the grave–digger, who has survived from colonial times, carries us back involuntarily to the burial scene in "Hamlet." Alcott, whose name is changed to Colcord, is not treated realistically, but rather idealized in such kindly sympathetic manner as might prevent all possibility of offence at the artistic theft of his personality. The plot, too, is a most ingenious one, turning and winding like a hare, and even diving out of sight for a time; but only to reappear again, as the school- master Colcord does, with a full and satisfactory explanation of its mysterious course. To judge from the appearance of the manuscript, this romance was written very rapidly, and there are places in the text which intimate this; but it vies in power with "The Scarlet Letter," and why Hawthorne should have become dissatisfied with it,—why he should have failed to complete, revise, and publish it—can only be accounted for by the mental or nervous depression which was now fastening itself upon him.

It is noticeable, however, that where the plot is transferred to English ground Hawthorne's writing has much the same tone and quality that we find in "Our Old Home." External appearances seem to impede his insight there; but this is additional proof of the authenticity of the work. [Footnote: There are many other evidences; such as, "after–dinner speeches on the necessity of friendly relations between England and the United States," and "the whistling of the railway train, *two* or *three* times a day."]

Shortly after the battle of Bull Run Hawthorne went with his boy to recuperate at Beverly Farms, leaving his wife and daughters at the Wayside, and the letters which passed between these two divisions of the family, during his absence, give some very pretty glimpses of their idyllic summer life. Mrs. Hawthorne "cultivated her garden," and gave drawing lessons to the neighbors' children, while her husband, forty miles away, was fishing and bathing. The Beverly shore has not a stimulating climate, but is very attractive in summer to those who do not mind a few sultry nights from land breezes. It was near enough to Salem for Hawthorne to revive the reminiscences of his youth (which become more and more precious after the age of fifty), without obtruding himself on the gaze of his former townsmen or of the young lady "who wished she could poison him." [Footnote: W. D. Howells' Memoirs.] It is to be hoped that he saw something of his sister Elizabeth again, the last remnant of his mother's household, who for some inscrutable reason had never visited him at Concord.

We note here a curious circumstance; namely, that Hawthorne appears to have lost the art of writing short sketches. It will be recollected that twenty years earlier he did not feel equal to anything beyond this, and that it cost him a strenuous effort to escape from the habit. Now when he would have liked to return to that class of composition he could not do so. Fields would have welcomed anything from his pen (so severe a critic he was of himself), but his name does not appear in the *Atlantic Monthly* from July, 1861, to June, 1862, and it cannot be doubted that with the education of his son before him, the remuneration would have been welcome. It was not until nearly a year later that he conceived the idea of cutting his English Note–book into sections, and publishing them as magazine articles.

From this time forth, one discouragement followed another. In the autumn of 1861 the illness of his daughter, which he had expected and predicted, came to pass in a violent form. The old Roman virus, kept under in her blood, for a time, by continual changes of air and climate, at last gained the mastery, and brought her once more in danger of her life. She had to be removed to the house of her aunt, Mrs. Mann, who lived in the centre of the town, on account of her father's nerves, so that the Concord doctor could attend her at night when necessary. It was the severest and most protracted case of fever that the physician had ever known to be followed by a recovery. Miss Una did recover, but the mental strain upon her father was even more exhausting than that which her previous illness had caused, and he was not in an equal condition to bear it.

"Septimius Felton" may have been written about this time (perhaps during his daughter's convalescence), but his family knew nothing of it, until they discovered the manuscript after his death. When it was published ten years later, the poet Whittier spoke of it as a failure, and Hawthorne would seem to have considered it so; for he left it in an unfinished condition, and immediately began a different story on the same theme,—the elixir of life. It has no connection with the sketch already mentioned, in which Alcott's personality becomes the mainspring, but with another abortive romance, called "The Ancestral Footstep," which Hawthorne commenced while he was in England. It is invaluable for the light it throws on his method of working. Descriptive passages are mentioned in it "to be inserted" at a later time, meanwhile concentrating his energy on more important portions of the narrative. Half way through the story he changed his original plan, transforming the young woman who previously had been Septimius's sweetheart to Septimius's sister; and it may have been the difficulty of adjusting this change to the portion previously written, that discouraged Hawthorne from completing the romance. But the work suffers also from a tendency to exaggeration. The name of Hagburn is unpleasantly realistic, and Doctor Portsoaken, with his canopy of spider–webs hanging in noisome festoons above his head, is closely akin to the repulsive. The amateur critic who averred that he could not read Hawthorne without feeling a sensation as if cobwebs were drawn across his face, must have had "Septimius Felton" in mind. Yet there are refreshing passages in it, and the youthful English officer who kisses Septimius's sweetheart before his eyes, and afterward fights an impromptu duel with him, dying as cheerfully as he had lived, is an original and charming character. The scene of the story has a peculiar interest, from the fact that it is laid at Hawthorne's own door; the Feltons are supposed to have lived at the Wayside and the Hagburns in the Alcott house.

The firm of Ticknor &Fields now began to feel anxious on Hawthorne's account, and the last of the winter the senior partner proposed a journey to Washington, which was accordingly accomplished in the second week of March. Horatio Bridge was now chief of a bureau in the Navy Department, and was well qualified to obtain for his veteran friend an inside position for whatever happened to be going on. In the midst of the turmoil and excitement of war, Hawthorne attracted as much attention as the arrival of a new ambassador from Great Britain. Secretary Stanton appointed him on a civil commission to report concerning the condition of the Army of the Potomac. He was introduced to

President Lincoln, and made excursions to Harper's Ferry and Fortress Monroe. Concerning General McClellan, he wrote to his daughter on March 16:

"The outcry opened against Gen. McClellan, since the enemy's retreat from Manassas, is really terrible, and almost universal; because it is found that we might have taken their fortifications with perfect ease six months ago, they being defended chiefly by wooden guns. Unless he achieves something wonderful within a week, he will be removed from command, at least I hope so; I never did more than half believe in him. By a message from the State Department, I have reason to think that there is money enough due me from the government to pay the expenses of my journey. I think the public buildings are as fine, if not finer, than anything we saw in Europe." [Footnote: J. Hawthorne, ii. 309.]

General McClellan was not a great man, and Hawthorne's opinion of him is more significant from the fact that at that time McClellan was expected to be the Joshua who would lead the Democratic party out of its wilderness. On his return to Concord, Hawthorne prepared a commentary on what he had seen and heard at the seat of war, and sent it to the *Atlantic Monthly*; but, although patriotic enough, his melancholy humor was prominent in it, and Fields particularly protested against his referring to President Lincoln as "Old Abe," although the President was almost universally called so in Washington; and the consequence of this was that Hawthorne eliminated everything that he had written about Lincoln in his account,—which might be called "dehamletizing" the subject. In addition to this he wrote a number of foot-notes purporting to come from the editor, but really intended to counteract the unpopularity of certain statements in the text. This was not done with any intention to deceive, but, with the exception of Emerson and a few others who could always recognize Hawthorne's style, the readers of the *Atlantic* supposed that these foot-notes were written by either James T. Fields or James Russell Lowell, who had been until recently the editor of the Magazine,—a practical joke which Hawthorne enjoyed immensely when it was discovered to him.

This contribution, essay, or whatever it may be called, had only a temporary value, but it contained a prediction, which has been often recollected in Hawthorne's favor; namely, that after the war was over "one bullet-headed general after another would succeed to the presidential chair." In fact, five generals, whether bullet-headed or not, followed after Lincoln and Johnson; and then the sequence came to an end apparently because the supply of politician generals was exhausted. Certainly the Anglo-Saxon race yields to no other in admiration for military glory.

The Life and Genius of Nathaniel Hawthorne

Fields afterward published Hawthorne's monograph on President Lincoln, and, although it is rather an unsympathetic statement of the man, it remains the only authentic pen—and—ink sketch that we have of him. Most important is his recognition of Lincoln as "essentially a Yankee" in appearance and character; for it has only recently been discovered that Lincoln was descended from an old New England family, and that his ancestors first emigrated to Virginia and afterward to Kentucky. [Footnote: Essay on Lincoln in "True Republicanism."] Hawthorne says of him:

"If put to guess his calling and livelihood, I should have taken him for a country schoolmaster as soon as anything else. [Footnote: The country school—master of that time.—Ed.] He was dressed in a rusty black frock—coat and pantaloons, unbrushed, and worn so faithfully that the suit had adapted itself to the curves and angularities of his figure, and had grown to be the outer skin of the man. He had shabby slippers on his feet. His hair was black, still unmixed with gray, stiff, somewhat bushy, and had apparently been acquainted with neither brush nor comb that morning, after the disarrangement of the pillow; and as to a nightcap, Uncle Abe probably knows nothing of such effeminacies. His complexion is dark and sallow, betokening, I fear, an insalubrious atmosphere around the White House; he has thick black eyebrows and impending brow; his nose is large, and the lines about his mouth are very strongly denned.

"The whole physiognomy is as coarse a one as you would meet anywhere in the length and breadth of the States; but, withal, it is redeemed, illuminated, softened, and brightened by a kindly though serious look out of his eyes, and an expression of homely sagacity, that seems weighted with rich results of village experience. A great deal of native sense; no bookish cultivation, no refinement; honest at heart, and thoroughly so, and yet, in some sort, sly,—at least, endowed with a sort of tact and wisdom that are akin to craft.... But on the whole, I liked this sallow, queer, sagacious visage, with the homely human sympathies that warmed it; and, for my small share in the matter, would as lief have Uncle Abe for a ruler as any man whom it would have been practicable to put in his place." [Footnote: "Yesterdays with Authors," 99.]

This is not a flattered portrait, like those by Lincoln's political biographers; neither is it an idealized likeness, such as we may imagine him delivering his Gettysburg Address. It is rather an external description of the man, but it is, after all, Lincoln as he appeared in the White House to the innumerable visitors, who, as sovereign American citizens, believed they had a right to an interview with the people's distinguished servant.

The Life and Genius of Nathaniel Hawthorne

Hawthorne's European letter–bag in 1862 is chiefly interesting for Henry Bright's statement that the English people might have more sympathy with the Union cause in the War if they could understand clearly what the national government was fighting for; and that Lord Houghton and Thomas Hughes were the only two men he had met who heartily supported the Northern side. Perhaps Mr. Bright would have found it equally as difficult to explain why the British Government should have made war upon Napoleon for twelve consecutive years.

Henry Bright, moreover, seemed to be quite as much interested in a new American poet, named J. G. Holland, and his poem called "Bitter–Sweet." Lord Houghton agreed with him that it was a very remarkable poem, and they wished to know what Hawthorne could tell them about its author. As Holland was not recognized as a poet by the Saturday Club, Hawthorne's answer on this point would be very valuable if we could only obtain a sight of it. Holland was in certain respects the counterpart of Martin F. Tupper.

In the summer of this year Hawthorne went to West Goldsboro', Maine, an unimportant place opposite Mount Desert Island, taking Julian with him; a place with a stimulating climate but a rather foggy atmosphere. He must have gone there for his health, and it is pathetic to see how the change of climate braced him up at first, so that he even made the commencement of a new diary, and then, as always happens in such cases, it let him down again to where he was before. He did not complain, but he felt that something was wrong with him and he could not tell what it was.

Wherever he went in passing through the civilized portion of Maine, he found the country astir with recruits who had volunteered for the war, so that it seemed as if that were the only subject which occupied men's minds. He says of this in his journal:

"I doubt whether any people was ever actuated by a more genuine and disinterested public spirit; though, of course, it is not unalloyed with baser motives and tendencies. We met a train of cars with a regiment or two just starting for the South, and apparently in high spirits. Everywhere some insignia of soldiership were to be seen,— bright buttons, a red stripe down the trousers, a military cap, and sometimes a round–shouldered bumpkin in the entire uniform. They require a great deal to give them the aspect of soldiers; indeed, it seems as if they needed to have a good deal taken away and added, like the rough clay of a sculptor as it grows to be a model."

Such is the last entry in his journal. Hawthorne was not carried off his feet by the excitement of the time, but looked calmly on while others expended their patriotism in hurrahing for the Union. What he remarks concerning the volunteers was perfectly true Men cannot change their profession in a day, and soldiers are not to be made out of farmers' boys and store clerks simply by clothing them in uniform, no matter how much courage they may have. War is a profession like other professions, and requires the severest training of them all.

CHAPTER XVIII. IMMORTALITY

In the autumn of 1862 there was great excitement in Massachusetts. President Lincoln had issued his premonitory proclamation of emancipation, and Harvard College was stirred to its academic depths. Professor Joel Parker, of the Law School, pronounced Lincoln's action unconstitutional, subversive of the rights of property, and a most dangerous precedent. With Charles Eliot Norton and other American Tories, Parker headed a movement for the organization of a People's Party, which had for its immediate object the defeat of Andrew for Governor and the relegation of Sumner to private life. The first they could hardly expect to accomplish, but it was hoped that a sufficient number of conservative representatives would be elected to the Legislature to replace Sumner by a Republican, who would be more to their own minds; and they would be willing to compromise on such a candidate as Honorable E. R. Hoar,—although Judge Hoar was innocent of this himself and was quite as strongly anti–slavery as Sumner. The movement came to nothing, as commonly happens with political movements that originate in universities, but for the time being it caused a great commotion and nowhere more so than in the town of Concord. Emerson was never more emphatic than in demanding the re–election of Andrew and Sumner.

How Hawthorne felt about this and how he voted in November, can only be conjectured by certain indications, slight, it is true, but all pointing in one direction. As long since explained, he entertained no very friendly feeling toward the Cotton Whigs; his letter to his daughter concerning Gen. McClellan, who set himself against the proclamation and was removed in consequence, should be taken into consideration; and still more significant is the letter to Horatio Bridge, in which Hawthorne proposed the enlistment of negro soldiers. Doctor George B. Loring, of Salem, always a loyal friend to the Hawthorne family, came to Concord in September to deliver an address at the annual cattle–show, and visited at the Wayside. He had left the Democratic party and become a member of the Bird Club, which was then the centre of political influence in the State. As a matter of course he explained his new position to Hawthorne. He had long felt attracted to the Republican party, and but for his influential position among his fellow–Democrats, he would have joined it sooner. Parties were being reconstructed. Half the Democrats had become Republicans; and a considerable portion of the Whigs had joined the Democratic party. The interests of the Republic were in the hands of the Republican party and it ought to be supported. We can believe that Hawthorne listened to him with close attention.

It was in the spring of 1862 that I first became well acquainted with the Hawthorne family, which seemed to exist in an atmosphere of purity and refinement derived from the man's own genius. Julian visited me at our house in Medford during the early summer, where he made great havoc among the small fruits of the season. We boxed, fenced, skated, played cricket and studied Cicero together. As my father was one of the most revolutionary of the Free–Soilers, this may have amused Hawthorne as an instance of the Montagues and Capulets; but I found much sympathy with my political notions in his household. When the first of January came there was a grand celebration of the Emancipation in Boston Music Hall. Mrs. Hawthorne and Una were very desirous to attend it, and I believe they both did so—Miss Una at all events. If Mrs. Hawthorne's opinions could be taken in any sense as a reflection of her husband's mind, he was certainly drifting away from his old associations.

In October, 1862, Hawthorne published the first of a series of studies from English life and scenery, taken chiefly from his Note–book, and he continued this at intervals until the following summer, when Ticknor & Fields brought them out with some additions in book form as "Our Old Home;" a volume which has already been considered in these pages. It was not a favorable time for the publication of classic literature, for the whole population of the United States was in a ferment; and moreover the unfriendly attitude of the English educated classes toward the cause of the Union, was beginning to have its effect with us. In truth it seemed rather inconsistent that the philanthropic Gladstone, who had always professed himself the friend of freedom, should glorify Jefferson Davis as the founder of a new nation—a republic of slaveholders. In addition to this, Hawthorne insisted on dedicating the volume to President Pierce, and when his publishers protested that this would tend to make the book unpopular, he replied in a spirited manner, that if that was the case it was all the more reason why Pierce's friends should signify their continued confidence in him. This may have made little difference, however, for comparatively few readers notice the dedication of a book until after they have purchased it; and we like Hawthorne for his firmness in this instance.

In England the book produced a sensation of the unfavorable sort. Hawthorne's attack on the rotundity of the English ladies, whatever may have been his reason for it, was, to speak reservedly, somewhat lacking in delicacy. It stirred up a swarm of newspaper enemies against him; and proved a severe strain to the attachment of his friends there. Henry Bright wrote to him:

"It really was too bad, some of the things you say. You talk like a cannibal. Mrs. Heywood says to my mother, 'I really believe you and I were the only ladies he knew in Liverpool, and we are not like beefsteaks.' So all the ladies are furious." [Footnote: J. Hawthorne, ii. 280. Good Mrs. Alcott also objected stoutly to the reflections on her sex.]

But Hawthorne was no longer what he had been, and allowance should be made for this.

Hawthorne's chief interest at this time, however, lay in the preparation of his son for Harvard College. Julian was sixteen in August and, considering the itinerant life he had lived, well advanced in his studies. He was the best–behaved boy in Concord, in school or out, and an industrious though not ambitious scholar. He was strong, vigorous and manly; and his parents had sufficient reason to be proud of him. To expect him, however, to enter Harvard College at the age of seventeen was somewhat unreasonable. His father had entered Bowdoin at that age, but the requirements at Harvard were much more severe than at Bowdoin; enough to make a difference of at least one year in the age of the applicant. For a boy to enter college in a half–fitted condition is simply to make a false start in life, for he is only too likely to become discouraged, and either to drag along at the foot of the class or to lose his place in it altogether. Hawthorne may have felt that the end of earthly affairs was close upon him, and wished to see his son started on the right road before that came; but Emerson also had an interest in having Julian go to college at exactly this time; namely, to obtain him as a chum for his wife's nephew, with the advantage of a tutor's room thrown in as an extra inducement. He advised Hawthorne to place Julian in charge of a Harvard professor who was supposed to have a sleight–of–hand faculty for getting his pupils through the examinations. Julian worked bravely, and succeeded in entering Harvard the following July; but he was nine months (or a good school year), younger than the average of his class.

The Life and Genius of Nathaniel Hawthorne

Hawthorne did not leave home this summer (1863), and the only letter we have of his was the one to James T. Fields concerning the dedication of "Our Old Home," which was published in the autumn. Julian states that his father spent much of his time standing or walking in his narrow garden before the house, and looking wistfully across the meadows to Walden woods. His strength was evidently failing him, yet he could not explain why—nor has it ever been explained.

One bright day in November two of us walked up from Cambridge with Julian and lunched at his father's. Mr. Hawthorne received us cordially, but in a tremulous manner that betrayed the weakness of his nerves. As soon as Julian had left the room, he said to us, "I suppose it would be of little use to ask you young gentlemen what sort of a scholar Julian is." H——replied to this, that we were neither of us in the division with him, but that he had heard nothing unfavorable in regard to his recitations; and I told him that Julian went to the gymnasium with me every evening, and appeared to live a very regular kind of life. This seemed to please Mr. Hawthorne very much, and he soon produced a decanter of port, and, his son having entered the room again, he said, "I want to teach Julian the taste of good wine, so that he will learn to avoid those horrible punches, which I am told you have at Harvard." We all laughed greatly at this, which was afterward increased by Julian's saying that the only punches he had yet seen were those which the sophomores gave us in the foot–ball fight,—or some such statement. It was a bright occasion for all of us, and when Mrs. Hawthorne and her daughters entered the room, such a beautiful group as they all formed together! And Hawthorne himself seemed ten years younger than when he first greeted us.

He was the most distinguished–looking man that I ever beheld, and no sensible person could meet him without instantly recognizing his superior mental endowment. His features were not only classic but grandly classic; and his eyes large, dark, luminous, unfathomable— looking into them was like looking into a deep well. His face seemed to give a pictorial reflection of whatever was taking place about him; and again became like a transparency through which one could see dim vistas of beautiful objects. The changes of expression on it were like the sunshine and clouds of a summer day—perhaps thunder clouds sometimes, with flashes of lightning, which his son may still remember; for where there is a great heart there will always be great heat.

"THE DOLLIVER ROMANCE"

According to James T. Fields, the ground–plan of this work was laid the preceding winter, but Hawthorne became dissatisfied with the way in which the subject developed itself and so set the manuscript aside until he could come to it again with fresh inspiration. With the more bracing weather of September he commenced on it again, and wrote during the next two months that portion which we now have. On December 1 he forwarded two chapters to Ticknor &Fields, requesting to have them set up so that he could see them in print and obtain a retrospective view of his work before he proceeded further. Yet on December 15 he wrote again, saying that he had not yet found courage to attack the proofs, and that all mental exertion had become hateful to him. [Footnote: "Yesterdays with Authors," 115.] He was evidently feeling badly, and for the first time Mrs. Hawthorne was seriously anxious for him. Four days later she wrote to Una, who was visiting in Beverly:

"Papa is comfortable to–day, but very thin and pale and weak. I give him oysters now. Hitherto he has had only toasted crackers and lamb and beef tea. I am very impatient that he should see Dr. Vanderseude, but he wants to go to him himself, and he cannot go till it be good weather.... The splendor and pride of strength in him have succumbed; but they can be restored, I am sure. Meanwhile he is very nervous and delicate; he cannot bear anything, and he must be handled like the airiest Venetian glass." [Footnote: J. Hawthorne, ii. 333.]

He divided his time between lying on a sofa and sitting in an arm–chair; and he did not seem very comfortable in either position. It was long since he had attended meetings of the Saturday Club.

It is clear from this that Hawthorne had not recently consulted a doctor concerning his condition, and perhaps not at all. He may have been right enough in supposing that no common practitioner could give him help, but there was at that time one of the finest of physiologists in Boston, Dr. Edward H. Clark, who cured hundreds of sick people every year, as quietly and unostentatiously as Dame Nature herself. He was a graduate of the University of Pennsylvania, and as such not generally looked upon with favor by the Boston medical profession, but when Agassiz's large brain gave way in 1868, Dr. Brown–Sequard telegraphed to him from Europe to consult Edward Clark, and Doctor Clark so improved his health that Agassiz afterward enjoyed a number of years of useful work. Perhaps he might have accomplished as much for Hawthorne; but how was Hawthorne in his retired and uncommunicative life to know of him? There are decided advantages in living in the great world, and in knowing what goes on there,—if one only can.

It is doubtful if Hawthorne ever opened the proof of "The Dolliver Romance." In February he wrote to Fields that he could not possibly go on with it, and as it had already been advertised for the *Atlantic Monthly*, a notification had to be published concerning the matter, which startled Longfellow, Whittier and other old friends of Hawthorne, who were not in the way of knowing much about him. The fragment that we now have of it was printed in the *Atlantic* many years after his death.

It was the last expiring ember of Hawthorne's genius, blazing up fitfully and momentarily with the same brightness as of old, and then disappearing like Hawthorne himself into the unknown and the unknowable. It is a fragment, and yet it seems complete, for it is impossible to imagine how the story could have been continued beyond its present limits; and Hawthorne left no word from which we can conjecture his further intentions in regard to it.

There was an old apothecary in Concord, named Reynolds, a similar man to, but not so aged as, Hawthorne's Doctor Dolliver; and he also had a son, a bright enterprising boy,—too bright and spirited to suit Boston commercialism,—who went westward in 1858 to seek his fortune, nor have I ever heard of his return. The child Pansie, frisking with her kitten —a more simple, ingenuous, and self–centred, but also less sympathetic nature than the Pearl of Hester Prynne—may have been studied from Hawthorne's daughter Rose. There also lived at Concord in Hawthorne's time a man with the title of Colonel, a pretentious, self–satisfied person, who corresponded fairly to his description of Colonel Dabney, in "The Dolliver Romance." Neither is it singular that the apothecary's garden should have bordered on a grave–yard, for there are two old cemeteries in Concord in the very centre of the town.

I know of no such portrait of an old man as Doctor Dolliver in art or literature,—except perhaps Tintoretto's portrait of his aged self, in the Louvre. We not only see the customary marks of age upon him, but we feel them so that it seems as if we grew old and stiff and infirm as we read of him; and the internal life of old age is revealed to us, not by confessions of the man himself, but by every word he speaks and every act he does as if the writer were a skilful tragedian upon the stage. It seems as if Hawthorne must have felt all this himself during the last year of his life, to describe it so vividly; but he ascends by these infirm steps to loftier heights than ever before, and the scene in which he represents Doctor Dolliver seated at night before the fire in his chamber after Pansie had been put to bed, is the noblest passage in the whole cycle of Hawthorne's art; one of those rare passages written in moments of gifted insight, when it seems as if a higher power guided the writer's hand. It is given here entire, for to subtract a word from it would be an irreparable injury.

"While that music lasted, the old man was alive and happy. And there were seasons, it might be, happier than even these, when Pansie had been kissed and put to bed, and Grandsir Dolliver sat by his fireside gazing in among the massive coals, and absorbing their glow into those cavernous abysses with which all men communicate. Hence come angels or fiends into our twilight musings, according as we may have peopled them in by-gone years. Over our friend's face, in the rosy flicker of the fire-gleam, stole an expression of repose and perfect trust that made him as beautiful to look at, in his high-backed chair, as the child Pansie on her pillow; and sometimes the spirits that were watching him beheld a calm surprise draw slowly over his features and brighten into joy, yet not so vividly as to break his evening quietude. The gate of heaven had been kindly left ajar, that this forlorn old creature might catch a glimpse within. All the night afterwards, he would be semi-conscious of an intangible bliss diffused through the fitful lapses of an old man's slumber, and would awake, at early dawn, with a faint thrilling of the heart-strings, as if there had been music just now wandering over them."

So Jacob in the desert saw angels descending and ascending on a ladder from Heaven. Discouraged, depressed, the door closed upon his earthly hopes, not only for himself, but for those whom he loves much better than himself, so far as he could ever be a help and a providence to them, Hawthorne finds a purer joy and a higher hope in the depths of his own spirit.

In the second chapter, or fragment, of this romance, Doctor Dolliver, followed by Pansie, goes out into the garden one frosty October morning, and while the apothecary is digging at his herbs, the imitative child, with an instinctive repulsion for everything strange and morbid, pulls up the fatal plant from which the elixir of life was distilled, and frightened at her grandfather's chiding, runs with it into the cemetery where it is lost among the graves and never seen again. This account stands by itself, having no direct connection with what precedes or follows; but the delineation is so vivid, the poetic element in it so strong, that it may be said to stand without assistance, and does not require the name of

Hawthorne to give it value.

In the conclusion, the elixir of life proves to be an elixir of death; extremes meet and are reconciled. As he says in "The Marble Faun," joy changes to sorrow and sorrow is laughed away; the experience of both being that which is really valuable. Doctor Dolliver and Pansie are figures for the end and the beginning of life; the Old Year and the New. Such is the sum of Hawthorne's philosophy—the ultimate goal of his thought. There could have been no more fitting consummation of his work. The cycle of his art is complete, and death binds the laurel round his brow.

A HERO'S END

After Hawthorne's letter of February 25, Fields felt that he ought to make an effort in his behalf. Fields's partner, W. D. Ticknor, was also ailing, and it was arranged that he and Hawthorne should go on a journey southward as soon as the weather permitted. Doctor Holmes was consulted, and the last of March Hawthorne came to Boston and met Holmes at Fields's house. Holmes made an examination, which was anything but satisfactory to his own mind; in fact, he was appalled at the condition in which he found his former companion of the Saturday Club. "He was very gentle," Holmes says; "very willing to answer questions, very docile to such counsel as I offered him, but evidently had no hope of recovering his health. He spoke as if his work were done, and he should write no more." [Footnote: *Atlantic Monthly*, July, 1864.] The doctor, however, must have been mistaken in supposing that Hawthorne was suffering from the same malady that carried off General Grant, for no human being could die in that manner without suffering greater pain than Hawthorne gave any indication of; and the sedatives which Holmes prescribed for him could only have resulted in a weakening of the nerves. He even warned Hawthorne against the use of alcoholic stimulants, to which for some time he had been more or less accustomed.

Hawthorne and Ticknor went to New York, and two days later Ticknor was able to write to Mrs. Hawthorne that her husband appeared to be much improved. How cruelly disappointing to meet him at their own door four days later, haggard, weary and more dispirited than when he had left the Wayside on March 26! He had proceeded to Philadelphia with Ticknor, and there at the Continental Hotel Ticknor was suddenly seized with a mortal malady and died almost in Hawthorne's arms, before the latter could notify his family in Boston that he was ill. What a severe ordeal for a man who was strong and well, but to a person in Hawthorne's condition it was like a thunderbolt. Ticknor's son came to him at once, and together they performed the necessary duties of the occasion, and made their melancholy way homeward. Nothing, perhaps, except a death in his own family, could have had so unfavorable an effect upon Hawthorne's condition.

Some good angel now notified Franklin Pierce of the serious posture of affairs, and he came at once to Concord to offer his services in Hawthorne's behalf. However, he could propose nothing more hopeful than a journey in the uplands of New Hampshire, and for this it would be necessary to wait for settled weather. So Hawthorne remained at home for the next month without his condition becoming apparently either better or worse. At length, on May 13, the ex–President returned and they went together the following day.

We will not linger over that leave–taking on the porch of the Wayside; so pathetic, so full of tenderness, even of despair, and yet with a slender ray of hope beneath the leaden cloud of anxiety. To Hawthorne it must have seemed even more discouraging than to his wife and children, though none of them could have suspected that the end would be so soon.

* * * * *

On the morning of May 20, I had just returned from my first recitation when Julian Hawthorne appeared at my room in the Massachusetts dormitory, and said, like a man gasping for breath, "My father is dead, and I want you to come with me." Fields had sent him word through Professor Gurney, who knew how to deliver such a message in the kindliest manner. We went at once to Fields's house on Charles Street, where Mrs. Fields gave Julian the little information already known to them through a dispatch from Franklin Pierce,—that his father died during his sleep in the night of May 18, at the Pemmigewasset House, Plymouth, New Hampshire. After this we wandered about Boston, silent and aimless, until the afternoon train carried him to Concord. He greatly dreaded meeting the gaze of his fellow–townsmen, and confessed that he wanted to hide himself in the woods like a wounded deer. [Footnote: The passage in "A Fool of Nature," in which he describes Murgatroyd's discovery of his father's death, must have been a reminiscence of this time—a passage of the finest genius.]

The Life and Genius of Nathaniel Hawthorne

On Wednesday, May 18, Hawthorne and Pierce drove from Centre Harbor to Plymouth, a long and rather rough journey to be taken in a carriage. Hawthorne, however, did not make much complaint of this, nor did he seem to be unusually fatigued. He retired to his room soon after nine o'clock, and was sleeping comfortably an hour later. Pierce was evidently nervous about him, for he went in to look at him at two in the morning, and again at four; and the last time he discovered that life was extinct. Hawthorne had died in his sleep as quietly and peacefully as he had lived. There is the same mystery in his death that there was in his life, and it is difficult to assign either an immediate or a proximate cause for it. With such a physique, and his simple, regular habits of life, he ought to have reached the age of ninety. General Pierce believed that he died of paralysis, and that is the most probable explanation; but it was not like the usual cases of paralysis at Hawthorne's age; for, as we have seen, the process of disintegration and failure of his powers had been going on for years. Nor did this follow, as commonly happens, a protracted period of adversity, but it came upon him during the most prosperous portion of his life. The first ten years following upon his marriage were years of anxiety, self–denial and even hardship; but other men, Alcott, for example, have suffered as much and yet lived to a good old age. It may have been "the old dull pain" which Longfellow associated with him, filing perpetually on the vital cord. It was part of the enigmatic side of his nature.

The last ceremonies of respect to the earthly remains of Hawthorne were performed at Concord on May 23, 1864, in the Unitarian Church, a commodious building, [Footnote: In 1899 this building was burned to the ground, and a new church has been erected on the same spot.] well adapted to the great concourse of mourners who gathered there on this occasion. Reverend James Freeman Clarke, who had united Hawthorne and Sophia Peabody in marriage twenty–two years before, was now called upon to preside over the last act in their married life. The simple eloquence of his address penetrated to the heart of every person present. "Hawthorne had achieved a twofold immortality,—and his immortality on earth would be a comforting presence to all who mourned him. The noblest men of the age had gathered there, to testify to his worth as a man as well as to his genius as a writer." Faces were to be seen in that assembly that were never beheld in Concord before. Among these was the soldierly figure and flashing eye of the poet Whittier. Longfellow, Emerson, Lowell, Agassiz, Alcott and Hillard were present; and ex–President Pierce shook hands with Judge Hoar over Hawthorne's bier. After the services the assembly of mourners proceeded to Sleepy Hollow cemetery, and there the mortal remains of Hawthorne were buried under the pine trees on the same hill–side where he and Emerson and Margaret Fuller conversed together on the summer afternoon twenty years before. He needs no monument, for he has found a place in the universal pantheon of art and literature.

* * * * *

It would seem advisable at this parting of the ways to say something of Hawthorne's religious convictions. He went as a boy with his mother and sisters to the East Church in Salem, a society of liberal tendencies and then on the verge of Unitarianism. All the Manning family attended service there, but at a later time Robert Manning separated from it and joined an orthodox society. Hawthorne's mother and his sister Louisa became Unitarians, and at Madam Hawthorne's death in 1848 the funeral services were conducted by Reverend Thomas T. Stone, of the First Salem Church. It is presumable that Nathaniel Hawthorne also became a Unitarian, so far as he can be considered a sectarian at all; but certain elements of the older faith still remained in his mental composition. It cannot be questioned that the strong optimism in Emerson's philosophy was derived from Doctor Channing's instruction, and it is equally certain that Hawthorne could never agree to this. Whatever might be the origin of evil or its abstract value, he found it too potent an element in human affairs to be quietly reasoned out of existence. Whatever might be the ultimate purpose of Divine Providence, the witchcraft prosecutions were an awful calamity to those who were concerned in them. In this respect he resembled David A. Wasson, one of the most devout religious minds, who left the church of Calvin (as it was in his time), without ever becoming a Unitarian or a radical. Miss Rebecca Manning says:

"I never knew of Hawthorne's going to church at all, after I remember about him, and do not think he was ever in the habit of going. I think he may have gone sometimes when he was in England, but I do not know about it. Somewhere in Julian or Rose Hawthorne's reminiscences, there is mention made of his reading family prayers, when he was in England. He, as also his mother and sisters were people of deeply religious natures, though not always showing it by outward observances."

A Concord judge and an old Free–Soil politician once attended a religious convention, and after the business of the day was over they went to walk together. The politician confessed to the judge that he had no very definite religious belief, for which the judge thought he did himself great injustice; but is not that the most advanced and intelligent condition of a man's religious faith? How can we possess clear and definite ideas of the grand mystery of Creation? Consider only this simple metaphysical fact, that space has no limit, and that we can neither conceive a beginning of time nor imagine time without a beginning. What is there outside of the universe? The brain reels as we think of it. The time has gone by when a man can say to himself definitely, I believe this or I believe that; but we know at least that we, "the creature of a day," cannot be the highest form of intelligence in this wonderful world. We thought that we lived in solid bodies, but electric rays have been discovered by which the skeletons inside of us become visible. The correlation and conservation of forces brings us very close to the origin of all force; and yet in another sense we are as far off as ever from the perception of it.

This would seem to have been also Hawthorne's position in regard to religious faith. What do we know of the religious belief of Michel Angelo, of Shakespeare, or of Beethoven? We cannot doubt that they were sincerely and purely religious men; but neither of them made any confession of their faith. Vittoria Colonna may have known something of Michel Angelo's belief, but Vasari does not mention it; and Beethoven confessed it was a subject that he did not like to talk about. The deeper a man's sense of the awe and mystery which underlies Nature, the less he feels inclined to expose it to the public gaze. Hawthorne's own family did not know what his religious opinions were—only that he was religious. One may imagine that the reticent man would be more reticent on this subject than on any other; but we can feel confident that at least he was not a sceptic, for the confirmed sceptic inevitably becomes a chatterer. He walks to Walden Pond with Hillard and Emerson on Sunday, and confesses his doubts as to the utility of the Church (in its condition at that time), for spiritual enlightenment; but in regard to the great omnipresent fact of spirituality he has no doubt. In "The Snow Image" he makes a statue come to life, and says in conclusion that if a new miracle is ever wrought in this world it will be in some such simple manner as he has described.

To the poetic mind, which is after all the highest form of intellect, the grand fact of existence is a sufficient miracle. The rising of the sun, the changes of the seasons, the blooming of flowers and the ripening of the grain, were all miracles to Hawthorne, and none the less so because they are continually being repeated. The scientists tell us that all these happen according to natural laws: perfectly true, but WHO was it that made those laws? WHO is it that keeps the universe running? Laws made for the regulation of human affairs by the wisest of men often prove ineffective, and inadequate to the purpose for which they were intended; but the laws of Nature work with unfailing accuracy. The boy solves his problem in algebra, finding out the unknown quantity by those values which are given him; and can we not also infer something of the *unknown* from the great panorama that passes unceasingly before us? The one thing that Hawthorne could not have understood was, how gifted minds like Lucretius and Auguste Comte could recognize only the evidence of their senses, and deliberately blind themselves to the evidence of their intellects. He who denies the existence of mind as a reality resembles a person looking for his spectacles when they are on his nose; but it is the imagination of the poet that leads civilization onward to its goal.

College life is rather generally followed by a period of scepticism, partly owing in former times to the enforced attendance at morning prayers, and still more perhaps to the study of Greek and Latin authors. During what might be called Hawthorne's period of despair, he could not very well have obtained consolation from the traditional forms of divine worship; at least, such has been the experience of all those who have passed through the Wertherian stage, so far as we know of them. It is a time when every man has to strike the fountain of spiritual life out of the hard rock of his own existence; and those are fortunate who, like Moses and Hawthorne, strike forcibly enough to accomplish this. It is the "new birth from above," in the light of which religious forms seem of least importance.

One effect of matrimony is commonly a deepening of religious feeling, but it is not surprising that Hawthorne should not have attended church after his marriage. His wife had not been accustomed to church–going, on account of the uncertainty of her health; the Old Manse was a long distance from the Concord tabernacle; Hawthorne's associates in Concord, with the exception of Judge Keyes, were not in the habit of going to church; and the officiating minister, both at that time and during his later sojourn, was not a person who could have been intellectually attractive to him. Somewhat similar reasons may have interfered with his attendance after his return to Salem; and during the last fifteen years of his life, he was too much of a wanderer to take a serious interest in the local affairs of the various places he inhabited; but he was desirous that his children should go to church and should be brought up in honest Christian ways.

Little more need to be said concerning Hawthorne's character as a man. It was not so perfect as Longfellow's, to whom all other American authors should bow the head in this respect—the Washington of poets; and yet it was a rare example of purity, refinement, and patient endurance. His faults were insignificant in comparison with his virtues, and the most conspicuous of them, his tendency to revenge himself for real or fancied injuries, is but a part of the natural instinct in us to return the blows we receive in self–defence. Wantonly, and of his own accord, he never injured human being. His domestic life was as pure and innocent as that which appeared before the world; and Mrs. Hawthorne once said of him in my presence that she did not believe he ever committed an act that could properly be considered wrong. It was like his writing, and his "wells of English undefiled" were but as a synonym for the clear current of his daily existence.

The ideality in Hawthorne's face was so conspicuous that it is recognizable in every portrait of him. It was not the cold visionary expression of the abstract thinker, but a human poetic intelligence, which resolved all things into a spiritual alembic of its own. It is this which elevates him above all writers who only deal with the outer world as they find it, and add nothing to it from their own natures.

George Brandes, the Danish critic and essayist, speaks of Hawthorne somewhere as "the baby poet;" but we suspect that if he had ever met the living Hawthorne, he would have stood very much in awe of him. It would not have been like meeting Ernest Renan or John Stuart Mill. Although Hawthorne was not splenetic or rash, there was an occasional look in his eye which a prudent person might beware of. He was emphatically a man of courage.

The wide and liberal interest which German scholars and writers have so long taken in the literature of other nations, has resulted in founding an informal literary tribunal in Germany, to which the rest of the world is accustomed to appeal. A. E. Schonbach, one of the most recent German writers on universal literature, gives his impression of Hawthorne in the following statement:

"I find the distinguishing excellence of Hawthorne's imaginative writings in the union of profound, keen, psychological development of characters and problems with the most lucid objectivity and a joyous modern realism. Occasionally there appears a light and delicate humor, sometimes hidden in a mere adjective, or little phrase which lights up the gloomiest situation with a gentle ray of hope. Far from unimportant do I rate the charm of his language, its purity, its melody, its graceful flexibility, the wealth of vocabulary, the polish which rarely betrays the touch of the file. After, or with George Eliot, Hawthorne is the first English prose writer of our century. At the same time he sacrifices nothing of his peculiar American quality. Not only does he penetrate into the most secret inner movements of the old colonial life, as no one else has done, and reproduces the spirit of his forefathers with a power of intuition which no historical work could equal; but in all his other works, from the biography of General Pierce, to the 'Marble Faun,' Hawthorne shows the freshness and keenness, the precision and lucidity, and other qualities not easy to describe, which belong to American literature. He is its chief representative." [Footnote: "Gesammelte Aufsatze zur neueren Litteratur," p. 346.]

Hawthorne has always been accorded a high position in literature, and as time goes on I believe this will be increased rather than diminished. In beauty of diction he is the first of American writers, and there are few that equal him in this respect in other languages. It is a pleasure to read him, simply for his form of expression, and apart from the meaning which he conveys in his sentences. It is like the grace of the Latin races,—like Dante and Chateaubriand; and the adaptation of his words is so perfect that we never have to think twice for his meaning. In those editions called the Elzevirs, which are so much prized by book collectors, the clearness and legibility of the type result from such a fine proportion of space and line that no other printer has succeeded in imitating it; and there is something similar to this in the construction of Hawthorne's sentences.

He is the romance writer of the English language; and there is no form of literature which the human race prizes more. How many translations there have been of "The Vicar of Wakefield," and of "The Sorrows of Werther"! The latter is not one of Goethe's best, and yet it made him famous at the age of twenty–eight. The novel deals with what is new and surprising; the romance with what is old and universal. In "The Vicar of Wakefield" we have the old story of virtue outwitted by evil, which is in its turn outwitted by wisdom. There is nothing new in it except the charming exposition which Goldsmith's genius has given to the subject. Thackeray ridiculed "The Sorrows of Werther," and in the light of matured judgment the tale appears ridiculous; but it strikes home to the heart, because we all learn wisdom through such experiences, of which young Werther's is an extreme instance. It was only another example of the close relation that subsists between comedy and tragedy.

It cannot be questioned that "The Scarlet Letter" ranks above "The Sorrows of Werther;" nor is it less evident that "The Marble Faun" falls short of "Wilhelm Meister" and "Don Quixote." [Footnote: See "Cervantes" in *North American Review*, May, 1905] Hawthorne's position, therefore, lies between these two—nearer perhaps to "Werther" than to "Wilhelm Meister." In certain respects he is surpassed by the great English novelists: Fielding, Scott, Thackeray, Dickens and Marian Evans; but he in turn surpasses them all in the perfection and poetic quality of his art. There is much poetry in Scott and

Dickens, a little also in Thackeray and Miss Evans, but Hawthorne's poetic vein has a more penetrating tone, and appeals more deeply than Scott's verses. If power and versatility of characterization were to be the test of imaginative writing, Dickens would push closely on to Shakespeare; but we do not go to Shakespeare to read about Hamlet or Falstaff, or for the sake of the story, or even for his wisdom, but for the *tout ensemble*—to read Shakespeare. Raphael painted a dozen or more pictures on the same subject, but they are all original, interesting and valuable, because Raphael painted them. If it were not for the odd characters and variety of incident in Dickens's novels they would hardly be worth reading. Hawthorne's *dramatis persona* is not a long one, for his plots do not admit of it, but his characters are finely drawn, and the fact that they have not become popular types is rather in their favor. There are Dombeys and Shylocks in plenty, but who has ever met a Hamlet or a Rosalind in real life?

A certain English writer promulgated a list of the hundred superior authors of all times and countries. There were no Americans in his catalogue, but he admitted that if the number was increased to one hundred and eighteen Hawthorne and Emerson might be included in it. Doubtless he had not heard of Webster or Alexander Hamilton, and many of his countrymen would be inclined to place Longfellow before Emerson.

I have myself frequently counted over the great writers of all times and languages, weighing their respective values carefully in my mind, but I have never been able to discover more than thirty–five authors who seem to me decidedly superior to Hawthorne, nor above forty others who might be placed on an equality with him. [Footnote: Appendix C.] This, of course, is only an individual opinion, and should be accepted for what it is worth; but there are many ancient writers, like Hesiod, Xenophon, and Catullus, whose chief value resides in their antiquity, and a much larger number of modern authors, such as Balzac, Victor Hugo, Freytag, and Ruskin, who have been over–estimated in their own time. Petrarch, and the author of "Gil Bias," might be placed on a level with Hawthorne, but certainly not above him. Those whom he most closely resembles in style and subject matter are Goldsmith, Manzoni, and Auerbach.

Yet Hawthorne is essentially a domestic writer,—a poetizer of the hearth–stone. Social life is always the proper subject for works of fiction, and political life should never enter into them, except as a subordinate element; but there is a border–land between the two, in which politics and society act and react on each other, and it is from this field that the great subjects for epic and dramatic poetry have always been reaped. Hawthorne only knew of this by hearsay. Of the strenuous conflict that continually goes on in political centres like London and New York, a struggle for wealth, for honor, and precedence; of plots and counterplots, of foiled ambition and ruined reputations,— with all this Hawthorne had but slight acquaintance. We miss in him the masculine vigor of Fielding, the humanity of Dickens, and the trenchant criticism of Thackeray; but he knew that the true poetry of life (at the present time) was to be found in quiet nooks and in places far off from the turbulent maelstrom of humanity, and in his own line he remains unrivalled.

PORTRAITS OF HAWTHORNE

Hawthorne had no more vanity in his nature than is requisite to preserve a good appearance in public, but he always sat for his portrait when asked to do so, and this was undoubtedly the most sensible way. He was first painted by Charles Osgood in 1840, a portrait which has at least the merit of a fine poetic expression. He was afterward painted by Thompson, Healy, and Emanuel Leutze, and drawn in crayon by Rowse and Eastman Johnson. Frances Osborne also painted a portrait of him from photographs in 1893, an excellent likeness, and notable especially for its far–off gaze. Of all these, Rowse's portrait is the finest work of art, for Rowse was a man of genius, but there is a slight tendency to exaggeration in it, and it does not afford so clear an idea of Hawthorne as he was, as the Osborne portrait. Healy was not very successful with Hawthorne, and Miss Lander's bust has no merit whatever. The following list contains most of the portraits and photographs of Hawthorne now known to exist, with their respective ownerships and locations.

Oil portrait painted by Charles Osgood, in 1840. Owned by Mrs. Richard C. Manning.

Crayon portrait drawn by Eastman H. Johnson, in 1846. Owned by Miss Alice M. Longfellow.

Oil portrait painted by George P. A. Healy, in 1850. Now in the possession of Kirk Pierce, Esq.

Oil portrait by Miss H. Frances Osborne, after a photograph by Silsbee, Case &Co., Boston.

Crayon portrait drawn by Samuel W. Rowse, in 1866. Owned by Mrs. Annie Fields.

Engraving after the portrait painted in 1850 by Cephas G. Thompson. Owned by Hon. Henry C. Leach.

The Grolier Club bronze medallion, made in 1892, by Ringel d'Illzach. Owned by B. W. Pierson.

Cabinet photograph, bust, by Elliott &Fry, London. Owned by Mrs. Richard C. Manning.

Card photograph, full length, seated, with book in right hand, by Black &Case, Boston.

Cabinet photograph, three–quarter length, standing beside a pillar, copy by Mackintire of the original photograph.

Card photograph, three–quarter length, seated, from Warren's Photographic Studio, Boston.

Card photograph, bust, by Brady, New York, with autographic signature. Owned by Hon. Henry C. Leach.

Bust in the Concord (Massachusetts) Public Library, by Miss Louise Lander.

Card photograph, bust, from Warren's Photographic Studio, Boston. Owned by Mrs. Richard C. Manning.

Oil portrait by Emanuel Leutze, painted in April, 1852. Owned by Julian Hawthorne.

Photograph by Mayall, London. The so–called "Motley photograph."

Two photographs by Brady, full length; one seated, the other standing.

Photograph showing Hawthorne, Ticknor and Fields standing together.

Editions of Nathaniel Hawthorne's Books published under his own Direction

Fanshawe: A Tale, Boston, 1828.
Twice–Told Tales, Boston, 1837.
   Another edition, Boston, 1842.
Peter Parley's Universal History, Boston, 1837.
The Gentle Boy: A Thrice–Told Tale, Boston, 1839.
Grandfather's Chair: A History for Youth, Boston, 1841.
Famous Old People: or Grandfather's Chair II, Boston, 1841.
Liberty Tree: The Last Words of Grandfather's Chair, Boston, 1841.
Biographical Stories for Children, Boston, 1842.
Historical Tales for Youth, Boston, 1842.
The Celestial Railroad, Boston, 1843.
Mosses from an Old Manse, New York, 1846, 1851.
The Scarlet Letter, Boston, 1850.
True Stories from History and Biography, Boston, 1851.
The House of the Seven Gables, Boston, 1852.
A Wonder–Book for Girls and Boys, Boston, 1851.
   Another edition, Boston, 1857.
The Snow–Image and Other Tales, Boston, 1852.
   Another edition, Boston, 1857.
The Blithedale Romance, Boston, 1852.
Life of Franklin Pierce, Boston, 1852.
Tanglewood Tales for Girls and Boys, Boston, 1853.
Transformation, or the Romance of Monte Beni, Smith &Elder, London, 1860.
The Marble Faun, or the Romance of Monte Beni, Boston, 1860.
Our Old Home, Boston, 1863.

A complete list of Hawthorne's contributions to American magazines will be found in the appendix to Conway's "Life of Hawthorne."

Mrs. Emerson and Mrs. Hawthorne [Footnote: Read at the Emerson Club, at Boston, January 2, 1906]

The Life and Genius of Nathaniel Hawthorne

In 1892, when I was constructing the volume known as "Sketches from Concord and Appledore," I said in comparing Emerson with Hawthorne that one was like *day*, and the other like *night*. I was not aware that four years earlier M. D. Conway had made a similar statement in his Life of Hawthorne, which was published in London. Miss Rebecca Manning, Hawthorne's own cousin, still living at the age of eighty and an admirable old lady, distinctly confirms my statement, that "wherever Hawthorne went he carried twilight with him." Emerson, on the contrary, was of a sanguine temperament and an essentially sunny nature. His writings are full of good cheer, and the opening of his Divinity School Address is as full of summer sunshine as the finest July day. It was only necessary to see him look at the sunshine from his own porch to recognize how it penetrated into the depths of his nature.

It would seem consistent with the rational order of things, that *day* should be supplemented by *night*, and *night* again by *day*; and here we are almost startled by the completeness of our allegory. We sometimes come across faces in the streets of a large city, which show by their expression that they are more accustomed to artificial light than to the light of the sun. Mrs. Emerson was one of these. She never seemed to be fully herself, until the lamps were lighted. Her pale face seemed to give forth moonlight, and its habitual expression was much like that of a Sister of Charity. It was said of her that she was the last in the house to retire at night, always reading or busying herself with household affairs, until twelve or one o'clock; but this mode of life would appear to have been suited to her organization, for in spite of her colorless look she lived to be over ninety.

So far I can tread upon firm earth, without drawing upon my imagination, but in regard to Mrs. Hawthorne I cannot speak with the same assurance, for I only became acquainted with her after her husband's health had begun to fail, and the anxiety in her face was strongly marked; yet I have reason to believe that her temperament was originally sanguine and optimistic, and that she alternated from dreamy, pensive moods to bright vivacious ones. She certainly was very different from her husband. Her sister, Elizabeth Peabody, was the most sanguine person of her time, and her introduction of the kindergarten into America was accomplished through her unbounded hopefulness. The Wayside, where Mrs. Hawthorne lived, has an extended southern exposure. The house was always full of light, which is not often the case with New England country houses; and when she lived at Liverpool, where sunshine is a rare commodity, she became unwell, so that Mr. Hawthorne was obliged to send her to Madeira in order to avert a dangerous illness.

These two estimable ladies were alike in the excellence of their housekeeping, the purity of their manners, their universal kindliness, and their devotion to the welfare of their husbands and children. It was a pleasure to pass them on the road–side; the fare at their tables was always of the nicest, even if it happened to be frugal; and people of all classes could have testified to their helpful liberality. In these respects they might almost have served as models, but otherwise they were as different as possible. Mrs. Emerson was of a tall, slender, and somewhat angular figure (like her husband), but she presided at table with a grace and dignity that quite justified his favorite epithet of "Queenie." There was even more of the Puritan left in her than there was in him, and although she encouraged the liberal movements and tendencies of her time, one always felt in her mental attitude the inflexibility of the moral law. To her mind there was no shady border–land between right and wrong, but the two were separated by a sharply defined line, which was never to be crossed, and she lived up to this herself, and, in theory at least, she had but little mercy for sinners. On one occasion I was telling Mr. Emerson of a fraudulent manufacturing company, which had failed, as it deserved to, and which was found on investigation to have kept two sets of books, one for themselves, and another for their creditors. Mrs. Emerson listened to this narrative with evident impatience, and at the close of it she exclaimed, "This world has become so wicked that if I were the maker of it, I should blow it up at once." Emerson himself did not like such stories; and although he once said that "all deaf children ought to be put in the water with their faces downward," he was not always willing to accept human nature for what it really is.

Mrs. Emerson did not agree with her husband's religious views; neither did she adopt the transcendental faith, that the idea of God is innate in the human mind, so that we cannot be dispossessed of it. She belonged to the conservative branch of the Unitarian Church, which was represented by Reverend James Freeman Clarke and Doctor Andrew P. Peabody. The subject was one which was permitted to remain in abeyance between them, but Mrs. Emerson was naturally suspicious of those reverend gentlemen who called upon her husband, and this may have been the reason why he did not encourage the visits of clergymen like Samuel Johnson, Samuel Longfellow, and Professor Hedge, whom he greatly respected, and who should have been by good rights his chosen companions. I suppose all husbands are obliged to make these domestic compromises.

Mrs. Emerson had also something of the spirit–militant in her. When David A. Wasson came to dine at Mr. Emerson's invitation, she said to him, by way of grace before meat: "I see you have been carrying on a controversy with Reverend Mr. Sears, of Wayland, and you will excuse me for expressing my opinion that Mr. Sears had the best of it." But after sounding this little nourish of trumpets, she was as kindly and hospitable as any one could desire. She was one of the earliest recruits to the anti–slavery cause,—not only a volunteer, but a recruiting officer as well,—and she made this decision entirely of her own mind, without any special encouragement from her husband or relatives. At the time of John Brown's execution she wanted to have the bells tolled in Concord, and urged her husband energetically to see that it was done. Mrs. Emerson was always thoroughly herself. There never was the shadow of an affectation upon her; nor more than a shadow of self–consciousness—very rare among conscientious persons. One of her fine traits was her fondness for flowers, which she cultivated in the little garden between her house and the mill–brook, with a loving assiduity. She is supposed to have inspired Emerson's poem, beginning:

> "O fair and stately maid, whose eyes
> Were kindled in the upper skies
>   At the same torch that lighted mine:
> For so I must interpret still
> Thy sweet dominion o'er my will,
>   A sympathy divine."

There are other references to her in his published writings, which only those who were personally acquainted with her would recognize.

* * * * *

Mrs. Hawthorne belonged to the class of womankind which Shakespeare has typified in Ophelia, a tender–hearted, affectionate nature, too sensitive for the rough strains of life, and too innocent to recognize the guile in others. This was at once her strength and her weakness; but it was united, as often happens, with a fine artistic nature, and superior intelligence. Her face and manners both gave the impression of a wide and elevated culture. One could see that although she lived by the wayside, she had been accustomed to enter palaces. Her long residence in England, her Italian experience, her visit to the Court of Portugal, her enjoyment of fine pictures, poetry, and architecture, the acquaintance of distinguished men and women in different countries, had all left their impress upon her, combined in a quiet and lady–like harmony. Her conversation was cosmopolitan, and though she did not quite possess the narrative gift of her sister Elizabeth, it was often exceedingly interesting.

Hawthorne has been looked upon as the necrologist of the Puritans, and yet a certain coloring of Puritanism adhered to him to the last. It was his wife who had entirely escaped from the old New England conventicle. Severity was at the opposite pole from her moral nature. Tolerant and charitable to the faults of others, her only fault was the lack of severity. She believed in the law of love, and when kind words did not serve her purpose she let matters take what course they would, trusting that good might fall, "At last far off at last to all."

I suspect her pathway was by no means a flowery one. Mrs. Emerson's life had to be as stoical as her husband's, and Mrs. Hawthorne's, previous to the Liverpool consulate,—the consulship of Hawthorne,—was even more difficult. No one knew better than she the meaning of that heroism which each day requires. A writer in the *Atlantic Monthly*, reviewing Julian Hawthorne's biography of his father, emphasizes, "the dual selfishness of Mr. and Mrs. Hawthorne." Insensate words! There was no room for selfishness in the lives they led. In a certain sense they lived almost wholly for one another and for their children; but Hawthorne himself lived for all time and for all mankind, and his wife lived through him to the same purpose. The especial form of their material life was as essential to its spiritual outgrowth as the rose–bush is to the rose; and it would be a cankered selfishness to complain of them for it.

APPENDIX A

There is at least one error in the Symmes diary, which is however explainable, and need not vitiate the whole of it. It has been ascertained that the drowning of Henry Jackson in Songo River by being kicked in the mouth by another boy while swimming, took place in 1828, so that the statement to that effect in the diary, must have been interpolated. As it happened, however, another Henry Jackson was drowned in the Songo River, so Mr. Pickard says, more than twenty years before that, and it is quite possible that young Hawthorne overheard some talk about that catastrophe, and mistook it for a recent event; and that Symmes afterwards confounding the two Jacksons and the difference in time, amended Hawthorne's statement as we now have it. Mr. Pickard says in a recent letter:

"This item alone led me to doubt. But I cannot doubt, the more I reflect upon it, that H. himself had a hand in most, if not all, the other items. Who but his uncle could have written that inscription? The negro Symmes could not have composed that—only a man of culture."... "The sketch of the sail on Sebago Lake surely was written by some one who was in that party. Symmes *might* have been there, but he was a genius deserving the fame of a Chatterton if he really did this. Three of that party I personally knew—one (Sawyer) was a cousin of my grandfather. His sleight of hand, his skill with rifle, his being a 'votary of chance,' are traditions in my family."

This does not differ essentially from the opinion I have already expressed in Chapter II. F. B. Sanborn, who is one of the best-informed of living men in regard to Hawthorne, takes a similar view.

APPENDIX B

In February, 1883, a review of "Nathaniel Hawthorne and his Wife" was published in the *Atlantic Monthly*, evidently written by a person with no good-will toward the family. Editors ought to beware of such reviews, for their character is easily recognized, and the effect they produce often reacts upon the publication that contains them. In the present instance, the ill-humor of the writer had evidently been bottled up for many years.

To place typographical errors to the debit of an author's account—not very numerous for a work of eight hundred pages—suggests either an inexperienced or a strongly prejudiced critic. This is what the *Atlantic* writer begins with, and he (or she) next proceeds to complain that the book does not contain a complete bibliography of Hawthorne's works; although many excellent biographies have been published without this, and it is quite possible that Hawthorne's son preferred not to insert it. No notice is taken of the many fine passages in the book, like the apostrophe upon Hawthorne's marriage, [Footnote: J. Hawthorne, i. 242,] and that excellent description of the performances of a trance medium at Florence, but continues in an ascending climax of fault-finding until he (or she) reaches the passage from Hawthorne's Roman diary concerning Margaret Fuller. [Footnote: J. Hawthorne, i. 30–35.]

If public opinion has any value, this passage concerning Margaret Fuller's marriage ought not to have been published; but what can Margaret Fuller's friends and admirers expect? Do they think that a young American woman can go to a foreign country, and live with a foreign gentleman, in defiance of the customs of modern society, without subjecting herself to the severest criticism? It is true that she married Count d'Ossoli before her child was born, and her friends, who were certainly an enlightened class, always believed that she acted throughout from the most honorable motives (my own opinion is, that she acted in imitation of Goethe), but how can they expect the great mass of mankind to think so? Hawthorne had a right to his opinion, as well as Emerson and Channing, and although it was certainly not a very charitable opinion, we cannot doubt that it was an honest one. In regard to the marriage tie, Hawthorne was always strict and conservative.

This is the climax of the *Atlantic* critique, and its anti–climax is an excoriation of Hawthorne's son for neglecting to do equal and exact justice to James T. Fields. This truly is a grievous accusation. Fields was Hawthorne's publisher and would seem to have taken a personal and friendly interest in him besides, but we cannot look on it as a wholly unselfish interest. It was not like Hillard's, Pierce's, and Bridge's interest in Hawthorne. If Fields had not been his publisher, it is not probable that Hawthorne would have made his acquaintance; and if his son has not enlarged on Fields's good offices in bringing "The Scarlet Letter" before the public, there is an excellent reason for it, in the fact that Fields had already done so for himself in his "Yesterdays with Authors." That Fields's name should have been omitted in the index to "Nathaniel Hawthorne and his Wife," may have been an oversight; but, at all events, it is too microscopic a matter to deserve consideration in a first–class review.

Are we become such babies, that it is no longer possible for a writer to tell the plain, ostensible truth concerning human nature, without having a storm raised about his head for it? George P. Bradford and Martin F. Tupper are similar instances, and like Boswell have suffered the penalty which accrues to men of small stature for associating with giants.

APPENDIX C

The great poets and other writers of all nations whom I conceive to be superior to Hawthorne, may be found in the following list: Homer, Aschylus, Sophocles, Euripides,

Pindar, Thucydides, Plato, Aristotle, Demosthenes, Theocritus, Plutarch; Horace, Virgil, Cicero, Tacitus; Dante, Tasso, Petrarch; Cervantes, Calderon, Camoens; Moliere, Racine, Descartes, Voltaire; Lessing, Goethe, Schiller, Kant; Swedenborg; Chaucer, Shakespeare, Bacon, Milton, and perhaps Burns and Byron; Alexander Hamilton, Napoleon.

These also may be placed more on an equality with Hawthorne, although there will of course always be wide differences of opinion on that point: Hesiod, Herodotus, Menander, Aristophases; Livy, Casar, Lucretius, Juvenal; Ariosto, Macchiavelli, Manzoni, Lope de Vega, Buthas Pato; Corneille, Pascal, Rousseau; Wieland, Klopstock, Heine, Auerbach; Spenser, Ben Jonson, Fletcher, Fielding, Pope, Scott, Wordsworth, Shelley, Carlyle, Browning, Tennyson, Froude; Webster, Emerson, Wasson. Sappho, Bion, Moschus, and Cleanthes were certainly poets of a high order, but only some fragments of their poetry have survived. Gottfried of Strassburg, the Minnesinger, might be included, and some of the finest English poetry was written by unknown geniuses of the fourteenth and fifteenth centuries. Ballads like "Chevy Chace" and the "Child of Elle" deserve a high place in the rank of poetry; and the German "Reineke Fuchs" is in its way without a rival. There may be other French, German, and Spanish writers of exceptional excellence with whom I am unacquainted, but I do not feel that any French or German novelists of the last century ought to be placed on a level with Hawthorne—only excepting Auerbach. Victor Hugo is grandiloquent, and the others all have some serious fault or limitation. I suppose that not one in ten of Emerson's readers has ever heard of Wasson, but he was the better prose writer of the two, and little inferior as a poet. More elevated he could not be, but more profound, just, logical and humane—that is, more like Hawthorne. Emerson could not have filled his place on the *Atlantic Monthly* and the *North American Review*.

9 781419 169335